*For Caroline*

# THE TOP 10 OF EVERYTHING

## RUSSELL ASH

Macdonald
Queen Anne Press

A Queen Anne Press BOOK

© Queen Anne Press and Russell Ash 1989. First Published in Great Britain in 1989 by Queen Anne Press, a division of Macdonald & Co (Publishers) Ltd, Orbit House, 1 New Fetter Lane, London, EC4A 1AR; A member of Maxwell Pergamon Publishing Corporation plc

Reprinted 1989

**British Library Cataloguing in Publication Data**

Ash, Russell, *1946–*
   Top ten of everything.
   1. Records of achievement
   I. Title
   032'.02

ISBN 0-356-15983-3

Typeset by Tradespools Ltd, Frome, Somerset
Printed and bound in Great Britain
by Butler and Tanner Ltd, Frome, Somerset

# CONTENTS

· · · · · · · · · · · · · · · · · · · · · · · · · · ·

# ABOUT THE AUTHOR

After obtaining a Joint Honours degree in Geography and Anthropology, Russell Ash worked briefly as an aviation insurance broker before his move into book publishing, which has occupied him for the past 20 years. He has been a director of several major publishing companies, among them Weidenfeld & Nicolson and Pavilion Books. He has contributed to numerous publications, including *Punch* and *The Observer,* and has written nearly 40 books in the fields of art and biography (he is the official biographer of Paddington Bear) as well as humour and offbeat reference books, such as *The Cynic's Dictionary* and *The Londoner's Almanac,* and is the co-author of *Bizarre Books.*

# INTRODUCTION

· · · · · · · · · · · · · · · · · · · · · · · · · ·

'Figures often beguile me, particularly when I have the arranging of them myself', wrote Mark Twain, while warning his readers that 'There are three kinds of lies: lies, damned lies, and statistics.'

Yet, lies or not, we are constantly presented with statistics; a news item will refer to a rail crash as the seventh worst, describe Margaret Thatcher as the sixth woman to become a Prime Minister, or we will be told that Neptune is the fifth largest planet. My reaction is always to ask, 'What about the others?'

In an attempt to put such data into some sort of perspective, I came up with **THE TOP 10 OF EVERYTHING.** There are ten points I ought to make about it:

1. Why 10? Firstly, it's a manageable number – I can remember 10 telephone numbers, but not 100. Traditionally we have Top 10 records and bestselling books, and we count in tens, have 10 fingers and 10 toes, and there happen to be 10 Commandments. There is a nice roundedness about 10 that just doesn't apply to any other number.

2. This is not strictly a 'Book of Lists' in the style of those published over the past dozen years or so. Much as I enjoy them – and they have undoubtedly extended our obsession with trivia – they usually arbitrarily contain lists of ten, or more or fewer, as well as lists that represent some personality or other's personal opinion (10 Favourite Films, 10 Best Restaurants, etc); all very entertaining, but these are qualitative lists. Those in **THE TOP 10 OF EVERYTHING** are entirely quantitative. Even lists that might appear to be qualitative (such as British Students' 10 Favourite Music Films) are measurable, since they are derived from the opinions of not one, but many (in this instance 24,000!) people.

3. Some lists are solidly factual and deadly serious; others definitely fall into the category of 'trivia' because I like solid facts, and I like trivia, and there's a place for both of them. That's why I have included such oddities as the 10 Commonest Phobias, the 10 Most Irritating Women in the Public Eye, the 10 Countries· Where Sheep Most Outnumber People and the 10 Largest Cheeses.

4. This is the first **TOP 10 OF EVERYTHING,** and compiling it has revealed a good deal about information sources. When I started, I thought a sensible approach would be, firstly, to prepare the lists that I assumed were firmly established and not liable to change (the heights of the tallest mountains, the largest islands and so on) before moving on to those that change from year to year. I was surprised, however, to discover that there is no international agreement on just what are the tallest mountains or the largest islands, and that a debate still rages over the lengths of the longest rivers. Some such disagreements derive from varying methods of measurement and definitions (where does a river actually start? How do you measure the speed of a bird? Do you include or exclude inland water in calculating the area of a country? What are the precise boundaries of a city?), others from the immense difficulty of calculating certain statistics (how many Christians are there in the world? How many people in the USA are called 'Smith'?).

5. Short of setting off with a theodolite to measure the tallest mountains, or whatever, one inevitably relies a good deal on previously published material. One then has to decide which data to trust. A major problem has been the often alarming inaccuracy of supposedly authoritative sources. Here is a test you can carry out for yourself: take an encyclopaedia or geography book and check the area of a country such as Pakistan. Now look it up in another reference book. Chances are the two figures will be completely different. Which one do you believe? I have had to ask myself this question every time I have found two or more divergent figures. As well as published information, I have turned to specialist organizations, research bodies and experts who are credited on page 253. A number of individuals were generous enough to supply lists that would have taken me a month of Sundays to compile – The 10 Oldest Pillar Boxes and 10 Highest-scoring Scrabble Words, for instance. Just occasionally I have found sources secretive (citing 'commercial confidentiality'), demanding huge fees for relatively straightforward information, or sometimes deliberately obstructive. This is sadly often truer in this country than elsewhere; it is often frustrating to be able to obtain superb

up-to-date information promptly from a United States source – often by fax the same day – but then to come up against their counterpart in this country who refuses to cooperate.

6. There is often a time-lag in the compilation of statistics – especially government figures - sometimes of several years. You should assume that those I have presented are the latest available, and, unless otherwise stated, not more than a year old. Of course, many of the lists are in constant flux; the birth of Princess Beatrice threw out the list of 10 in Line to the Throne, and The Queen is steadily moving up the list of 10 Longest-reigning Monarchs, (although she has a long way to go to overtake Queen Victoria). Because fashions change and new products are introduced, the lists of 10 Bestselling Toys or the 10 Most-rented Videos will be quite different next year.

7. Since this is a British book, I make no apologies for the preponderance of British lists. Some feature the United Kingdom, some Great Britain, some England & Wales only, depending on how the statistics are prepared. However, apart from specific British lists for UK products and the like, the UK is also given whatever place it warrants in global lists. Sometimes it appears prominently, and occasionally this is unsurprising – we are well known as the world's leading tea-drinkers, for instance; but we are also the world's major champagne importer, the leading consumers of Heinz baked beans, have some of the world's largest advertising agencies and banks and feature high in the lists of 10 longest bridges, TV-ownership, wheat-growers and egg-producers. We can be proud that, for example, Bournemouth appears in the list of the 10 Longest Rail Platforms in the World – but less that we are so well up in the league table of heart attack and lung cancer deaths. Occasionally the UK does not appear at all in the Top 10, but is added for the purposes of comparison. The USA features throughout, however, showing interesting similarities, and often bizarre anomalies.

8. Despite the 'Everything' of the title there are certain lists you won't find. There are those that simply don't reach ten, and are therefore omitted (some are in by the skin of their teeth – if there had been a couple fewer lunar missions, there wouldn't have been 10 moonwalkers!). The paucity of sporting records is deliberate. Partly this is a reflection of the fact that books of such data exist for every conceivable sport, and to repeat even the most important here would have doubled the size of the book. Also, in all sports, everyone avowedly sets out to be first, and it's a case of 'winner takes all'. Once a record has been broken (some of them so frequently that such lists are immediately out of date), the nine 'also-rans' are of relatively little interest – although longer-term historical achievements do occasionally have a place. Another omission that may seem strange is that of The Queen from the list of Britain's 10 richest. Apart from the virtual impossibility of calculating her wealth, along with other hereditary rulers, she is only a custodian of riches that she is expected to leave to her heirs (the idea of The Queen selling off her Rembrandts or putting Windsor Castle up for sale being somewhat unlikely), so placing her alongside billionaires with free rein over their coffers is pretty meaningless. I have largely avoided lists of '10 Rarest' – anything of which there is only one is rare, so a list of, say, 10 stamps of which there is a single example of each is not of enormous interest. Just occasionally, a list defeated me: the 10 Largest Statues in the World, for example.

9. Rates of exchange are an eternal bugbear. Often one is forced to make comparisons based on different currencies in the same list, for instance in those that relate to worldwide auction prices. Where this is done, I have attempted to convert at the rate prevailing at the time or at a date that is clearly stated. Now and again, there are two entries in equal 10th position, which means the Top 10 becomes a Top 11: the extra entry is supplied with my compliments at no additional charge...

10. Finally, although I have done my best to achieve 100% accuracy, with a project of this magnitude and covering such a wide range of data, it seems inevitable that there will be mistakes, for which I apologise. I would be delighted to have these pointed out to me to ensure that future editions of **THE TOP 10 OF EVERYTHING** are even more precise. If you want to do so, or wish to suggest new ideas for Top 10 lists, please write to:

Russell Ash
c/o Queen Anne Press
Headway House
66-73 Shoe Lane
London EC4P 4AB

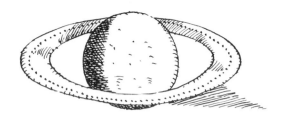

# The Universe

Sirius, in the constellation of Canis Major. Although the 'Dog Star' is 8.65 light years away, it is the brightest seen from earth.

*B*ased on apparent visual magnitude from Earth. At its brightest, the star Betelgeuse is brighter than some of these, but as it is variable its average brightness disqualifies it from the Top 10. If the Sun is excluded, the 10th brightest star is Hadar.

## THE 10 STARS NEAREST TO EARTH

| Star | light years | Distance km | miles |
|------|-------------|-------------|-------|
| 1. Proxima Centauri | 4.22 | 33,923,310,000,000 | 24,805,160,000,000 |
| 2. Alpha Centauri | 4.35 | 41,153,175,000,000 | 25,569,300,000,000 |
| 3. Barnard's Star | 5.98 | 56,790,790,000,000 | 35,150,440,000,000 |
| 4. Wolf 349 | 7.75 | 73,318,875,000,000 | 45,554,500,000,000 |
| 5. Lalande 21185 | 8.22 | 77,765,310,000,000 | 48,317,160,000,000 |
| 6. Luyten 726-8 | 8.43 | 79,752,015,000,000 | 49,551,540,000,000 |
| 7. Sirius | 8.65 | 81,833,325,000,000 | 50,844,700,000,000 |
| 8. Ross 154 | 9.45 | 89,401,725,000,000 | 55,547,100,000,000 |
| 9. Ross 248 | 10.40 | 98,389,200,000,000 | 61,131,200,000,000 |
| 10. Epsilon Eridani | 10.80 | 102,173,400,000,000 | 63,482,400,000,000 |

**THE UNIVERSE**

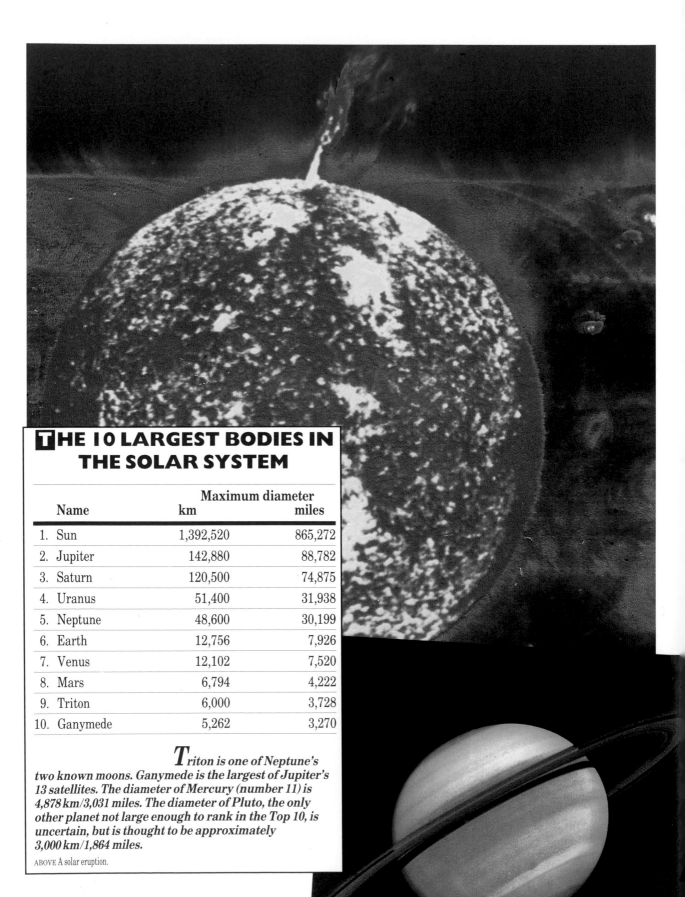

# THE 10 LARGEST BODIES IN THE SOLAR SYSTEM

| | | Maximum diameter | |
|---|---|---|---|
| | Name | km | miles |
| 1. | Sun | 1,392,520 | 865,272 |
| 2. | Jupiter | 142,880 | 88,782 |
| 3. | Saturn | 120,500 | 74,875 |
| 4. | Uranus | 51,400 | 31,938 |
| 5. | Neptune | 48,600 | 30,199 |
| 6. | Earth | 12,756 | 7,926 |
| 7. | Venus | 12,102 | 7,520 |
| 8. | Mars | 6,794 | 4,222 |
| 9. | Triton | 6,000 | 3,728 |
| 10. | Ganymede | 5,262 | 3,270 |

*T*riton is one of Neptune's
two known moons. Ganymede is the largest of Jupiter's
13 satellites. The diameter of Mercury (number 11) is
4,878 km/3,031 miles. The diameter of Pluto, the only
other planet not large enough to rank in the Top 10, is
uncertain, but is thought to be approximately
3,000 km/1,864 miles.

ABOVE A solar eruption.

THE UNIVERSE

# THE 10 COMMONEST ELEMENTS IN THE UNIVERSE

1. Hydrogen
2. Helium
3. Oxygen
4. Carbon
5. Nitrogen
6. Silicon
7. Magnesium
8. Neon
9. Sulphur
10. Iron

*Hydrogen comprises 90% of all matter in the universe.*

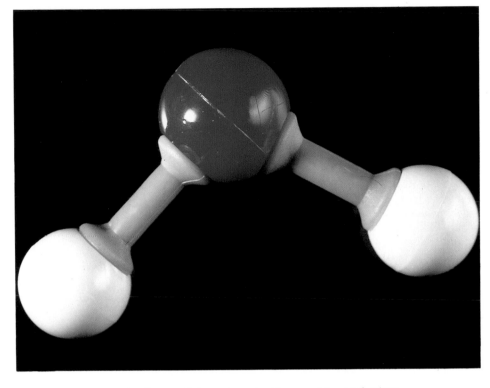

A model of a molecule of water, which combines atoms of hydrogen and oxygen, two of the commonest elements in the universe.

# THE 10 LARGEST ASTEROIDS IN THE SOLAR SYSTEM

| Name | Year discovered | Diameter km | miles |
|---|---|---|---|
| 1. Ceres | 1801 | 1,001 | 622 |
| 2. Pallas | 1802 | 607 | 377 |
| 3. Vesta | 1807 | 537 | 334 |
| 4. Hygeia | 1849 | 450 | 280 |
| 5. Euphrosyne | 1854 | 370 | 230 |
| 6. Interamnia | 1910 | 349 | 217 |
| 7. Davida | 1903 | 322 | 200 |
| 8. Cybele | 1861 | 308 | 191 |
| 9. Europa | 1858 | 288 | 179 |
| 10. Patienta | 1899 | 275 | 171 |

*Asteroids are fragments of rock orbiting between Mars and Jupiter. The first (and largest) to be discovered was Ceres, which was found by Giuseppi Piazzi, director of the observatory in Palermo, Sicily, on New Year's Day, 1801. Since then, over 3,000 have been recorded. All have been numbered according to the order in which they were discovered. Some have only code numbers, but most also have names: girls' names are especially popular and include Marilyn (No. 1,486), Sabrina (No. 2,264) and Samantha (No. 3,147). Among asteroids named after men are Mark Twain (No. 2,362) and Brian (No. 3,254). Numbers 3,350–3,356 were named after the seven astronauts killed in the 1986 Challenger space shuttle disaster, No. 2,309 is called Mr Spock after the character in Star Trek and numbers 435, 1,896 and 2,683 have the odd names, respectively, of Tea, Beer and Bus.*

LEFT A photograph taken by *Voyager I* showing Saturn, the third largest body in the Solar system.

# THE 10 LARGEST PLANETARY MOONS

|    | Moon | Planet | Diameter km | miles |
|----|------|--------|-------------|-------|
| 1. | Triton | Neptune | 6,000 | 3,728 |

*D*iscovered on 10 October 1846 by a 19th-century brewer, amateur astronomer William Lassell, 17 days after he had discovered Neptune itself, Triton is the only known satellite in the Solar System that revolves around its planet in the opposite direction to the planet's rotation. It is getting progressively closer to Neptune, and it is believed that in several million years the force of the planet's gravity may pull it apart.

|    | Moon | Planet | Diameter km | miles |
|----|------|--------|-------------|-------|
| 2. | Ganymede | Jupiter | 5,262 | 3,270 |

*D*iscovered by Galileo in 1609–10 and long thought to be the largest moon in the Solar System, Ganymede is believed to have a surface of ice about 97 km/60 miles thick. The 1979 Voyager probe failed to detect evidence of any atmosphere.

|    | Moon | Planet | Diameter km | miles |
|----|------|--------|-------------|-------|
| 3. | Titan | Saturn | 5,150 | 3,200 |

*T*itan, the largest of Saturn's 20 or more moons, is actually larger than two of the planets in the Solar System, Mercury and Pluto. It was discovered by the Dutch astronomer Christian Huygens in 1655. We have no idea what its surface looks like because it has a dense atmosphere containing numerous gases which shroud its surface.

|    | Moon | Planet | Diameter km | miles |
|----|------|--------|-------------|-------|
| 4. | Callisto | Jupiter | 4,820 | 2,995 |

*P*ossessing a similar composition to Ganymede, Callisto is heavily pitted with craters – one of them, known as Valhalla, measures 2,993 km/1,860 miles in diameter.

|    | Moon | Planet | Diameter km | miles |
|----|------|--------|-------------|-------|
| 5. | Io | Jupiter | 3,632 | 2,257 |

*M*ost of what we know about Io was reported back by the 1979 Voyager probe, which revealed a crust of solid sulphur with massive volcanic eruptions in progress.

|    | Moon | Planet | Diameter km | miles |
|----|------|--------|-------------|-------|
| 6. | Moon | Earth | 3,476 | 2,160 |

*O*ur own satellite is a quarter of the size of Earth, the 6th largest in the Solar System and, to date, the only one to have been explored by man.

|    | Moon | Planet | Diameter km | miles |
|----|------|--------|-------------|-------|
| 7. | Europa | Jupiter | 3,126 | 1,942 |

*A*lthough Europa's ice-covered surface is crater-free, it is covered with mysterious black lines, some of them 64 km/40 miles wide and resembling canals.

|    | Moon | Planet | Diameter km | miles |
|----|------|--------|-------------|-------|
| 8. | Titania | Uranus | 1,610 | 1,000 |

*T*he largest of Uranus's 15 moons, Titania was discovered by William Herschel in 1787 and has a snowball-like surface of ice.

|    | Moon | Planet | Diameter km | miles |
|----|------|--------|-------------|-------|
| 9. | Oberon | Uranus | 1,550 | 963 |

*A*lso discovered by Herschel, this was given the name of the fairy king husband of Queen Titania, both characters in A Midsummer Night's Dream.

|     | Moon | Planet | Diameter km | miles |
|-----|------|--------|-------------|-------|
| 10. | Rhea | Saturn | 1,530 | 951 |

*S*aturn's second-largest moon was discovered by 17th-century Italian-born French astronomer Giovanni Cassini. Its icy surface is pitted with craters, one of them 225 km/140 miles in diameter.

Jupiter's giant satellites: Io, Europa, Ganymede and Callisto, four of the ten largest planetary moons, photographed by *Voyager I*.

# Planet Earth

## THE AIR WE BREATHE: THE 10 PRINCIPAL COMPONENTS

*These ten, together with Xenon (0.0000087%), are the main constant components of dry air. Water vapour, ozone and various pollutants are also present in variable amounts.*

ABOVE Oxygen, vital for life and the second major component of the atmosphere, seen here in less familiar liquid form at −180°C.

| Component | Volume % |
|---|---|
| 1. Nitrogen | 78.110 |
| 2. Oxygen | 20.953 |
| 3. Argon | 0.934 |
| 4. Carbon dioxide | 0.01–0.10 |
| 5. Neon | 0.001818 |
| 6. Helium | 0.000524 |
| 7. Methane | 0.0002 |
| 8. Krypton | 0.000114 |
| 9= Hydrogen | 0.00005 |
| 9= Nitrous oxide | 0.00005 |

PLANET EARTH

# THE 10 LAYERS OF CLOUDS

| Cloud type | Level m | ft |
|---|---|---|
| 1. Stratus | <450 | <1,456 |
| 2= Cumulus | 450–2,000 | 1,476–6,562 |
| 2= Stratocumulus | 450–2,000 | 1,476–6,562 |
| 2= Cumulonimbus | 450–2,000 | 1,476–6,562 |
| 5. Nimbostratus | 900–3,000 | 2,953–9,843 |
| 6= Altostratus | 2,000–7,000 | 6,562–22,966 |
| 6= Altocumulus | 2,000–7,000 | 6,562–22,966 |
| 8= Cirrus | 5,000–13,500 | 16,404–44,291 |
| 8= Cirrostratus | 5,000–13,500 | 16,404–44,291 |
| 8= Cirrocumulus | 5,000–13,500 | 16,404–44,291 |

# THE 10 COMMONEST ELEMENTS IN THE EARTH'S CRUST

| Element | % |
|---|---|
| 1. Oxygen | 46.60 |
| 2. Silicon | 27.72 |
| 3. Aluminium | 8.13 |
| 4. Iron | 5.00 |
| 5. Calcium | 3.63 |
| 6. Sodium | 2.83 |
| 7. Potassium | 2.59 |
| 8. Magnesium | 2.09 |
| 9. Titanium | 0.44 |
| 10. Hydrogen | 0.14 |

Based on the average constituents by weight of igneous rock.

**PLANET EARTH**

# THE 10 HEAVIEST ELEMENTS

| Element | Year discovered | Density per cubic cm at 20°C (grams) |
|---|---|---|
| 1. Osmium | 1804 | 22.59 |
| 2. Iridium | 1804 | 22.56 |
| 3. Platinum | 1748 | 21.45 |
| 4. Rhenium | 1925 | 21.01 |
| 5. Neptunium | 1940 | 20.47 |
| 6. Plutonium | 1940 | 20.26 |
| 7. Gold | Prehistoric | 19.29 |
| 8. Tungsten | 1783 | 19.26 |
| 9. Uranium | 1789 | 19.05 |
| 10. Tantalium | 1802 | 16.67 |

*The two heaviest elements, the metals osmium and iridium, were discovered at the same time by the British chemist Smithson Tennant (1761–1815), who was also the first to prove that diamonds are made of carbon. A cubic foot of osmium weighs 640 kg/1,410 lb – equivalent to ten people each weighing ten stone.*

# THE 10 DEGREES OF HARDNESS

1. Talc
2. Gypsum
3. Calcite
4. Fluorite
5. Apatite
6. Orthoclase
7. Quartz
8. Topaz
9. Corundum
10. Diamond

*The Mohs Scale, named after German mineralogist Friedrich Mohs (1773–1839), is used for comparing the relative hardness of minerals. Each item on the scale is capable of being scratched by all those below it. To help remember the scale, several mnemonics have been devised, each word's initial letter corresponding to one of the levels of hardness, such as: 'Those girls can flirt and other queer things can do'.*

ABOVE Crystals of calcite, a type of calcium rated third on the Mohs Scale of hardness.
LEFT A layer of stratus clouds, encountered at the lowest level in the atmosphere.

## PLANET EARTH

# THE 10 LARGEST METEORITE CRATERS IN THE WORLD

| Name | Location | Diameter km | miles |
|---|---|---|---|
| 1= Sudbury | Ontario, Canada | 140 | 87 |
| 1= Vredefort | South Africa | 140 | 87 |
| 3= Manicouagan | Quebec, Canada | 100 | 62 |
| 3= Popigai | USSR | 100 | 62 |
| 5. Puchezh-Katunki | USSR | 80 | 50 |
| 6. Kara | USSR | 60 | 37 |
| 7. Siljan | Sweden | 52 | 32 |
| 8. Charlevoix | Quebec, Canada | 46 | 29 |
| 9. Araguainha Dome | Brazil | 40 | 25 |
| 10. Carswell | Saskatchewan, Canada | 37 | 23 |

*O*ne of the great debates in geology is whether or not certain crater-like structures are of meteoric origin, since some may be long-extinct volcanoes. All the above giant meteorite craters are believed to be so by the International Union of Geological Sciences Commission on Comparative Planetology. The relatively small Barringer Crater in Arizona (1.265 km/0.79 miles) is the largest that all scientists agree is indisputably a collision site.

The Hoba meteorite, found in South Africa in 1920.

# THE 10 LARGEST METEORITES EVER FOUND

| Location | Estimated weight tonnes |
|---|---|
| 1. Hoba West, Grootfontein, South Africa | 60 |
| 2. Ahnighito ('The Tent'), Cape York, West Greenland | 30.4 |
| 3. Bacuberito, Mexico | 27 |
| 4. Mbosi, Tanganyika | 26 |
| 5. Agpalik, Cape York, West Greenland | 20.1 |
| 6. Armanti, Western Mongolia | 20 |
| 7= Willamette, Oregon | 14 |
| 7= Chupaderos, Mexico | 14 |
| 9. Campo del Cielo, Argentina | 13 |
| 10. Mundrabila, Western Australia | 12 |

• • • • • • • • • • • • • • • •

# THE 10 LARGEST METEORITES FOUND IN THE UK

| Location | Date found | Approx. weight kg | lb |
|---|---|---|---|
| 1. Barwell, Leicestershire | 24 December 1965 | 46 | 101 |
| 2= Appley Bridge, Lancashire | 13 October 1914 | 33 | 73 |
| 2= Hatford, Berkshire (3 rocks) | 9 April 1628 | 33 | 73 |
| 4. Wold Cottage, Yorkshire | 13 December 1795 | 25.4 | 56 |
| 5. Strathmore, Tayside (4 rocks) | 3 December 1917 | 13 | 29 |
| 6. Strechleigh, Devon | 10 January 1623 | 12 | 26 |
| 7. Perth | 17 May 1830 | 11 | 24 |
| 8. High Possil, Strathclyde | 5 April 1804 | 4.5 | 10 |
| 9. Crumlin, Antrim | 13 September 1902 | 4.1 | 9 |
| 10. Rowton, Shropshire | 20 April 1876 | 3.2 | 7 |

**PLANET EARTH**

# THE 10 LARGEST OCEANS AND SEAS IN THE WORLD

The Californian coast of the Pacific, the world's largest ocean.

| | Ocean/Sea | Approx. area | |
|---|---|---|---|
| | | sq km | sq miles |
| 1. | Pacific Ocean | | |
| | (with adjacent seas) | 181,343,000 | 70,017,000 |
| | (without adjacent seas) | 166,241,000 | 64,186,000 |
| 2. | Atlantic Ocean | | |
| | (with adjacent seas) | 94,314,000 | 36,415,000 |
| | (without adjacent seas) | 86,557,000 | 33,420,000 |
| 3. | Indian Ocean | | |
| | (with adjacent seas) | 74,118,000 | 28,617,000 |
| | (without adjacent seas) | 73,426,000 | 28,350,000 |
| 4. | Arctic Ocean | | |
| | (with adjacent seas) | 12,256,000 | 4,732,000 |
| | (without adjacent seas) | 9,485,000 | 3,662,000 |
| 5. | Coral Sea | 4,791,000 | 1,850,000 |
| 6. | Arabian Sea | 3,864,000 | 1,492,000 |
| 7. | South China Sea | 3,686,000 | 1,423,000 |
| 8. | Caribbean Sea | 2,753,000 | 1,063,000 |
| 9. | Mediterranean Sea | 2,515,000 | 971,000 |
| 10. | Bering Sea | 2,305,000 | 890,000 |

# THE 10 DEEPEST OCEANS AND SEAS

| | Ocean/Sea | Greatest depth m | ft | Average depth m | ft |
|---|---|---|---|---|---|
| 1. | Pacific Ocean | 10,918 | 35,820 | 4,028 | 13,215 |
| 2. | Indian Ocean | 7,455 | 24,460 | 3,963 | 13,002 |
| 3. | Atlantic Ocean | 9,219 | 30,246 | 3,926 | 12,880 |
| 4. | Caribbean Sea | 6,946 | 22,788 | 2,647 | 8,685 |
| 5. | South China Sea | 5,016 | 16,456 | 1,652 | 5,419 |
| 6. | Bering Sea | 4,773 | 15,659 | 1,547 | 5,075 |
| 7 | Gulf of Mexico | 3,787 | 12,425 | 1,486 | 4,874 |
| 8. | Mediterranean Sea | 4,632 | 15,197 | 1,429 | 4,688 |
| 9. | Japan Sea | 3,742 | 12,276 | 1,350 | 4,429 |
| 10. | Arctic Ocean | 5,625 | 18,456 | 1,205 | 3,953 |
| | *North Sea* | *660* | *2,165* | *94* | *308* |

# THE 10 DEEPEST CAVES IN THE WORLD

| | Cave system | Location | Depth m | ft |
|---|---|---|---|---|
| 1. | Résneau Gouffe Jean Bernard | France | 1,535 | 5,036 |
| 2. | Atea Kananda | Papua New Guinea | 1,500 | 4,920 |
| 3. | Snezhnaya | USSR | 1,470 | 8,823 |
| 4. | Sima de las Puertas de Illamina | Spain | 1,338 | 4,390 |
| 5. | Gouffe de la Pierre-Saint-Martin | France | 1,332 | 4,370 |
| 6. | Sistema Huautla | Mexico | 1,246 | 4,088 |
| 7. | Mammuthöhle | Austria | 1,219 | 3,999 |
| 8. | Sumidero de Cellagua | Spain | 970 | 3,182 |
| 9= | Antro di Corchia | Italy | 950 | 3,117 |
| 9= | Kieveskaya | USSR | 950 | 3,117 |
| | *Ogof Ffynnon Ddu* | *Wales* | *308* | *1,010* |

*T*he extent of the world's cave systems is undergoing constant revision as new branches are discovered and mapping improved. The most extensive cave system in the world is that of the limestone Mammoth Cave, Kentucky, which extends some 530 km/329 miles.

## PLANET EARTH

Greenland (Kalaatdlit Nunaat), by far the largest island in the world.

# THE 10 LARGEST ISLANDS IN THE WORLD

| Island | Approx. area* | |
| --- | --- | --- |
| | sq km | sq miles |
| 1. Greenland (Kalaatdlit Nunaat) Arctic Ocean | 2,175,590 | 840,000 |
| 2. New Guinea, West Pacific | 789,900 | 304,980 |
| 3. Borneo, Indian Ocean | 751,000 | 289,961 |
| 4. Madagascar (Malagasy Republic) Indian Ocean | 587,041 | 226,657 |
| 5. Baffin Island, Canada, Arctic Ocean | 507,451 | 195,926 |
| 6. Sumatra, Indonesia, Indian Ocean | 422,200 | 163,011 |
| 7. Honshu, Japan, Northwest Pacific | 230,092 | 88,839 |
| 8. Great Britain, North Atlantic | 218,041 | 84,186 |
| 9. Victoria Island, Canada, Arctic Ocean | 217,290 | 83,896 |
| 10. Ellesmere Island, Canada, Arctic Ocean | 196,236 | 75,767 |

*of mainlands, including areas of inland water, but excluding offshore islands

*A*ustralia is regarded as a continental land mass rather than an island; otherwise it would rank first, at 7,618,493 sq km/2,941,517 sq miles, or 35 times the size of Great Britain.

# THE 10 LARGEST ISLANDS OF GREAT BRITAIN

| Island | sq km | sq miles | population |
| --- | --- | --- | --- |
| 1. Lewis with Harris, Outer Hebrides | 2,225.30 | 859.19 | 23,390 |
| 2. Skye, Hebrides | 1,666.08 | 643.27 | 8,139 |
| 3. Mainland, Shetland | 967.00 | 373.36 | 22,184 |
| 4. Mull, Inner Hebrides | 899.25 | 347.20 | 2,605 |
| 5. Anglesey | 713.80 | 275.60 | 68,500 |
| 6. Islay, Inner Hebrides | 638.79 | 246.64 | 3,997 |
| 7. Isle of Man | 571.66 | 220.72 | 64,679 |
| 8. Mainland, Orkney | 536.10 | 206.99 | 14,299 |
| 9. Arran | 435.32 | 168.08 | 4,726 |
| 10. Isle of Wight | 380.99 | 147.10 | 120,400 |

Neistpoint, the most westerly point of the Isle of Skye, Britain's second largest island.

# THE 10 LONGEST RIVERS IN THE WORLD

| River | Length km | miles |
|---|---|---|
| 1. Nile (Tanzania, Uganda, Sudan, Egypt) | 6,670 | 4,145 |
| 2. Amazon (Brazil) | 6,448 | 4,007 |
| 3. Mississippi-Missouri-Red Rock (USA) | 5,970 | 3,710 |
| 4. Yenisey-Algara-Selenga (USSR) | 5,540 | 3,442 |
| 5. Yangtze Kiang (China) | 5,530 | 3,436 |
| 6. Ob-Irtysh (USSR) | 5,410 | 3,362 |
| 7. Huang Ho (China) | 4,830 | 3,001 |
| 8. Zaire (Congo, Angola) | 4,700 | 2,920 |
| 9. Lena-Kiringa (USSR) | 4,400 | 2,734 |
| 10. Amur-Argun (China, USSR) | 4,345 | 2,700 |

RIGHT An aerial photograph of the Nile Delta, the terminus of the world's longest river.

# THE 10 LONGEST RIVERS IN THE USA

| River | Length km | miles |
|---|---|---|
| 1. Missouri-Red Rock | 4,088 | 2,540 |
| 2. Mississippi | 3,779 | 2,348 |
| 3. Missouri | 3,726 | 2,315 |
| 4. Yukon | 3,185 | 1,979 |
| 5. Rio Grande | 2,832 | 1,760 |
| 6. Arkansas | 2,348 | 1,459 |
| 7. Colorado | 2,334 | 1,450 |
| 8. Ohio-Allegheny | 2,102 | 1,306 |
| 9. Red | 2,076 | 1,290 |
| 10. Columbia | 2,000 | 1,243 |

*T*he Mississippi, Missouri *and Red Rock rivers are often combined, thus becoming the 3rd longest river in the world at 5,970 km/3,710 miles.*

LEFT 'Old Man River' – the Mississippi, part of the third longest in the world and itself the second longest in the USA.

## PLANET EARTH

# THE 10 LONGEST RIVERS IN THE UK

| | River | km | miles |
|---|---|---|---|
| | | | **Length** |
| 1. | Severn | 354 | 220 |
| 2. | Thames | 346 | 215 |
| 3. | Trent | 298 | 185 |
| 4. | Aire | 259 | 161 |
| 5. | Great Ouse | 230 | 143 |
| 6. | Wye | 217 | 135 |
| 7. | Tay | 188 | 117 |
| 8. | Nene | 161 | 100 |
| 9. | Clyde | 159 | 98.5 |
| 10. | Spey | 158 | 98 |

*During their courses, some rivers change their names, for example, Trent/Humber, Thames/Isis.*

Victoria, Africa's largest and the world's third biggest lake.

# THE 10 LARGEST LAKES IN THE UK

| | Lake | Country | Area sq km | sq miles |
|---|---|---|---|---|
| 1. | Lough Neagh | Northern Ireland | 381.74 | 147.39 |
| 2. | Lower Lough Erne | Northern Ireland | 105.08 | 40.57 |
| 3. | Loch Lomond | Scotland | 71.22 | 27.50 |
| 4. | Loch Ness | Scotland | 56.64 | 21.87 |
| 5. | Loch Awe | Scotland | 38.72 | 14.95 |
| 6. | Upper Loch Erne | Northern Ireland | 31.73 | 12.25 |
| 7. | Loch Maree | Scotland | 28.49 | 11.00 |
| 8. | Loch Morar | Scotland | 26.68 | 10.30 |
| 9. | Loch Tay | Scotland | 26.39 | 10.19 |
| 10. | Loch Shin | Scotland | 22.53 | 8.70 |

*The largest lake in England is Windermere, 14.74 sq km/5.69 sq miles.*

# THE 10 LARGEST LAKES IN THE WORLD

| | Lake | Location | Approx. area sq km | sq miles |
|---|---|---|---|---|
| 1. | Caspian Sea | Iran/USSR | 371,800 | 143,552 |
| 2. | Superior | Canada/USA | 82,350 | 31,795 |
| 3. | Victoria | Kenya/Tanzania/ Uganda | 69,500 | 26,834 |
| 4. | Aral Sea | USSR | 65,500 | 25,290 |
| 5. | Huron | Canada/USA | 59,600 | 23,012 |
| 6. | Michigan | USA | 58,000 | 22,394 |
| 7. | Tanganyika | Burundi/Tanzania/ Zaire/Zambia | 32,900 | 12,703 |
| 8. | Great Bear | Canada | 31,800 | 12,278 |
| 9. | Baikal | USSR | 30,500 | 11,776 |
| 10. | Nyasa (Malawi) | Malawi/Mozambique/ Tanzania | 29,600 | 11,429 |

# THE 10 HIGHEST WATERFALLS IN THE WORLD

| | Waterfall | River | Location/Country | Drop m | ft |
|---|---|---|---|---|---|
| 1. | Angel | Carrao | Venezuela | 979 | 3,212 |
| 2. | Tugela | Tugela | South Africa | 948 | 3,110 |
| 3. | Utigård | Jostedal Glacier | Nesdale, Norway | 800 | 2,625 |
| 4. | Mongefossen | Monge | Mongebekk, Norway | 774 | 2,540 |
| 5. | Yosemite | Yosemite Creek | California, USA | 739 | 2,425 |
| 6. | Østre Mardøla Foss | Mardals | Eikisdal, Norway | 657 | 2,154 |
| 7. | Tyssestrengane | Tysso | Hardanger, Norway | 646 | 2,120 |
| 8. | Cuquenán | Arabopo | Venezuela | 610 | 2,000 |
| 9. | Sutherland | Arthur | South Island, New Zealand | 580 | 1,904 |
| 10. | Kjellfossen | Naero | near Gudvangen, Norway | 561 | 1,841 |

The Tugela Falls in the Drakensberg Mountains, the highest in Africa and second highest in the world.

# THE 10 HIGHEST WATERFALLS IN THE UK

| | Waterfall | Country | m | ft |
|---|---|---|---|---|
| 1. | Eas Coul Aulin | Scotland | 201 | 658 |
| 2. | Falls of Glomach | Scotland | 113 | 370 |
| 3. | Pistyll y Lyn | Wales | 91 | 300 |
| 4. | Pistyll Rhaeadr | Wales | 73 | 240 |
| 5. | Falls of Foyers | Scotland | 62.5 | 205 |
| 6. | Falls of Clyde | Scotland | 62.2 | 204 |
| 7= | Falls of the Bruar | Scotland | 61 | 200 |
| 7= | Caldron Snout | England | 61 | 200 |
| 7= | Grey Mare's Tail | Scotland | 61 | 200 |
| 10. | Falls of Measach | Scotland | 46 | 150 |

# THE 10 LONGEST GLACIERS IN THE WORLD

| | Glacier | Location | Length km | miles |
|---|---|---|---|---|
| 1. | Lambert-Fisher | Antarctica | 515 | 320 |
| 2. | Novaya Zemala | USSR | 418 | 260 |
| 3. | Arctic Institute | Antarctica | 362 | 225 |
| 4. | Nimrod-Lennox-King | Antarctica | 290 | 180 |
| 5. | Denman | Antarctica | 241 | 150 |
| 6= | Beardmore | Antarctica | 225 | 140 |
| 6= | Recovery | Antarctica | 225 | 140 |
| 8. | Petermanns | Greenland | 200 | 124 |
| 9. | Unnamed | Antarctica | 193 | 120 |
| 10. | Slessor | Antarctica | 185 | 115 |

PLANET EARTH

# THE 10 LARGEST DESERTS IN THE WORLD

|   | Desert | Location | Approx. area sq km | sq miles |
|---|--------|----------|--------------------|----------|
| 1. | Sahara | North Africa | 9,000,000 | 3,474,920 |
| 2. | Australian | Australia | 3,830,000 | 1,478,771 |
| 3. | Arabian | Southwest Asia | 1,300,000 | 501,933 |
| 4. | Gobi | Central Asia | 1,295,000 | 500,002 |
| 5. | Kalahari | Southern Africa | 520,000 | 200,772 |
| 6. | Turkestan | Central Asia | 450,000 | 173,745 |
| 7. | Takla Makan | China | 327,000 | 126,255 |
| 8= | Sonoran | USA/Mexico | 310,000 | 119,691 |
| 8= | Namib | Southwest Africa | 310,000 | 119,691 |
| 9= | Thar | Northwest India/Pakistan | 260,000 | 100,386 |
| 9= | Somali | Somalia | 260,000 | 100,386 |

# THE 10 DEEPEST DEPRESSIONS IN THE WORLD

|   | Depression | Country | Maximum depth below sea-level m | ft |
|---|-----------|---------|--------------------------------|----|
| 1. | Dead Sea | Israel/Jordan | 400 | 1,312 |
| 2. | Turfan Depression | China | 154 | 505 |
| 3. | Munkhafed el Qattâra | Egypt | 133 | 436 |
| 4. | Poloustrov Mangyshlak | USSR | 132 | 433 |
| 5. | Danakil Depression | Ethiopia | 117 | 383 |
| 6. | Death Valley | USA | 86 | 282 |
| 7. | Salton Sink | USA | 72 | 235 |
| 8. | Zapadny Chink Ustyurta | USSR | 70 | 230 |
| 9. | Prikaspiyskaya Nizmennost | USSR | 67 | 220 |
| 10. | Ozera Sarykamysh | USSR | 45 | 148 |

*The list is of visible depressions only; there are deeper depressions beneath the Antarctic ice-cap, and the beds of many lakes are below sea-level.*

# THE 10 HIGHEST ACTIVE VOLCANOES IN THE WORLD

|   | Volcano | Country | Height m | ft |
|---|---------|---------|----------|----|
| 1. | Antofalla | Argentina | 6,450 | 21,161 |
| 2. | Guallatiri | Argentina/Chile | 6,060 | 19,882 |
| 3. | Cotopaxi | Ecuador | 5,897 | 19,347 |
| 4. | Sangay | Ecuador | 5,320 | 17,454 |
| 5. | Kluchevskaya | USSR | 4,850 | 15,912 |
| 6. | Wrangell | Alaska | 4,269 | 14,006 |
| 7. | Mauna Loa | Hawaii | 4,171 | 13,684 |
| 8. | Galeras | Ecuador | 4,083 | 13,392 |
| 9. | Cameroun | Cameroun | 4,070 | 13,353 |
| 10. | Acatenango | Guatemala | 3,959 | 12,989 |

Cotopaxi, Ecuador, among the world's highest active volcanoes.

## PLANET EARTH

# THE 10 HIGHEST MOUNTAINS IN THE USA

| Mountain | Height m | ft |
|---|---|---|
| 1.  McKinley | 6,194 | 20,320 |
| 2.  St Elias | 5,489 | 18,008 |
| 3.  Foraker | 5,304 | 17,400 |
| 4.  Bona | 5,044 | 16,550 |
| 5.  Blackburn | 4,996 | 16,390 |
| 6.  Kennedy | 4,964 | 16,286 |
| 7.  Sanford | 4,949 | 16,237 |
| 8.  South Buttress | 4,842 | 15,885 |
| 9.  Vancouver | 4,785 | 15,700 |
| 10.  Churchill | 4,766 | 15,638 |

*All ten tallest mountains in the United States are in Alaska or on the Alaska/Canada border. Mt Logan in Canada is the second tallest peak in the North American continent at 6,050 m/19,850 ft. Colorado and California also have a number of mountains over 5,000 m/14,000 ft. Only one other state – Washington – has a mountain in the Top 80: Mt Rainier at 4,392 m/14,410 ft.*

# THE 10 HIGHEST MOUNTAINS IN THE WORLD

| Mountain | Country | Height m | ft |
|---|---|---|---|
| 1.  Everest | Nepal/Tibet | 8,848 | 29,028 |
| 2.  K2 (Chogori or Godwin-Austen) | Kashmir/China | 8,611 | 28,250 |
| 3.  Kanchenjunga | Nepal/Sikkim | 8,598 | 28,208 |
| 4.  Lhotse | Nepal/Tibet | 8,501 | 27,890 |
| 5.  Makalu | Nepal/Tibet | 8,470 | 27,790 |
| 6.  Dhaulagiri I | Nepal | 8,172 | 26,810 |
| 7.  Manaslu | Nepal | 8,156 | 26,760 |
| 8.  Cho Oyu | Nepal | 8,153 | 26,750 |
| 9.  Nanga Parbat | Kashmir | 8,126 | 26,660 |
| 10.  Annapurna I | Nepal | 8,078 | 26,504 |

*All ten of the world's highest mountains are in the Himalayas, but the peak of Chimborazo in Ecuador, which is not even one of the Top 30 highest mountains in the world, is 2,151 m/7,057 ft further from the centre of the earth than Everest's. This is because it is nearer the Equator, where the earth bulges more. No two sources agree on the precise heights of the world's tallest mountains, partly because of the inaccuracy of measuring instruments, which are affected by the gravitational attraction of the mountains, partly because the ice-caps on their peaks vary in depth from season to season, and partly because many of them are inaccessible. In recent years, satellite surveys have provided some new data, but even this is hotly disputed – especially when the result of one recent survey suggested that K2 was actually 8,859 m/29,064 ft, some 11 m/36 ft higher than Everest!*

Despite rival claims, Mount Everest is still believed to be the world's tallest mountain.

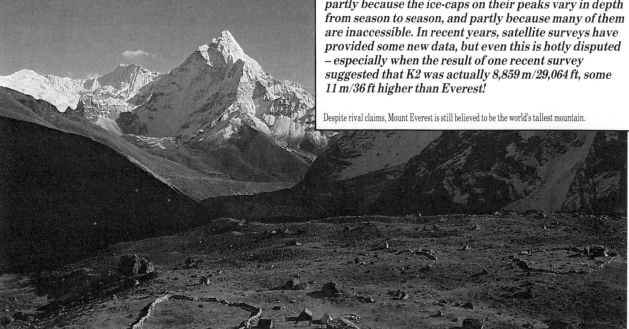

# Plants & Crops

· · · · · · · · · · · · · · · · · · · · · · · ·

## THE TOP 10 TREES PLANTED BY THE FORESTRY COMMISSION

1. Sitka spruce
2. Scots pine
3. Lodgepole pine
4. Larch
5. Norway spruce
6. Corsican pine
7. Douglas fir
8. Beech
9. Oak
10. Birch

*In 1988 the Forestry Commission planted 23,853 hectares/ 58,941 acres of conifers and 4,822 hectares/11,915 acres of broadleaved trees with an average density respectively of 2,000 and 1,000 trees per hectare/2.47 acres – a total of approximately 47,706,000 conifers and 4,822,000 broadleaved trees, or almost one tree for every person in Great Britain.*

The Kielder Forest, the largest in Great Britain.

## BRITAIN'S 10 LARGEST FORESTS

| | Forest | Hectares | Acres |
|---|---|---|---|
| 1. | Kielder | 39,380 | 97,310 |
| 2. | Newton Stewart | 35,275 | 87,166 |
| 3. | Dornoch | 35,180 | 86,932 |
| 4. | Ayrshire & Arran | 29,189 | 72,127 |
| 5. | Castle Douglas | 27,415 | 67,774 |
| 6. | Kintyre | 26,287 | 64,956 |
| 7. | Loch Awe | 25,202 | 62,275 |
| 8. | Aberfoyle | 24,431 | 60,370 |
| 9. | Easter Ross | 23,795 | 58,799 |
| 10. | Cowal | 23,521 | 58,122 |

Based on the Forestry Commission's largest tended blocks of land under plantation.

## THE TOP 10 TEA-PRODUCING COUNTRIES

| Country | Annual production tonnes |
|---|---|
| 1. India | 673,000 |
| 2. China | 517,000 |
| 3. Sri Lanka | 214,000 |
| 4. Kenya | 160,000 |
| 5. Turkey | 152,000 |
| 6. USSR | 150,000 |
| 7. Indonesia | 130,000 |
| 8. Japan | 95,000 |
| 9= Argentina | 40,000 |
| 9= Iran | 40,000 |

*The top three producers are responsible for nearly 60% of the total world tea production, which is estimated to be 2,413,000 tonnes.*

A tea plantation in India, the world's leading tea producer, under the supervision of the British, the world's leading tea consumers.

## BRITAIN'S TOP 10 VEGETABLE CROPS

| Crop | Annual production tonnes |
|---|---|
| 1. Potatoes | 6,760,000 |
| 2. Cabbages | 689,800 |
| 3. Carrots | 566,900 |
| 4. Cauliflowers | 384,400 |
| 5. Peas | 317,600 |
| 6. Onions | 305,100 |
| 7. Lettuces | 170,700 |
| 8. Brussels sprouts | 165,100 |
| 9. Turnips and swedes | 158,900 |
| 10. Tomatoes | 131,600 |

## BRITAIN'S 10 MOST POPULAR VEGETABLES (GROWN FROM SEED)

| Vegetable | Variety |
|---|---|
| 1. Beetroot | Globe |
| 2. Onion | White Lisbon |
| 3. Parsley | Imperial Curled |
| 4. Parsnip | Tender and True |
| 5. Beetroot | Boltardy |
| 6. Lettuce | Webbs Wonderful |
| 7. Runner bean | Scarlet Emperor |
| 8. Leek | Musselburgh |
| 9. Runner bean | Best of All |
| 10. Carrot | Favourite |

## THE TOP 10 COFFEE-GROWING COUNTRIES

| Country | Annual production tonnes |
|---|---|
| 1. Brazil | 2,112,000 |
| 2. Colombia | 654,000 |
| 3. Indonesia | 330,000 |
| 4. Mexico | 315,000 |
| 5. Ivory Coast | 260,000 |
| 6. Uganda | 205,000 |
| 7. Ethiopia | 178,000 |
| 8. Guatemala | 159,000 |
| 9. El Salvador | 141,000 |
| 10. India | 140,000 |

*W*orld total coffee production is 6,145,000 tonnes. Surprisingly, Kenya does not appear in the Top 10 as its annual production is only 109,000 tonnes.

## THE TOP 10 SUGAR PRODUCERS

| Country | Annual production tonnes |
|---|---|
| 1. USSR | 9,500,000 |
| 2. India | 9,250,000 |
| 3. Brazil | 8,649,000 |
| 4. Cuba | 7,218,000 |
| 5. United States | 6,645,000 |
| 6. China | 6,273,000 |
| 7. Mexico | 4,031,000 |
| 8. France | 3,973,000 |
| 9. Australia | 3,450,000 |
| 10. West Germany | 2,960,000 |
| *United Kingdom* | *1,343,000* |

## PLANTS & CROPS

# THE TOP 10 POTATO-GROWING COUNTRIES

| Country | Annual production tonnes |
|---|---|
| 1. USSR | 75,900,000 |
| 2. Poland | 36,252,000 |
| 3. China | 29,048,000 |
| 4. United States | 17,498,000 |
| 5. India | 12,731,000 |
| 6. East Germany | 11,300,000 |
| 7. Romania | 7,800,000 |
| 8. Netherlands | 7,478,000 |
| 9. France | 7,200,000 |
| 10. West Germany | 7,150,000 |
| *11. Great Britain* | *6,760,000* |

*The estimated total world production is 285,009,000 tonnes. It should be noted that dividing a country's population by the weight of potatoes grown will not reveal who eats the most, since a great deal of the world's potato harvest is used in the manufacture of alcohol and other products.*

# THE TOP 10 RICE-GROWING COUNTRIES

| Country | Annual production tonnes |
|---|---|
| 1. China | 176,530,000 |
| 2. India | 77,960,000 |
| 3. Indonesia | 38,676,000 |
| 4. Bangladesh | 22,250,000 |
| 5. Thailand | 17,650,000 |
| 6. Vietnam | 15,300,000 |
| 7. Burma | 13,722,000 |
| 8. Japan | 13,300,000 |
| 9. Brazil | 10,460,000 |
| 10. Philippines | 8,683,000 |

*World total annual production of paddy rice is estimated to be 454,320,000 tonnes. China thus produces over 38% of the total world crop.*

# THE TOP 10 ORANGE-GROWING COUNTRIES

| Country | Annual production tonnes |
|---|---|
| 1. Brazil | 14,978,000 |
| 2. United States | 7,019,000 |
| 3. Spain | 2,359,000 |
| 4. Mexico | 2,200,000 |
| 5. China | 2,180,000 |
| 6. Italy | 1,416,000 |
| 7. India | 1,350,000 |
| 8. Egypt | 1,300,000 |
| 8. Pakistan | 1,050,000 |
| 10. Israel | 861,000 |

# THE TOP 10 WHEAT-GROWING COUNTRIES

| Country | Production tonnes |
|---|---|
| 1. China | 85,000,000 |
| 2. USSR | 78,100,000 |
| 3. United States | 66,002,000 |
| 4. India | 44,069,000 |
| 5. France | 28,890,000 |
| 6. Canada | 24,252,000 |
| 7. Turkey | 17,032,000 |
| 8. Australia | 16,127,000 |
| 9. United Kingdom | 12,050,000 |
| 10. Pakistan | 11,703,000 |
| *World total* | *505,671,000* |

## PLANTS & CROPS

Tobacco leaves drying in Maryland. The USA's huge production places it second in the world league, but considerably behind China.

# THE TOP 10 APPLE-GROWING COUNTRIES

| Country | Annual production tonnes |
|---|---|
| 1. USSR | 5,200,000 |
| 2. United States | 4,511,000 |
| 3. China | 3,008,000 |
| 4. France | 2,424,000 |
| 5. Italy | 2,144,000 |
| 6. Turkey | 1,650,000 |
| 7. Argentina | 1,078,000 |
| 8. West Germany | 1,077,000 |
| 9. Spain | 1,039,000 |
| 10. Japan | 1,003,000 |
| *United Kingdom* | *340,000* |

# THE TOP 10 TOBACCO-GROWING COUNTRIES

| Country | Annual production tonnes |
|---|---|
| 1. China | 1,926,000 |
| 2. United States | 559,000 |
| 3. India | 460,000 |
| 4. Brazil | 401,000 |
| 5. USSR | 381,000 |
| 6. Turkey | 177,000 |
| 7. Italy | 156,000 |
| 8. Greece | 145,000 |
| 9. Indonesia | 131,000 |
| 10. Zimbabwe | 128,000 |

PLANTS & CROPS

A sweet pea – top of the crops among Britain's flower-growers.

32% of houseplant owners admit to owning at least one geranium.

## BRITAIN'S 10 MOST POPULAR FLOWERS (GROWN FROM SEED)

| | Flower | Variety |
|---|---|---|
| 1. | Sweet Pea | Special Mixed |
| 2. | Nasturtium | Jewel Mixed |
| 3. | Dwarf Godetia | Selected Mixed |
| 4. | Wallflower | Choice Mixed |
| 5. | Nasturtium | Tall Single Mixed |
| 6. | Lobelia | Crystal Palace |
| 7. | Alyssum | Snow Carpet |
| 8. | Wallflower | Persian Carpet |
| 9. | Dwarf Candythrift | Fairy Mixed |
| 10. | Nemesia | Carnival Mixed |

## BRITAIN'S 10 MOST POPULAR HOUSEPLANTS

| | Type | % |
|---|---|---|
| 1. | Cactus/succulent | 48 |
| 2. | Geranium | 32 |
| 3. | Spider plant | 31 |
| 4. | Busy Lizzie | 25 |
| 5. | Ivy | 23 |
| 6. | African violet | 19 |
| 7. | Begonia | 18 |
| 8. | Rubber plant | 17 |
| 9. | Fern | 16 |
| 10. | Tradescantia | 13 |

The percentages relate to houseplant owners surveyed who own one or more specimens of each variety.

# Animals & Birds

An unequal contest: a cheetah, the world's fastest runner, in pursuit of a zebra.

## THE 10 FASTEST MAMMALS IN THE WORLD

| Mammal | Maximum recorded speed | |
| --- | --- | --- |
| | kph | mph |
| 1.  Cheetah | 104 | 65 |
| 2.  Pronghorn Antelope | 88 | 55 |
| 3= Mongolian Gazelle | 80 | 50 |
| 3= Springbok | 80 | 50 |
| 5= Thomson's Gazelle | 75 | 47 |
| 5= Grant's Gazelle | 75 | 47 |
| 7.  Brown Hare | 72 | 45 |
| 8.  Horse | 69 | 43 |
| 9= Red Deer | 67 | 42 |
| 9= Greyhound | 67 | 42 |

## THE 10 FASTEST FISH IN THE WORLD

| Fish | Maximum recorded speed | |
| --- | --- | --- |
| | kph | mph |
| 1.  Sailfish | 110 | 68 |
| 2.  Marlin | 80 | 50 |
| 3.  Wahoo | 78 | 48 |
| 4.  Tunny | 74 | 46 |
| 5.  Bluefish Tuna | 70 | 44 |
| 6.  Great Blue Shark | 69 | 43 |
| 7= Bonefish | 64 | 40 |
| 7= Swordfish | 64 | 40 |
| 9= Four-winged flying fish | 56 | 35 |
| 9= Tarpon | 56 | 35 |

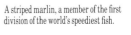

A striped marlin, a member of the first division of the world's speediest fish.

## ANIMALS & BIRDS

A Frigate Bird, one of the world's fastest fliers. During the mating season, the male inflates his scarlet throat to attract the female.

Three new additions to the Wren population explosion.

# THE 10 FASTEST BIRDS IN THE WORLD

| | | Maximum recorded speed | |
|---|---|---|---|
| | Bird | kph | mph |
| 1. | Spine-tailed Swift | 171 | 106 |
| 2. | Frigate Bird | 153 | 95 |
| 3. | Spur-winged Goose | 142 | 88 |
| 4. | Red-breasted Merganser | 129 | 80 |
| 5. | White-rumped Swift | 124 | 77 |
| 6. | Canvasback Duck | 116 | 72 |
| 7. | Eider Duck | 113 | 70 |
| 8. | Teal | 109 | 68 |
| 9= | Pintail | 105 | 65 |
| 9= | Mallard | 105 | 65 |

# THE 10 COMMONEST BIRDS IN GREAT BRITAIN

| | Bird | Estimated number of breeding pairs |
|---|---|---|
| 1. | Wren | 10,000,000 |
| 2= | Blackbird | 7,000,000 |
| 2= | Chaffinch | 7,000,000 |
| 4. | Starling | 5,500,000 |
| 5= | Bluetit | 5,000,000 |
| 5= | Hedge Sparrow | 5,000,000 |
| 5= | House Sparrow | 5,000,000 |
| 5= | Robin | 5,000,000 |
| 9. | Wood Pigeon | 4,000,000 |
| 10. | Song Thrush | 3,500,000 |

*Y*ou may well wonder how these estimates are produced. The answer is that groups of volunteers go out and count them! Estimates made in sample areas are then multiplied up to produce national data.

ANIMALS & BIRDS

A White-tailed Eagle (ABOVE) and a male Ruff (ABOVE RIGHT) – representatives of Britain's rarest bird species.

# THE 10 LARGEST BIRDS IN GREAT BRITAIN

|  | Bird | Height cm | in |
|---|---|---|---|
| 1= | Whooper Swan | 145–160 | 57–63 |
| 1= | Mute Swan | 145–160 | 57–63 |
| 3. | Bewick's Swan | 116–128 | 45½–50½ |
| 4. | Canada Goose | up to 110 | up to 43½ |
| 5. | Grey Heron | 90–100 | 35½–39½ |
| 6. | Cormorant | 84–98 | 33–38½ |
| 7. | Gannet | 86–96 | 34–38 |
| 8. | White-tailed Sea Eagle | 69–91 | 27–36 |
| 9. | Capercaillie (male) | 82–90 | 32–35½ |
| 10. | Golden Eagle | 76–90 | 30–35½ |

# THE 10 RAREST BRITISH BIRDS

|  | Bird | Estimated number of pairs |
|---|---|---|
| 1= | Red-necked Grebe | 1 |
| 1= | Red-backed Shrike | 1 |
| 3. | Ruff | 1 to 2 |
| 4= | Purple Sandpiper | up to 2 |
| 4= | Fieldfare | up to 2 |
| 6= | Wood Sandpiper | up to 3 |
| 6= | Temminck's Stint | up to 3 |
| 8. | White-tailed Eagle | up to 5 |
| 9= | Spotted Crake | up to 6 |
| 9= | Honey Buzzard | up to 6 |

ANIMALS & BIRDS

# THE 10 LARGEST DINOSAURS

1. Seismosaurus

Length: 30–37 m/94–120 ft. Weight: an estimated 80 tonnes. A single skeleton was found in 1985 near Albuquerque and is currently being studied by New Mexico Museum of Natural History, which may establish its position as the largest dinosaur yet discovered. Its name means 'earthshaker'.

2. Ultrasaurus

Length: 30.5 m/100 ft. Height: 16–17 m/52–56 ft. Weight: an estimated 50 tonnes (though some authorities have claimed 100–140 tonnes). Ultrasaurus was discovered in Colorado in 1979 but has not yet been fully studied.

3. Antarctosaurus

Length: 30 m/98 ft. Weight: 80 tonnes. The thigh bone alone of this creature measures 2.3 m/7.5 ft.

4. Supersaurus

Length: 24–30 m/79–98 ft. Height: 15 m/49 ft. Weight: 75–100 tonnes. The remains of Supersaurus were found in Colorado in 1971.

5. Diplodocus

Length: 27 m/88.5 ft. Weight: only 10.6 tonnes, as he was long and thin. Diplodocus was probably one of the most stupid dinosaurs, having the smallest brain in relation to its body size. One skeleton was named *Diplodocus carnegii*, in honour of Scottish-American millionaire Andrew Carnegie, who financed the excavations that discovered it.

6. Brachiosaurus

Length: 23–27 m/75–88.5 ft. Height: 12 m/39 ft. Weight: 78 tonnes (190 tonnes according to some palaeontologists).

7. Barosaurus

Length: 22–27 m/72–88.5 ft. Barosaurus has been found in both North America and Africa, thus proving the existence of a land link in Jurassic times (205–140 million years ago).

8. Pelorosaurus

Length: 24 m/79 ft. The first pelorosaurus fragments were found in Sussex in 1850. Its name means 'monstrous reptile'.

9. Mamenchisaurus

Length: 22 m/72 ft. An almost complete skeleton was discovered in 1972 and named after the place in China where it was found. This showed that it had the longest neck ever of any animal, comprising half its total body length.

10. Apatosaurus

Length: 20–21 m/65–69 ft. Weight: 30 tonnes. Apatosaurus is better known as brontosaurus, or 'thunder reptile'.

*L*engths have often been estimated from only a few surviving fossilized bones, and there is much dispute, even among experts, about the true lengths and weights of most dinosaurs. Everyone's favourite dinosaur, Tyrannosaurus rex, *does not appear in the Top 10 list because, although it was the fiercest flesh-eating dinosaur, it was not as large as many of the herbivorous ones. However, measuring a probable 13.4 m/44 ft and weighing 8.5 tonnes certainly ranks it as the largest flesh-eating animal yet discovered.*

*To compare these sizes with living animals, note that the largest recorded crocodile measured 6.2 m/20.3 ft and the largest elephant 10.67 m/35 ft from trunk to tail and weighed about 12 tonnes. The largest living creature ever measured is the blue whale at 33.5 m/110 ft – slightly smaller than the size claimed for seismosaurus.*

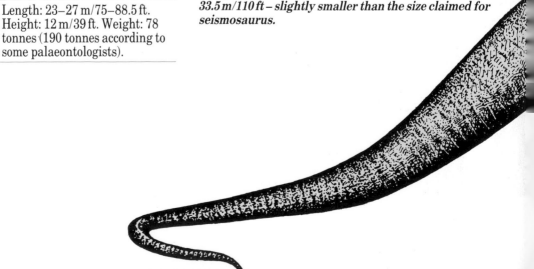

## ANIMALS & BIRDS

# THE 10 MOST RECENTLY EXTINCT ANIMAL SPECIES

1. Partula Tree Snails from Moorea, Polynesia
2. Palos Verde Blue Butterfly
3. Canary Islands Blackfly
4. Lord Howe Islands Phasmid Fly
5. Dusky Seaside Sparrow
6. Colombian Grebe and Atitlan Grebe
7. Glaucous Macaw
8. Hawaiian Honey Creeper
9. Pohmpei (Caroline Island bird)
10. Bali Tiger

*The saddest thing about this list is that by the time you read it, it will be out of date because yet another species will have become extinct, usually as a direct result of human intervention.*

LEFT *Partula mooreana*, the Moorean Tree Snail, now disappeared off the face of the earth.

BELOW A dinosaur of little brain, the Diploducus's 27-metre length was mainly neck and tail.

# BRITAIN'S 10 MOST-VISITED WILDLIFE ATTRACTIONS

| | | |
|---|---|---|
| 1. | London Zoo | 1,303,797 |
| 2. | Chester Zoo | 862,471 |
| 3. | Windsor Safari Park | 812,510 |
| 4. | Bristol Zoo | 575,000* |
| 5. | Twycross Zoo, Atherstone | 460,687* |
| 6. | Knowlsey Safari Park, Prescot | 422,605* |
| 7. | Whipsnade Park Zoo, Bedfordshire | 405,631 |
| 8. | Cotswold Wildlife Park, Burford | 362,209 |
| 9. | Paignton Zoo | 343,229 |
| 10. | Blackpool Zoo | 336,594 |

*estimated

# THE 10 MOST POPULAR CATS' NAMES IN GREAT BRITAIN

1. Sooty
2. Tiger
3. Smoky
4. Tigger
5. Whiskey
6. Kitty
7. Lucky
8. Suzie
9. Fluffy
10. Snowy

Based on a 1987 Kattomeat/Gallup Survey in which 4,000 people were questioned about their pets.

*In equal 11th place are: Suky, Thomas and Tabby.*

Dog tired? An estimated 6,000,000 dogs are kept as domestic pets in Great Britain alone.

# THE 10 MOST POPULAR BREEDS OF DOGS IN THE USA

| Breed | Number registered by American Kennel Club |
|---|---|
| 1. Cocker Spaniel | 105,236 |
| 2. Poodle | 85,400 |
| 3. Labrador Retriever | 81,987 |
| 4. Golden Retriever | 60,936 |
| 5. German Shepherd (Alsatian) | 57,612 |
| 6. Chow Chow | 49,096 |
| 7. Beagle | 41,972 |
| 8. Miniature Schnauzer | 41,462 |
| 9. Dachshund | 40,031 |
| 10. Shetland Sheepdog | 37,616 |

A pampered-looking poodle receives its final grooming before appearing at Cruft's.

# THE 10 MOST POPULAR BREEDS OF DOGS IN GREAT BRITAIN

| Breed | Number registered by Kennel Club |
|---|---|
| 1. German Shepherd (Alsatian) | 16,976 |
| 2. Labrador Retriever | 13,914 |
| 3. Golden Retriever | 11,290 |
| 4. Yorkshire Terrier | 10,241 |
| 5. Cavalier/King Charles Spaniel | 9,110 |
| 6. Rottweiler | 9,088 |
| 7. Cocker Spaniel | 6,490 |
| 8. Dobermann | 6,413 |
| 9. Staffordshire Bull Terrier | 6,233 |
| 10. English Springer Spaniel | 5,999 |

German Shepherds (Alsatians), one of the most popular breeds of dogs in Britain and the USA.

*This list represents only those dogs that are registered by the Kennel Club. An alternative Top 10 is that produced by the Gallup National Dog Survey:*

| | |
|---|---|
| 1. | Labrador Retriever |
| 2. | German Shepherd (Alsatian) |
| 3. | Jack Russell |
| 4. | Border Collie |
| 5. | Golden Retriever |
| 6. | Yorkshire Terrier |
| 7. | English Springer Spaniel |
| 8. | Cocker Spaniel |
| 9. | Poodle |
| 10. | Cavalier/King Charles Spaniel |

# THE 10 MOST POPULAR DOGS' NAMES IN GREAT BRITAIN

| | |
|---|---|
| 1. | Ben/Benny |
| 2. | Sam/Samuel/Sammy |
| 3. | Susie/Suzie/Sue |
| 4. | Benji/Bengy |
| 5. | Max/Maxwell |
| 6. | Lucy |
| 7. | Kim |
| 8. | Lady |
| 9. | Shelly |
| 10. | Judy |

*In the past decade there has been a definite move away from traditional dogs' names. Ten years ago, the Top 10 list included such evergreen (and specifically canine) names as Shep, Brandy, Whisky, Patch, Butch, Rex and, of course, Rover. Now most of the names could equally be those of people.*

# THE 10 MOST POPULAR DOGS' NAMES IN THE USA

| | |
|---|---|
| 1. | Lady |
| 2. | King |
| 3. | Duke |
| 4. | Peppy |
| 5. | Prince |
| 6. | Pepper |
| 7. | Snoopy |
| 8. | Princess |
| 9. | Heidi |
| 10= | Sam |
| 10= | Coco |

*A recent study of names appearing on dog licences in the USA produced a list that, with the exceptions of 'Lady' and 'Sam', is entirely different from the British Top 10. The same American list also exposed a number of bizarre dogs' names, including Beowulf, Bikini, Fag, Rembrandt and Twit.*

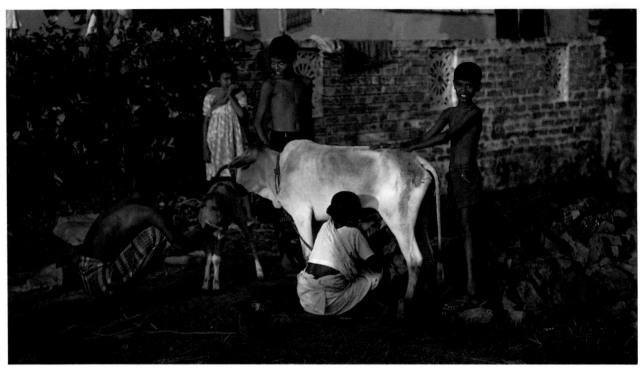

The cattle population in India numbers nearly 200,000,000.

## THE WORLD'S TOP 10 CATTLE COUNTRIES

| Country | Head of cattle |
|---------|---------------|
| 1. India | 199,300,000 |
| 2. Brazil | 131,503,000 |
| 3. USSR | 122,103,000 |
| 4. United States | 102,000,000 |
| 5. Argentina | 55,684,000 |
| 6. Mexico | 31,156,000 |
| 7. Ethiopia | 30,000,000 |
| 8. Colombia | 23,971,000 |
| 9. Bangladesh | 23,500,000 |
| 10. France | 22,803,000 |
| *United Kingdom* | *12,476,000* |

*The estimated world cattle population is 1,277,729,000.*

## THE WORLD'S TOP 10 EGG-PRODUCING COUNTRIES

| Country | Annual hen egg production |
|---------|---------------------------|
| 1. China | 102,833,000,000 |
| 2. USSR | 75,316,000,000 |
| 3. United States | 68,583,000,000 |
| 4. Japan | 39,250,000,000 |
| 5. Brazil | 18,333,000,000 |
| 6. India | 16,016,000,000 |
| 7. France | 15,000,000,000 |
| 8. Mexico | 14,333,000,000 |
| 9. West Germany | 12,416,000,000 |
| 10. United Kingdom | 12,266,000,000 |

*World total hen egg production is estimated to be 563,721,066,666.*

An egg market in China, the world's leading producer.

**ANIMALS & BIRDS**

# THE TOP 10 TYPES OF FISH CAUGHT BY BRITISH FISHERMEN

| Fish | Annual catch tonnes |
|------|--------------------:|
| 1.  Mackerel | 189,300 |
| 2.  Haddock | 102,100 |
| 3.  Herring | 100,300 |
| 4.  Cod | 92,500 |
| 5.  Whiting | 51,300 |
| 6.  Cockles | 39,000 |
| 7.  Plaice | 25,800 |
| 8.  Nephrop (Norway lobster) | 24,200 |
| 9.  Saithe (Coalfish) | 15,300 |
| 10. Dogfish | 13,600 |

A contribution to Britain's massive mackerel catch.

# THE WORLD'S TOP 10 MILK PRODUCERS

| Country | Annual production lit | pt |
|---------|---------------------:|---:|
| 1.  USSR | 102,879,897,049 | 181,043,388,600 |
| 2.  United States | 64,832,935,109 | 114,090,066,200 |
| 3.  France | 32,734,966,249 | 57,605,514,450 |
| 4.  West Germany | 24,747,975,238 | 43,550,367,240 |
| 5.  India | 17,699,982,292 | 31,147,628,100 |
| 6.  United Kingdom | 17,050,982,939 | 30,005,548,400 |
| 7.  Poland | 15,399,984,593 | 27,100,196,200 |
| 8.  Brazil | 12,349,987,644 | 21,732,949,550 |
| 9.  Netherlands | 11,671,988,319 | 20,539,837,010 |
| 10. Italy | 11,140,988,852 | 19,605,408,170 |

# THE WORLD'S TOP 10 CHICKEN COUNTRIES

| Country | Estimated chicken population |
|---------|----------------------------:|
| 1.  China | 1,796,000,000 |
| 2.  United States | 1,200,000,000 |
| 3.  USSR | 1,130,000,000 |
| 4.  Brazil | 520,000,000 |
| 5.  Indonesia | 400,000,000 |
| 6.  Japan | 351,000,000 |
| 7.  Mexico | 210,000,000 |
| 8.  France | 188,000,000 |
| 9= India | 175,000,000 |
| 9= Nigeria | 175,000,000 |
| *United Kingdom* | *119,000,000* |

*T*he world total chicken population is estimated to be 9,445,000,000 – almost twice the human population. In the United Kingdom chickens outnumber people more than twice over.

ANIMALS & BIRDS

A Chinese pig from the world's largest porcine population.

# THE WORLD'S TOP 10 PIG COUNTRIES

| | Country | Pigs |
|---|---|---|
| 1. | China | 344,248,000 |
| 2. | USSR | 79,501,000 |
| 3. | United States | 53,795,000 |
| 4. | Brazil | 32,000,000 |
| 5. | West Germany | 24,503,000 |
| 6. | Mexico | 18,662,000 |
| 7. | Poland | 18,546,000 |
| 8. | Romania | 14,711,000 |
| 9. | Netherlands | 14,349,000 |
| 10. | Spain | 14,000,000 |
| | *United Kingdom* | *7,955,000* |

*The estimated world pig population is 839,852,000.*

# THE WORLD'S TOP 10 SHEEP COUNTRIES

| | Country | Sheep |
|---|---|---|
| 1. | Australia | 159,177,000 |
| 2. | USSR | 142,210,000 |
| 3. | China | 99,009,000 |
| 4. | New Zealand | 66,400,000 |
| 5. | India | 55,482,000 |
| 6. | Turkey | 40,400,000 |
| 7. | Iran | 34,500,000 |
| 8. | South Africa | 29,728,000 |
| 9. | Argentina | 28,998,000 |
| 10. | Pakistan | 26,640,000 |
| 11. | *United Kingdom* | *25,976,000* |

Russian sheep comprise the largest flocks on earth.

*The world sheep population is estimated to be 1,157,643,000.*

# Human Body & Health

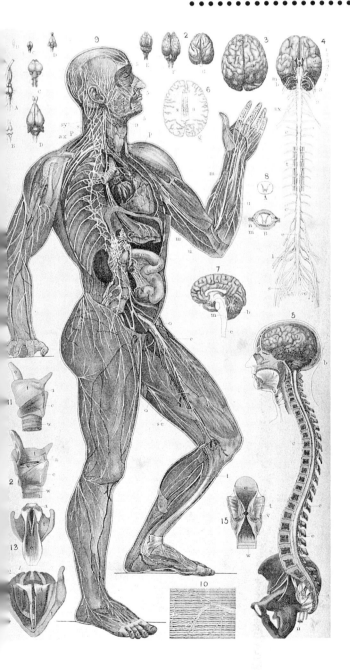

## THE 10 LARGEST HUMAN ORGANS

| Organ | | Weight g | oz |
|---|---|---|---|
| 1. Liver | | 1,560 | 55.0 |
| 2. Brain | male | 1,408 | 49.7 |
| | female | 1,263 | 44.6 |
| 3. Lungs | left | 510 | 18.0 |
| | right | 580 | 20.5 |
| | total | 1,090 | 38.5 |
| 4. Heart | male | 315 | 11.1 |
| | female | 265 | 9.3 |
| 5. Kidneys | left | 150 | 5.3 |
| | right | 140 | 4.9 |
| | total | 290 | 10.2 |
| 6. Spleen | | 170 | 6.0 |
| 7. Pancreas | | 98 | 3.4 |
| 8. Thyroid | | 35 | 1.2 |
| 9. Prostate | male only | 20 | .7 |
| 10. Adrenals | left | 6 | .2 |
| | right | 6 | .2 |
| | total | 12 | .4 |

*B*ased on average immediate post-mortem weights, as recorded by St Bartholemew's Hospital, London, and other sources during the past ten years. Various cases of organs far in excess of the average have been recorded, including male brains of over 2,000 g/70.5 oz.

The visible man and his principal parts.

# THE 10 COMMONEST AND STRANGEST PHOBIAS

1. Spiders (arachnephobia or arachnophobia)
2. People and social situations (anthropophobia or sociophobia)
3. Flying (aerophobia or aviatophobia)
4. Open space (agoraphobia, cenophobia or kenophobia)
5. Confined spaces (claustrophobia, cleisiophobia, cleithrophobia or clithrophobia)
6. Heights (acrophobia, altophobia, hypsophobia or hypsiphobia)
7. Cancer (carcinomaphobia, carcinophobia, carcinomatophobia, cancerphobia or cancerophobia)
8. Thunderstorms (brontophobia; related phobias are those associated with cyclones – anemophobia, and hurricanes and tornadoes – lilapsophobia)
9. Death (necrophobia or thanatophobia)
10. Heart disease (cardiophobia)

| |
| --- |
| Beards (pogonophobia) |
| Chickens (alektorophobia) |
| Chins (geniophobia) |
| Dolls (paedophobia) |
| Opening one's eyes (optophobia) |
| Eggshells (no scientific name) |
| Fish (ichthyophobia |
| Garlic (alliumphobia) |
| Purple (porphyrophobia) |
| Slime (blennophobia) |
| String (linonophobia) |
| Teeth (odontophobia) |
| The number thirteen (tridecaphobia, triakaidekaphobia or triskaidekaphobia) |

*A phobia is a morbid fear that is out of all proportion to the object of fear. There are many phobias that are much less common than those appearing in the Top 10. Often they arise from some incident in childhood when a person has been afraid of some object and has developed an irrational fear that persists into adulthood. Even if only one person has ever been observed with a specific phobia, psychologists have often given it a name – some more bizarre than others – as the next list shows:*

The fear of spiders is the commonest of all phobias.

*There are even several terms for the unfortunate condition of being afraid of everything: pantophobia, panophobia, panphobia or pamphobia. Nowadays, as well as the valuable work done by the Phobics' Society and other organizations, many phobias can be cured by taking special desensitization courses.*

## HUMAN BODY & HEALTH

"What shall we do with a drunken sailor?" – traditionally one of the heaviest-drinking occupations.

# THE 10 HEAVIEST-DRINKING OCCUPATIONS

| Occupational group | Mortality rate* |
|---|---|
| 1. Publicans | 1,017 |
| 2. Deck hands, engine-room hands, bargemen, lightermen, boatmen | 873 |
| 3. Barmen | 612 |
| 4. Ship engineering and radio officers and pilots | 417 |
| 5. Electrical engineers | 387 |
| 6. Hotel and residential club managers | 342 |
| 7. Innkeepers | 315 |
| 8. Fishermen | 296 |
| 9. Chefs and cooks | 265 |
| 10. Restaurateurs | 263 |

*base (average rate) = 100

*Research carried out over a number of years by the Office of Population Censuses and Surveys examined the number of people in various professions dying of liver cirrhosis – the classic disease of heavy drinkers. Taking the average as 100, it means that publicans are over ten times more likely to die from this cause than the average person. Such factors as access to drink at work, social and professional pressures and boredom all play their part in inclining members of such occupations to above-average drinking and its attendant health problems.*

# EUROPE'S 10 HEAVIEST-SMOKING NATIONS

| Country | Cigarettes per adult per annum |
|---|---|
| 1. Greece | 3,460 |
| 2. Poland | 3,300 |
| 3. Hungary | 3,260 |
| 4. Iceland | 3,100 |
| 5. Yugoslavia | 3,000 |
| 6. Switzerland | 2,960 |
| 7. Spain | 2,740 |
| 8= Austria | 2,560 |
| 8= Ireland | 2,560 |
| 10. Italy | 2,460 |
| *United Kingdom* | *2,120* |

*Figures are for the consumption of manufactured cigarettes by people aged 15 and over. The lowest annual consumption in Europe is that of Norway (710 per adult).*

The Greeks are Europe's heaviest smokers.

## HUMAN BODY & HEALTH

The lotions and potions of the chemists of yesteryear – a far cry from today's sophisticated pharmaceuticals.

# HEALTH SPENDING: THE 10 LEADING COUNTRIES

| | Country | Average annual health spending per person | |
|---|---|---|---|
| | | $ | £* |
| 1. | USA | 1,926 | 1,140 |
| 2. | Canada | 1,370 | 811 |
| 3. | Switzerland | 1,217 | 720 |
| 4. | Sweden | 1,195 | 707 |
| 5. | Iceland | 1,072 | 634 |
| 6. | France | 1,039 | 615 |
| 7. | West Germany | 1,031 | 610 |
| 8. | Norway | 1,021 | 604 |
| 9. | Netherlands | 984 | 582 |
| 10. | Luxembourg | 968 | 573 |
| | *United Kingdom* | *711* | *421* |

*calculated at rate prevailing in April 1989

*T*he USA not only spends the most per head on health care, but also the most as a percentage of Gross Domestic Product (11.8%, compared with the UK's 6.2%).

# THE 10 COUNTRIES WITH THE HIGHEST DOCTOR/PATIENT RATIO

| | Country | Doctors | Doctors per 1,000 population |
|---|---|---|---|
| 1. | Italy | 245,116 | 42.4 |
| 2. | USSR | 1,170,000* | 42.1 |
| 3. | Czechoslovakia | 55,871* | 35.5 |
| 4= | France | 173,116 | 31.9 |
| 4= | Hungary | 34,758* | 31.9 |
| 6. | Spain | 121,362 | 31.3 |
| 7. | Belgium | 29,776 | 30.2 |
| 8. | Israel | 11,895 | 29.0 |
| 9. | Greece | 28,212 | 28.5 |
| 10. | Bulgaria | 24,718 | 27.6 |
| | *United Kingdom* | *92,172* | *16.4* |

*T*he three countries marked * may not be as well off for doctors as the figures imply, since they include their dentists in the statistics (other countries list them separately). The worst ratios occur in such Third World countries as Ethiopia, where there are just 534 doctors – a ratio of 0.1 per 1,000 people.

## HUMAN BODY & HEALTH

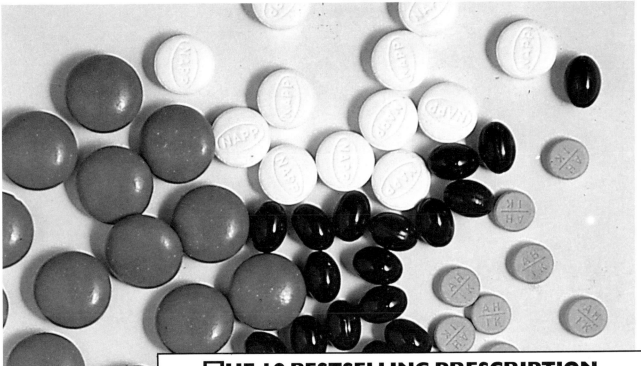

## THE 10 BESTSELLING PRESCRIPTION DRUGS IN THE WORLD

| | Brand name | Manufacturer | Prescribed for | Revenue $ | £* |
|---|---|---|---|---|---|
| 1. | Zantac | Glaxo/Sankyo | Ulcers | 1,479,000,000 | 875,000,000 |
| 2. | Tagamet | Smith Kline | Ulcers | 1,132,000,000 | 670,000,000 |
| 3. | Tenormin | ICI | High blood pressure | 867,000,000 | 513,000,000 |
| 4. | Capoten | Squibb | High blood pressure; heart failure | 779,000,000 | 461,000,000 |
| 5. | Vasotec | Merck & Co | High blood pressure; heart failure | 635,000,000 | 376,000,000 |
| 6. | Adalat | Bayer/Takeda | Angina; furring of arteries | 587,000,000 | 347,000,000 |
| 7. | Naprosyn | Syntex | Arthritis | 555,700,000 | 328,000,000 |
| 8. | Voltaren | Ciba-Geigy | Arthritis | 544,100,000 | 322,000,000 |
| 9. | Feldene | Pfizer | Arthritis | 524,000,000 | 310,000,000 |
| 10. | Ceclor | Eli Lilly | Infections | 515,000,000 | 305,000,000 |

*calculated at rate prevailing in April 1989

*T*he revenues of the international drug industry are among the world's largest. In 1987 the total income from the top 50 branded pharmaceutical products was $19,242,900,000,000 – more than the Gross Domestic Product of many large countries.

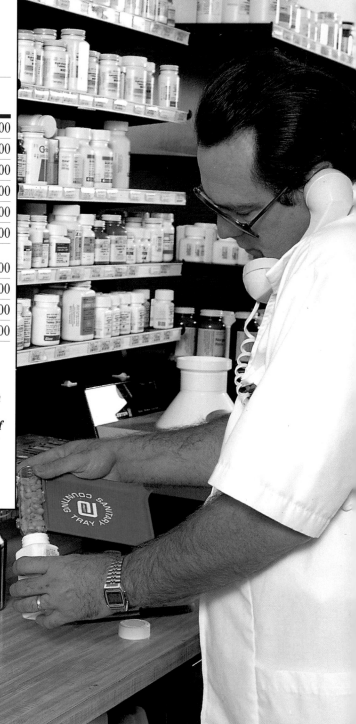

# THE 10 MOST POPULAR NON-PRESCRIPTION MEDICINES IN GREAT BRITAIN

| Medicine | Sales £ |
|---|---|
| 1. Vitamins | 144,000,000 |
| 2. Analgesics (painkillers such as aspirin) | 118,000,000 |
| 3. Sore throat remedies | 63,000,000 |
| 4. Cough remedies | 50,000,000 |
| 5. Cold remedies | 43,000,000 |
| 6. Indigestion remedies | 33,000,000 |
| 7. Skin treatments (other than acne products) | 26,000,000 |
| 8. Acne skin products | 20,000,000 |
| 9. Laxatives | 15,000,000 |
| 10. Stomach upset remedies | 14,000,000 |

*In 1988 we spent a total of £560,000,000 on non-prescription or 'over-the-counter' home remedies – approximately £10 for every person in the country. There is a noticeable increase in sales of cold and flu medicines when above average numbers of people succumb to such symptoms. Interestingly, after the BBC television QED programme suggested that vitamins contributed to increased intelligence among children, sales of vitamins generally increased by 12% and those of children's vitamins soared by 25%.*

## HUMAN BODY & HEALTH

Japanese men and women can look forward to the world's longest lifespans.

# THE 10 COUNTRIES WITH THE HIGHEST FEMALE LIFE EXPECTANCY

| Country | Life expectancy years |
|---|---|
| 1. Japan | 82.1 |
| 2. Switzerland | 81.0 |
| 3. Sweden | 80.2 |
| 4. France | 80.0 |
| 5= Canada | 79.9 |
| 5= Norway | 79.9 |
| 7= Netherlands | 79.8 |
| 7= Spain | 79.8 |
| 9. Australia | 79.6 |
| 10. Iceland | 79.0 |
| *United Kingdom* | *78.1* |

*T*he lowest female life expectancy is in Burkina Faso (formerly Upper Volta) – 31 years.

# THE 10 COUNTRIES WITH THE HIGHEST MALE LIFE EXPECTANCY

| Country | Life expectancy years |
|---|---|
| 1. Japan | 75.9 |
| 2. Iceland | 74.9 |
| 3. Greece | 74.1 |
| 4= Sweden | 74.0 |
| 4= Switzerland | 74.0 |
| 6. Israel | 73.4 |
| 7. Spain | 73.2 |
| 8= Canada | 73.1 |
| 8= Netherlands | 73.1 |
| 10. Australia | 73.0 |
| *United Kingdom* | *72.4* |

*T*he lowest male life expectancy is in Gabon – 25 years.

## HUMAN BODY & HEALTH

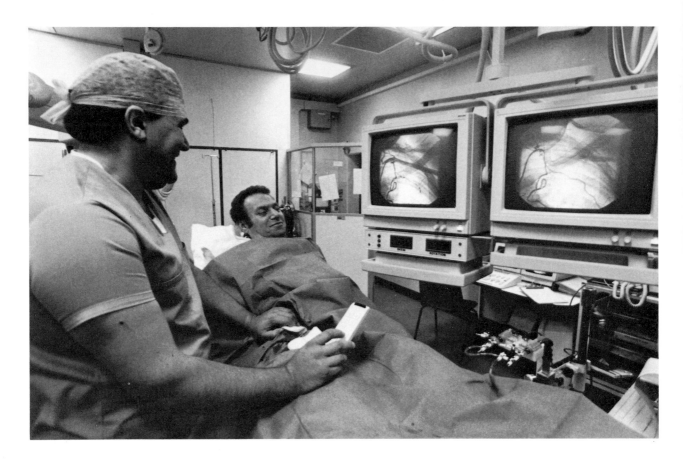

# THE 10 COMMONEST CAUSES OF DEATH IN THE UK

The most advanced technology can now be used to treat patients.

| Cause | England & Wales | Scotland | Northern Ireland | Total |
|---|---|---|---|---|
| 1. Diseases of circulatory system | 271,061 | 31,057 | 7,602 | 309,720 |
| 2. Cancer | 142,451 | 14,793 | 3,417 | 160,661 |
| 3. Diseases of respiratory system | 57,075 | 8,225 | 2,269 | 65,569 |
| 4. Accidents and violence | 17,823 | 2,686 | 762 | 21,271 |
| 5. Diseases of digestive system | 17,669 | 1,915 | 368 | 19,952 |
| 6. Mental disorders | 12,437 | 918 | 35 | 13,390 |
| 7. Diseases of nervous system | 10,953 | 788 | 174 | 11,915 |
| 8. Endocrine, nutritional and metabolic diseases and immunity disorders | 9,810 | 730 | 78 | 10,618 |
| 9. Diseases of the genito-urinary system | 7,696 | 842 | 237 | 8,775 |
| 10. Diseases of musculo-skeletal system | 5,192 | 252 | 46 | 5,490 |
| Totals: | 563,546 | 62,014 | 15,334 | 640,894 |

*Within category 1, heart disease is the principal killer (a UK total of 178,178); in category 2, lung cancer killed the most – 40,187 in 1987; in category 4, motor vehicle accidents account for most deaths (5,646).*

## HUMAN BODY & HEALTH

# DEATHS FROM HEART ATTACK: THE LEADING EUROPEAN NATIONS

| | Country | Death rate* per 100,000 population |
|---|---|---|
| 1. | Irish Republic | 89.25 |
| 2. | Finland | 82.73 |
| 3. | United Kingdom | 74.99 |
| 4. | Denmark | 58.81 |
| 5. | Norway | 58.61 |
| 6. | Sweden | 50.83 |
| 7. | Netherlands | 48.13 |
| 8. | Luxembourg | 45.04 |
| 9. | West Germany | 44.70 |
| 10. | Belgium | 39.49 |

*F*rance has one of the lowest rates – 21.35 per 100,000.

*Calculated on an annual basis

# THE TOP 10 DEATH RATES IN THE UK BY AGE GROUP

| | Age group | Deaths* per 1,000 |
|---|---|---|
| 1. | Males aged over 85 | 194.3 |
| 2. | Females aged over 85 | 159.9 |
| 3. | Males aged 75–84 | 97.3 |
| 4. | Females aged 75–84 | 60.8 |
| 5. | Males aged 65–74 | 42.0 |
| 6. | Females aged 65–74 | 23.3 |
| 7. | Males aged 55–64 | 16.4 |
| 8. | Males aged under 1 | 10.3 |
| 9. | Females aged 55–64 | 9.4 |
| 10. | Females aged under 1 | 7.9 |

*I*t is hardly surprising to find that old people are more likely to die than young people, but it is interesting to see that the relatively greater likelihood of males dying than females in the same age group remains consistent. It is similarly true for age groups not in the Top 10, except the age group 5–14, where the likelihood of death is equal.

# DEATHS FROM LUNG CANCER: THE 10 LEADING EUROPEAN NATIONS

| | Country | Death rate* per 100,000 population |
|---|---|---|
| 1. | Denmark | 26.49 |
| 2. | Belgium | 26.17 |
| 3. | United Kingdom | 24.47 |
| 4. | Netherlands | 23.83 |
| 5. | Irish Republic | 23.54 |
| 6. | Luxembourg | 22.98 |
| 7. | Finland | 18.26 |
| 8. | Greece | 18.22 |
| 9. | France | 17.47 |
| 10. | West Germany | 17.21 |

Scanning for cancer.

## THE 10 COMMONEST METHODS OF SUICIDE (ENGLAND & WALES)

| Method | Men | Women | Total |
|---|---|---|---|
| 1. Hanging, strangulation and suffocation | 967 | 295 | 1,262 |
| 2. Poisoning (liquids and solids) | 507 | 562 | 1,069 |
| 3. Poisoning (gases and vapours) | 760 | 88 | 848 |
| 4. Unspecified injury | 184 | 84 | 268 |
| 5. Drowning | 88 | 110 | 198 |
| 6. Injury by firearms or explosive | 183 | 11 | 194 |
| 7. Jumping from high place | 110 | 71 | 181 |
| 8. Injury by cutting or piercing instruments | 74 | 23 | 97 |
| 9. Poison by domestic gas | 6 | 1 | 7 |
| 10. After-effects of some earlier self-inflicted injury | 1 | 1 | 2 |
| Totals: | 2,880 | 1,246 | 4,126 |

## THE 10 MOST SUICIDAL NATIONS IN EUROPE

| Country | Rate per 100,000 population |
|---|---|
| 1. Denmark | 28.19 |
| 2. Finland | 24.75 |
| 3. Belgium | 22.65 |
| 4. France | 21.30 |
| 5. West Germany | 18.63 |
| 6. Sweden | 17.22 |
| 7. Norway | 14.52 |
| 8. Luxembourg | 14.27 |
| 9. Netherlands | 12.52 |
| 10. Portugal | 9.86 |
| *United Kingdom* | *8.53* |

The Romantic way to go: J.E. Millais's haunting painting depicting Ophelia's death by drowning.

Open 24 hours a day.

## THE SAMARITANS' 10 BUSIEST BRANCHES IN THE BRITISH ISLES

1. Central London
2. Dublin
3. Leeds
4. Manchester
5. Glasgow
6. Edinburgh
7. Birmingham
8. Hull
9. Newcastle
10. Liverpool

*The Samaritans was founded in 1953 by Prebendary Dr Chard Varah, OBE, to provide advice and counselling to the suicidal and desperate. Their switchboards are staffed 24 hours a day by some 20,000 volunteers.*

Help at the end of the line: a poster for the Samaritans.

# The Samaritans

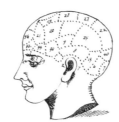

# Human Activities
# & Achievements

## THE 10 OLDEST TITLES IN BRITAIN

| Title | Date created |
|---|---|
| 1. Earl of Mar | 1115 |
| 2. Baron de Ros | 12 December 1264 |
| 3. Baron Mowbray and Stourton | 28 June 1283 |
| 4. Baron Hastings | before 1290 |
| 5. Baron Clinton | 6 February 1298 |
| 6= Baron de Clifford | 29 December 1299 |
| 6= Baron Strange of Knokin | 29 December 1299 |
| 8. Baron Zouche | 16 August 1308 |
| 9. Baron Beaumont | 4 March 1309 |
| 10. Baron Audley | 8 January 1313 |

*The Earldom of Mar is the premier earldom of Scotland. The current holder, Margaret, Countess of Mar, is the 31st to bear the title.*

## THE 10 OLDEST DUKEDOMS IN BRITAIN

| Dukedom | Order of succession | Date created |
|---|---|---|
| 1. Norfolk | 17th | 28 June 1483 |
| 2. Somerset | 19th | 16 February 1547 |
| 3. Richmond (Lennox and Gordon) | 9th | 9 August 1675 |
| 4. Grafton | 11th | 11 September 1675 |
| 5. Beaufort | 11th | 2 December 1682 |
| 6. St Albans | 13th | 10 January 1684 |
| 7. Bedford | 13th | 11 May 1694 |
| 8. Devonshire | 11th | 12 May 1694 |
| 9. Marlborough | 11th | 14 December 1702 |
| 10. Rutland | 10th | 29 March 1703 |

SOLA   VIRTUS   INVICTA

LEFT The arms of the Duke of Norfolk, founder of Britain's oldest-established dukedom.

RIGHT The 1st Duke of Norfolk.

## THE 10 YOUNGEST BRITISH MONARCHS

| | Monarch | Reign | Age at accession years | months |
|---|---|---|---|---|
| 1. | Henry VI | 1422–61 | 0 | 8 |
| 2. | Henry III | 1216–72 | 9 | 1 |
| 3. | Edward VI | 1547–53 | 9 | 3 |
| 4. | Richard II | 1377–99 | 10 | 5 |
| 5. | Edward V | 1483 | 12 | 5 |
| 6. | Edward III | 1327–77 | 14 | 2 |
| 7. | Jane | 1553 | 15 | 8 |
| 8. | Henry VIII | 1509–47 | 17 | 10 |
| 9. | Victoria | 1837–1901 | 18 | 1 |
| 10. | Charles II | 1649–85 | 18 | 8 |

## THE 10 OLDEST MONARCHS TO ASCEND THE BRITISH THRONE

| | Monarch | Reign | Age at accession |
|---|---|---|---|
| 1. | William IV | 1830–37 | 64 |
| 2. | Edward VII | 1901–10 | 59 |
| 3. | George IV | 1820–30 | 57 |
| 4. | George I | 1714–27 | 54 |
| 5. | James II | 1685–88 | 51 |
| 6. | George V | 1910–36 | 44 |
| 7. | George II | 1727–60 | 43 |
| 8. | George VI | 1936–52 | 40 |
| 9. | William I | 1066–87 | 39 |
| 10. | William III | 1689–1702 | 38 |

LEFT Henry III's ascent to the throne at the age of nine has been beaten only by the infant Henry VI.

# THE WORLD'S 10 LONGEST-REIGNING MONARCHS

| | Monarch | Country | Reign | Age at accession | Reign years |
|---|---|---|---|---|---|
| 1. | Louis XIV | France | 1643–1715 | 5 | 72 |
| 2. | John II | Liechtenstein | 1858–1929 | 18 | 71 |
| 3. | Franz-Josef | Austria-Hungary | 1848–1916 | 18 | 67 |
| 4. | Victoria | Great Britain | 1837–1901 | 18 | 64 |
| 5. | Hirohito | Japan | 1926–89 | 25 | 62 |
| 6. | George III | Great Britain | 1760–1820 | 22 | 60 |
| 7. | Louis XV | France | 1715–74 | 5 | 59 |
| 8= | Pedro II | Brazil | 1831–89 | 6 | 58 |
| 8= | Wilhelmina | Netherlands | 1890–1948 | 10 | 58 |
| 10. | Henry III | England | 1216–72 | 9 | 56 |

*S*ome authorities have claimed a 73-year reign for Alfonso I of Portugal, but his father, Henry of Burgundy, who conquered Portugal, ruled as Count, and it was this title that Alfonso inherited on 30 April 1112 – at the age of two. His mother, Theresa of Castile, ruled until he took power in 1128, but he did not assume the title of King until 25 July 1139 during the Battle of Ourique at which he vanquished the Moors. He thus ruled as king for 46 years until his death on 6 December 1185. Even more extravagant claims are sometimes made for long-reigning monarchs in the ancient world, such as the alleged 94 years of Phiops II, a 6th-dynasty Egyptian Pharaoh, but since it is uncertain when he was either born or died, he has not been included.

FAR LEFT The 'Sun King', Louis XIV of France, the longest-reigning monarch of all time.

LEFT George III, just pipped to the post as Britain's longest-lived monarch.

# THE 10 LONGEST-REIGNING BRITISH MONARCHS

| | Monarch | Reign | Age at accession | Age at death | Reign years |
|---|---|---|---|---|---|
| 1. | Victoria | 1837–1901 | 18 | 81 | 63 |
| 2. | George III | 1760–1820 | 22 | 81 | 59 |
| 3. | Henry III | 1216–72 | 9 | 64 | 56 |
| 4. | Edward III | 1327–77 | 14 | 64 | 50 |
| 5. | Elizabeth I | 1558–1603 | 25 | 69 | 44 |
| 6. | Henry VI | 1422-61 (deposed – d.1471) | 8 months | 49 | 39 |
| 7. | Henry VIII | 1509–47 | 17 | 55 | 38 |
| 8. | Elizabeth II | 1952– | 25 | – | 37 |
| 9. | Charles II | 1649–85 | 19 | 54 | 36 |
| 10. | Henry I | 1100–35 | 31/32* | 66/67 | 35 |

Still 14 years to go: Queen Victoria at the time of her Diamond Jubilee in 1887.

*Henry I's birthdate is unknown, so his age at accession and death are uncertain.

*T*his list excludes the reigns of monarchs before 1066, so omits such rulers as Ethelred II and his 37-year reign. Queen Elizabeth II has recently displaced Charles II from 8th position and pushed Edward I's 34-year reign out of the Top 10. If she is still on the throne on 11 September 2015, she will have beaten Queen Victoria's record by one day. She will then be 89 years old.

# THE 10 LONGEST-LIVED BRITISH MONARCHS

| | Monarch | Born | Reign | Age at death |
|---|---|---|---|---|
| 1. | Victoria | 1819 | 1837–1901 | 81 |
| 2. | George III | 1738 | 1760–1820 | 81 |
| 3. | Edward VIII | 1894 | 1936 (abdicated) | 77 |
| 4. | George II | 1683 | 1727–60 | 76 |
| 5. | William IV | 1765 | 1830–37 | 71 |
| 6. | George V | 1865 | 1910–36 | 70 |
| 7. | Elizabeth I | 1533 | 1558–1603 | 69 |
| 8. | Edward VII | 1841 | 1901–10 | 68 |
| 9. | Edward I | 1239 | 1272–1307 | 68 |
| 10. | James II | 1633 | 1685–88 | 67 |

*Q*ueen Victoria and George III are close rivals for the title of longest-lived British monarch, and George's dates might suggest that he lived slightly longer than Victoria. However, during his lifetime, in 1752, the Gregorian Calendar was adopted in Great Britain, as a result of which 11 days were lost. Taking this into account, Queen Victoria lived for 81 years 243 days and George III for 81 years 239 days. The difference between the lifetimes of Edward VII and Edward I is also very slight, with Edward VII the winner by just six months; furthermore, there is just a two-month difference between the lengths of reign of Edward I and James II, who ranks 10th.

## HUMAN ACTIVITIES & ACHIEVEMENTS

# BRITAIN'S 10 SHORTEST-REIGNING MONARCHS

| Monarch | Reign | Duration |
|---------|-------|----------|
| 1. Jane | 1553 | 14 days |
| 2. Edward V | 1483 | 75 days |
| 3. Edward VIII | 1936 | 325 days |
| 4. Richard III | 1483–85 | 2 years |
| 5. James II | 1685–88 | 3 years |
| 6. Mary I | 1553–58 | 5 years |
| 7. Mary II | 1689–94 | 5 years |
| 8. Edward VI | 1547–53 | 6 years |
| 9. William IV | 1830–37 | 7 years |
| 10. Edward VII | 1901–10 | 9 years |

# THE TOP 10 IN LINE TO THE BRITISH THRONE

1. HRH The Prince of Wales
   (Prince Charles Philip Arthur George)
   b. 14 November 1948

2. HRH Prince William of Wales
   (Prince William Arthur Philip Louis)
   b. 21 June 1982

3. HRH Prince Henry of Wales
   (Prince Henry Charles Albert David)
   b. 15 September 1984

4. HRH The Duke of York
   (Prince Andrew Albert Christian Edward)
   b. 19 February 1960

5. HRH Princess Beatrice of York
   (Princess Beatrice Elizabeth Mary)
   b. 8 August 1988

6. HRH Prince Edward
   (Prince Edward Antony Richard Louis)
   b. 10 March 1964

7. HRH The Princess Royal
   (Princess Anne Elizabeth Alice Louise)
   b. 15 August 1950

8. Master Peter Mark Andrew Phillips
   b. 15 November 1977

9. Miss Zara Anne Elizabeth Phillips
   b. 15 May 1981

10. HRH Princess Margaret, Countess of Snowdon
    (Princess Margaret Rose)
    b. 21 August 1930

*T*he birth in 1988 of Princess Beatrice altered the order of succession, ousting David Albert Charles Armstrong-Jones, Viscount Linley (b. 3 November 1961), from the number 10 position.

RIGHT New in at number five: Princess Beatrice plus proud parents The Duke and Duchess of York.

ABOVE LEFT Lady Jane Grey, Britain's shortest-reigning monarch.

LEFT Edward V, whose reign was only 61 days longer than Lady Jane's.

# THE 10 BEST-PAID MEMBERS OF THE ROYAL FAMILY

|   |   | 1988/89 | £ | 1989/90 |
|---|---|---|---|---|
| 1. | The Queen | 4,500,000 | | 4,658,000 |
| 2. | The Queen Mother | 390,300 | | 404,000 |
| 3. | The Duke of Edinburgh | 217,700 | | 225,300 |
| 4. | The Duke of York | 86,500 | | 155,400 |
| 5. | The Duke of Kent | 143,500 | | 148,500 |
| 6. | Princess Alexandra | 136,800 | | 141,600 |
| 7. | The Princess Royal | 135,600 | | 140,400 |
| 8. | Princess Margaret | 132,100 | | 136,700 |
| 9. | The Duke of Gloucester | 106,300 | | 110,000 |
| 10. | Princess Alice, Duchess of Gloucester | 53,500 | | 55,400 |

*T*he Civil List is not technically the Royal Family's 'pay', but the allowance made by the Government for their staff and costs incurred in the course of performing their public duties. The amount is announced annually at the time of the Budget. Of the total Civil List allocation of £5,795,200 for 1989 (£5,535,700 in 1988), the Queen refunds £400,100 (£386,600 in 1988). Prince Edward is number 11 on the list, receiving £20,000 (unchanged since 1988). The Prince of Wales receives nothing from the Civil List, his income deriving largely from the Duchy of Cornwall.

LEFT The Queen, the principal recipient from the Civil List.

FAR LEFT Prince Charles, first in line to the British throne.

# THE 10 LONGEST-SERVING MEMBERS OF PARLIAMENT

| Member of Parliament/ years in office | Constituency | Total years in office |
|---|---|---|
| 1. Sir Francis Knollys 1572–88 1597–1648 | Oxfordshire Berkshire | 67 |
| 2. Rt. Hon. Charles Pelham Villiers 1835–98 | Wolverhampton | 63 |
| 3. Sir Winston Churchill 1900–06 1906–22 1924–45 1945–64 | Oldham NW Manchester Epping Woodford | 62 |
| 4= William Aislabie 1721–81 | Ripon | 60 |
| 4= Christopher R. M. Talbot 1830–90 | Mid-Glamorganshire | 60 |
| 6. Sir John Aubrey 1768–1826 | (Seven different constituencies) | 58 |
| 7. Sir Charles Burrell 1806–62 | Shoreham | 56 |
| 8. Philips Gybbon 1707–62 | Rye, Sussex | 55 |
| 9. Hon. Henry Lowther 1812–67 | Westmorland | 55 |
| 10= Sir John Rushout 1713–68 | Malmesbury | 54 |
| 10= David Lloyd George 1890–1945 | Caernarvon | 54 |
| 10= Clement Tudway 1761–1815 | Wells | 54 |

ABOVE Sir Robert Walpole.

# THE 10 LONGEST-SERVING PRIME MINISTERS

| Prime Minister/dates | Periods in office | Total duration Years | months* |
|---|---|---|---|
| 1. Sir Robert Walpole (1676–1745) | 3 Apr 1721–8 Feb 1742 | 20 | 10 |
| 1. William Pitt the Younger (1759–1806) | 19 Dec 1783–14 Mar 1801<br>10 May 1804–23 Jan 1806 | 18 | 11 |
| 2. Earl of Liverpool (1770–1828) | 7 Jun 1812–17 Feb 1827 | 14 | 8 |
| 3. Marquess of Salisbury (1830–1903) | 23 Jun 1885–11 Aug 1892<br>25 Jun 1895–11 Jul 1902 | 13 | 9 |
| 4. William Gladstone (1809–98) | 4 Dec 1868–17 Feb 1874<br>23 Apr 1880–9 Jun 1885<br>1 Feb 1886–20 Jul 1886<br>15 Aug 1892–2 Mar 1894 | 12 | 4 |
| 5. Lord North (1732–79) | 28 Jan 1770–20 Mar 1782 | 12 | 2 |
| 6. Margaret Thatcher (1925– ) | 4 May 1979– | 10 | 0† |
| 7. Viscount Palmerston (1784–1865) | 6 Feb 1855–21 Feb 1858<br>12 Jun 1859–18 Oct 1865 | 9 | 5 |
| 8. Herbert Asquith (1852–1928) | 5 Apr 1908–5 Dec 1916<br>(coalition from 25 May 1915) | 8 | 8 |
| 9. Winston Churchill (1874–1965) | 10 May 1940–26 Jul 1945<br>(coalition – 23 May 1945)<br>26 Oct 1951–5 Apr 1955 | 8 | 8 |
| 10. Harold Wilson (1916– ) | 16 Oct 1964–19 Jun 1970<br>4 Mar 1974–5 Apr 1976 | 7 | 9 |

*total duration calculated to nearest month
†to June 1989

William Pitt.

Harold Wilson.

**S**ir Robert Walpole is usually regarded as the first Prime Minister, although the office was not officially recognized until 1905, most earlier Prime Ministers deriving their authority from their position as First Lords of the Treasury. It is arguable whether Walpole's ministry should be dated from the time he became First Lord of the Treasury and Chancellor of the Exchequer in 1721, or from 15 May 1730 when his brother-in-law, Lord Townshend, resigned as Secretary of State (in order to devote the remainder of his life to turnip farming!), leaving him in sole control of the Cabinet. Even if, on this basis, he is disqualified from the No. 1 position, his ministry from 1730 until 1742 still entitles him to 6th position.

FAR LEFT Winston Churchill.

CENTRE The Marquess of Salisbury.

ABOVE LEFT William Gladstone.

LEFT Viscount Palmerston.

# THE 10 MPs WITH THE LARGEST MAJORITIES*

| | Member of Parliament | Party | Constituency | Majority |
|---|---|---|---|---|
| 1. | Allan R. Rogers | Lab. | Rhondda | 30,754 |
| 2. | Edward Rowlands | Lab. | Merthyr Tydfil & Rhymney | 28,207 |
| 3. | Michael M. Foot | Lab. | Blaenau Gwent | 27,861 |
| 4. | John Major | Con. | Huntingdon | 27,044 |
| 5. | Patrick T. Cormack | Con. | Staffordshire South | 25,268 |
| 6. | John S. Cummings | Lab. | Easington | 24,639 |
| 7. | Allan Roberts | Lab. | Bootle | 24,477 |
| 8. | David Blunkett | Lab. | Sheffield Brightside | 24,191 |
| 9. | Sir Peter Hordern | Con. | Horsham | 23,907 |
| 10. | Michael J. Mates | Con. | Hampshire East | 23,786 |
| | *Margaret Hilda Thatcher* | *Con.* | *Finchley* | *8,913* |

*at the 11 June 1987 General Election

*The smallest majorities at the 1987 General Election were those of Alan Meale (Labour MP for Mansfield) and Richard Livsey (SLD MP for Brecon & Radnor), both of whom had majorities of just 56 votes. The highest ever majority was the 62,253 of Sir Cooper Rawson (Conservative MP for Brighton in 1931). Single vote majorities have been recorded more than once.*

# THE WORLD'S FIRST 10 FEMALE PRIME MINISTERS AND PRESIDENTS

| | Name | Country | Period in office |
|---|---|---|---|
| 1. | Sirimavo Bandaranaike (PM) | Ceylon (Sri Lanka) | 1960–64 1970–77 |
| 2. | Indira Gandhi (PM) | India | 1966–84 |
| 3. | Golda Meir (PM) | Israel | 1969–74 |
| 4. | Maria Estela Perón (President) | Argentina | 1974–75 |
| 5. | Elizabeth Domitien (PM) | Central African Republic | 1975– |
| 6. | Margaret Thatcher (PM) | United Kingdom | 1979– |
| 7. | Dr Maria Lurdes Pintasilgo (PM) | Portugal | 1979 (Aug–Nov) |
| 8. | Vigdis Finbogadottir (President) | Iceland | 1980– |
| 9. | Mary Eugenia Charles (PM) | Dominica | 1980– |
| 10. | Gro Harlem Brundtland (PM) | Norway | 1981 (Feb–Oct) 1986– |

*Mrs Bandaranaike of Sri Lanka (then called Ceylon), became the world's first female Prime Minister on 21 July 1960; Mrs Thatcher became Britain's first on 4 May 1979. The first ten have been followed by Corazón Aquino, who became President of the Philippines in 1986, and by Benazir Bhutto, Prime Minister of Pakistan (1988– ).*

Mrs Bandaranaike, the world's first woman Prime Minister.

# HUMAN ACTIVITIES & ACHIEVEMENTS

## VOTES FOR WOMEN: THE FIRST 10 COUNTRIES TO GIVE WOMEN THE VOTE

| Country | Year |
|---|---|
| 1. New Zealand | 1893 |
| 2. Australia (South Australia, 1894; Western Australia, 1898; Australia was united in 1901) | 1902 |
| 3. Finland (then a Grand Duchy under the Russian Crown) | 1906 |
| 4. Norway (restricted franchise 1907, all women over 25: 1913) | 1907 |
| 5. Denmark and Iceland (a Danish dependency until 1918) | 1915 |
| 6= USSR | 1917 |
| 6= Netherlands | 1917 |
| 8= Great Britain and Ireland (Ireland part of the UK until 1921; women over 30 only, 1918 – lowered to 21 in 1928) | 1918 |
| 8= Poland | 1918 |
| 8= Austria | 1918 |
| 8= Germany | 1918 |
| 8= Canada | 1918 |

*A*lthough not a country, the Isle of Man was the first place to give women the vote, in 1880. Until 1920 the only other European countries to enfranchise women were Sweden in 1919, and Czechoslovakia in 1920. Certain states of the USA gave women the vote at earlier dates (Wyoming in 1869, Colorado in 1894, Utah in 1895 and Idaho in 1896), but it was not granted nationally until 1920. A number of countries, such as France and Italy, did not give women the vote until 1945. Switzerland did not allow women to vote in elections to the Federal Council until 1971, and Liechtenstein was one of the last to relent, in 1984. In Saudi Arabia women are not allowed to vote at all – but neither can men.

TOP American Suffragettes march for the right to vote.

## HUMAN ACTIVITIES & ACHIEVEMENTS

# THE 10 LONGEST ENTRIES IN *WHO'S WHO*

| | Name | Occupation | Number of lines |
|---|---|---|---|
| 1. | Barbara Cartland | Author | 150 |
| 2. | Sir Peter Maxwell-Davies | Composer | 98 |
| 3. | Lord (Laurence) Olivier | Actor | 82 |
| 4. | Sir Karl Popper | Philosopher | 70 |
| 5= | Sir John Gielgud | Actor | 68 |
| 5= | Alan Bush | Composer, conductor, pianist | 68 |
| 7. | Eleanor Hibbert | Author | 64 |
| 8. | Professor William Mathias | Composer, conductor, pianist | 60 |
| 9= | John Frederick Harris | Curator | 55 |
| 9= | Sir Peter Hall | Theatre director | 55 |

*T*he publishers of **Who's Who** *include whatever data they receive from those eminent enough to be included. If authors with many books to their credit list them all, their entries tend to be very long. Barbara Cartland, Britain's most prolific romantic novelist, consequently has an entry some 38 cm/15 in long, more than twice that of Eleanor Hibbert, another novelist who writes under several pseudonyms, including Jean Plaidy and Victoria Holt. For comparison, Margaret Thatcher, Britain's first female Prime Minister, has a listing of just ten lines.*

# THE TOP 10 ACTIVITIES DURING A WORKING DAY

| | MEN | | |
|---|---|---|---|
| | Activity | hr | min |
| 1. | Sleeping | 7 | 43 |
| 2. | Working | 6 | 7 |
| 3. | Watching TV | 1 | 40 |
| 4. | Eating | 1 | 29 |
| 5. | Personal care | | 59 |
| 6. | Travel (other than commuting) | | 44 |
| 7. | Commuting | | 42 |
| 8. | Visiting | | 32 |
| 9. | Misc. household chores | | 29 |
| 10. | Reading newspaper | | 25 |

| | WOMEN | | |
|---|---|---|---|
| | Activity | hr | min |
| 1. | Sleeping | 7 | 47 |
| 2. | Working | 4 | 45 |
| 3. | Misc. household chores | 1 | 26 |
| 4. | Personal care | 1 | 17 |
| 5. | Eating | 1 | 12 |
| 6. | Watching TV | 1 | 3 |
| 7. | Cooking | | 48 |
| 8. | Visiting | | 39 |
| 9. | Travel (other than commuting) | | 42 |
| 10. | Commuting | | 30 |

*T*hese are the average times *spent on each activity by average employed people in the USA. The results are strange because in order to arrive at average figures, activities that occupy people only occasionally are included. Consequently, because few people visit the theatre regularly and some never go at all, we get an average figure for time spent at the theatre of one minute per day! And the leading 'activity' is sleeping . . .*

Novelist Barbara Cartland, whose entry in *Who's Who* runs to 150 lines.

## HUMAN ACTIVITIES & ACHIEVEMENTS

### THE 10 MOST IRRITATING MEN IN THE PUBLIC EYE

1. Derek Jameson
2. Terry Wogan
3. Arthur Scargill
4. Neil Kinnock
5. Paul Daniels
6. Bob Monkhouse
7. Barry Humphries
8. Jonathan Ross
9. Denis Thatcher
10. Ronald Reagan

### THE 10 MOST IRRITATING WOMEN IN THE PUBLIC EYE

1. Margaret Thatcher
2. Edwina Currie
3. Anne Diamond
4. The Duchess of York
5. Joan Collins
6. Anneka Rice
7. Su Pollard
8. Janet Street-Porter
9. Mary Whitehouse
10. Esther Rantzen

Based on *Slimming Magazine*'s 'Slimming Survey', 1988/89.

FAR RIGHT Twice as stunning or twice as irritating? Joan Collins ×2.

RIGHT A tearful crowning for Miss World 1977.

### THE 10 MOST STUNNING WOMEN IN THE PUBLIC EYE

1. The Princess of Wales
2. Elizabeth Taylor
3. Joan Collins
4. Victoria Principal
5. Cher
6. Linda Lusardi
7. Sophia Loren
8. Cybill Shepherd
9. Jane Seymour
10. Raquel Welch

### THE 10 SEXIEST MEN IN THE PUBLIC EYE

1. Tom Selleck
2. Richard Gere
3. Mel Gibson
4. Cliff Richard
5. Robert Redford
6. Paul Newman
7. Don Johnson
8. Sean Connery
9. Tom Cruise
10. Marty Pellow

### THE TOP 10 'MISS WORLD' COUNTRIES

| Country | Wins |
|---|---|
| 1. United Kingdom 1961, 64, 65, 74*, 83 | 5 |
| 2= Sweden 1951, 52, 77 | 3 |
| 2= Venezuela 1955, 81, 84 | 3 |
| 4= South Africa 1958, 74* | 2 |
| 4= Netherlands 1959, 62 | 2 |
| 4= Argentina 1960, 78 | 2 |
| 4= Jamaica 1963, 76 | 2 |
| 4= Australia 1968, 72 | 2 |
| 4= Austria 1969, 87 | 2 |
| 4= Iceland 1985, 88 | 2 |

*Helen Morgan later resigned and was replaced by Anneline Kriel of South Africa.

*W*est Germany would also have won twice, in 1956 and 1989, but in the latter contest Gabriella Brum was sacked after 18 hours, the shortest reign of any Miss World. Twelve other countries have each won once.

Irritating: Jameson.

Irritating: Mrs T.

Sexy: Tom Selleck.

Stunning: Princess Di.

## HUMAN ACTIVITIES & ACHIEVEMENTS

# THE TOP 10 GIRLS' AND BOYS' NAMES ANNOUNCED IN THE BIRTHS COLUMN OF *THE TIMES*

### FIRST NAME ONLY

| | Girls' names | No. | Boys' names | No. |
|---|---|---|---|---|
| 1= | Alice | 85 | James | 184 |
| 1= | Charlotte | 85 | Thomas | 176 |
| 3. | Sophie | 80 | William | 127 |
| 4= | Emma | 66 | Alexander | 124 |
| 4= | Emily | 66 | Edward | 100 |
| 6. | Lucy | 60 | Charles | 96 |
| 7= | Katherine | 59 | Oliver | 85 |
| 7= | Harriet | 59 | Nicholas | 78 |
| 9. | Alexandra | 56 | Christopher | 63 |
| 10. | Sarah | 54 | Henry/Robert | 55 |

### ALL NAMES (INCLUDING MIDDLE NAMES)

| | Girls' names | No. | Boys' names | No. |
|---|---|---|---|---|
| 1. | Elizabeth | 231 | James | 412 |
| 2. | Louise | 159 | William | 267 |
| 3. | Alice | 141 | Alexander | 237 |
| 4. | Charlotte | 139 | Thomas | 226 |
| 5. | Mary | 108 | Edward | 200 |
| 6. | Sophie | 102 | Charles | 198 |
| 7. | Rose | 99 | John | 197 |
| 8. | Alexandra | 96 | David | 147 |
| 9. | Lucy | 94 | Henry | 145 |
| 10. | Victoria | 91 | George | 132 |

*S*ince 1948, various people have carefully monitored the Births column of The Times *and listed the frequency of given names. In 1988 the paper listed 5,531 births – 2,659 girls and 2,872 boys.*

# THE TEN COMMONEST SURNAMES IN GREAT BRITAIN

1. Smith
2. Jones
3. Williams
4. Brown
5. Taylor
6. Davies/Davis
7. Evans
8. Thomas
9. Roberts
10. Johnson

# THE 10 COMMONEST SURNAMES IN THE USA

1. Smith
2. Johnson
3. Williams/Williamson
4. Brown
5. Jones
6. Miller
7. Davis
8. Martin/Martinez/ Martinson
9. Anderson
10. Wilson

## HUMAN ACTIVITIES & ACHIEVEMENTS

# THE 10 MOST POPULAR PET NAMES WOMEN USE FOR THEIR PARTNERS

1. Babes
2. Honey
3. Honeybunch
4. Puddin'
5. Cuddles
6. Sugar
7. Sexy Beast
8. Poochie
9. Sweetie
10. Petal

Based on *True Romances Magazine*'s 'True Romance Survey', 1988.

# THE 10 MOST POPULAR PET NAMES MEN USE FOR THEIR PARTNERS

1. Babes
2. Fatty
3. Petal
4. Darling
5. Sexy
6. Puddin'
7. Coochie
8. Cuddles
9. Princess
10. Sugar

Based on *True Romances Magazine*'s 'True Romance Survey', 1988.

# THE 10 COMMONEST AGE GROUPS IN GREAT BRITAIN

| | Age group | Total no. |
|---|---|---|
| 1. | 20–24 | 4,785,000 |
| 2. | 15–19 | 4,377,000 |
| 3. | 25–29 | 4,373,000 |
| 4. | 35–39 | 3,957,000 |
| 5. | 40–44 | 3,853,000 |
| 6. | 30–34 | 3,837,000 |
| 7. | 5–9 | 3,549,000 |
| 8. | 10–14 | 3,513,000 |
| 9. | 45–49 | 3,150,000 |
| 10. | 55–59 | 3,031,000 |

# THE 10 COUNTRIES WITH THE GREATEST NUMBER OF DIVORCES

| | Country | Divorces per annum |
|---|---|---|
| 1. | United States | 1,187,000 |
| 2. | USSR | 1,150,230 |
| 3. | Japan | 178,746 |
| 4. | Indonesia | 175,630 |
| 5. | Great Britain | 157,044 |
| 6. | West Germany | 130,744 |
| 7. | France | 103,700 |
| 8. | Canada | 68,567 |
| 9. | East Germany | 51,240 |
| 10. | Australia | 43,012 |

# THE TOP 10 LIVERY COMPANIES OF THE CITY OF LONDON

1. Mercers
2. Grocers
3. Drapers
4. Fishmongers
5. Goldsmiths
6/7 Merchant Taylors
7/6 Skinners
8. Haberdashers
9. Salters
10. Ironmongers

*The livery companies, so-called because of the distinctive costume, or livery, worn by their members, grew out of the city craft guilds of the 14th century, but today they function more as charitable, educational and social institutions than as trade associations. At one time all had halls and often extensive grounds, but as companies such as the Bonnet Makers, Virginals Makers and Heumers (helmet makers) were disbanded or absorbed and buildings were destroyed (many of them during the Blitz) or sold to raise funds, the number of halls has dwindled to 35. Today the liverymen elect the sheriffs of London and the Lord*

*Mayor. In the time of Henry VIII, long and bitter disputes over the rank of the various livery companies were resolved when their governing body, the Court of Aldermen, established a list in order of precedence, headed by the so-called 'Great*

*Twelve' (the other two are Vintners and Clothworkers). In 1484 an argument over precedence between the Skinners and Merchant Taylors was resolved by their order switching in alternate years. Over the centuries, the order of this list has remained the same, although many companies have left and new ones joined; in modern times these have included the Air Pilots' and Navigators' Guild (81 in precedence) and Chartered Accountants (86).*

FAR RIGHT White's Club, St James's, Britain's oldest club.

LEFT Mercers Hall in the City of London.

BELOW Uppark, Sussex, one of the properties owned by the National Trust.

## HUMAN ACTIVITIES & ACHIEVEMENTS

# THE TOP 10 ENVIRONMENTAL ORGANIZATIONS IN THE UK

| Organization | Membership |
|---|---|
| 1. National Trust | 1,700,000 |
| 2. Royal Society for the Protection of Birds | 540,000 |
| 3. Civic Trust | 300,000 |
| 4. English Heritage | 203,000 |
| 5. Royal Society for Nature Conservation | 186,000 |
| 6. National Trust for Scotland | 179,000 |
| 7. World Wide Fund for Nature | 155,000 |
| 8. Friends of the Earth | 70,000 |
| 9. Ramblers Association | 68,000 |
| 10. Woodland Trust | 62,000 |

*The Royal Society for Nature Conservation also has a junior body, WATCH, with 30,000 members. The figure for the Ramblers Association includes membership in the Republic of Ireland.*

# THE 10 OLDEST-ESTABLISHED CLUBS* IN GREAT BRITAIN

| Club | Location | Date established |
|---|---|---|
| 1. White's | London | 1693 |
| 2. Boodle's | London | 1762 |
| 3. Brooks's | London | 1764 |
| 4. Norfolk Club | Norwich | 1770 |
| 5. Royal Thames Yacht Club | London | 1775 |
| 6. New Club | Edinburgh | 1787 (Feb) |
| 7. Marylebone Cricket Club | London | 1787 (June) |
| 8. Athenaeum | Liverpool | 1797 |
| 9. Royal Anglesey Yacht Club | Beaumaris | 1802 |
| 10. City Club | Chester | 1807 |

*except golf clubs – see separate list, page 207

## HUMAN ACTIVITIES & ACHIEVEMENTS

American members of the Boy Scout Movement, which recently celebrated its eightieth anniversary.

# THE 10 COUNTRIES WITH THE HIGHEST SCOUT MEMBERSHIP

| | Country | Membership |
|---|---|---|
| 1. | United States | 3,825,117 |
| 2. | Philippines | 2,060,930 |
| 3. | Indonesia | 2,057,974 |
| 4. | India | 1,228,912 |
| 5. | United Kingdom | 681,257 |
| 6. | Thailand | 330,190 |
| 7. | Bangladesh | 312,237 |
| 8. | Canada | 304,138 |
| 9. | Japan | 284,957 |
| 10. | South Korea | 268,665 |

*The Scouting Movement was started in 1908 by Sir Robert Baden-Powell. There are now more than 16,000,000 Scouts in 150 countries and territories.*

# THE 10 COUNTRIES WITH THE HIGHEST GIRL GUIDE AND GIRL SCOUT MEMBERSHIP

| | Country | Membership |
|---|---|---|
| 1. | United States | 2,917,622 |
| 2. | Philippines | 1,596,856 |
| 3. | United Kingdom | 750,438 |
| 4. | India | 442,129 |
| 5. | Canada | 268,928 |
| 6. | Korea | 144,654 |
| 7. | Indonesia | 98,656 |
| 8. | Japan | 98,419 |
| 9. | Australia | 93,935 |
| 10. | Pakistan | 93,605 |

*The World Association of Girl Guides and Girl Scouts has 112 national member organizations with a total membership of more than 7,750,000.*

# THE TEN LARGEST TRADE UNIONS IN GREAT BRITAIN

| Union | Members |
|---|---|
| 1. Transport & General Workers' Union (TGWU) | 1,348,712 |
| 2. Amalgamated Engineering Union (AEU) | 815,072 |
| 3. General, Municipal Boilermakers and Allied Trades Union (GMW) | 803,319 |
| 4. National & Local Government Officers Association (NALGO) | 758,780 |
| 5. Manufacturing, Science & Finance (MSF)* | 653,000 |
| 6. National Union of Public Employees (NUPE) | 650,930 |
| 7. Union of Shop, Distributive & Allied Workers (USDAW) | 387,207 |
| 8. Electrical, Electronic, Telecommunications & Plumbing Union (EETPU) | 329,914 |
| 9. Royal College of Nursing (RCN) | 281,000 |
| 10. Union of Construction, Allied Trades & Technicians (UCATT) | 255,883 |

*formed by the amalgamation of the Association of Scientific, Technical and Managerial Staffs (ASTMS) and the Transport and Salaried Staffs' Association (TASS)

*I*n sharp contrast to these *huge unions, there are several tiny ones, such as the Military and Orchestral Musical Instrument Makers' Trade Society and the Society of Shuttlemakers (41 members each), and the Sheffield Wool Shearers' Union (17). But some of the smallest ones have been disbanded in recent years; the Spring Trapmakers' Society, for example, was dissolved in 1988. Total trade union membership is currently just over 9,000,000.*

# THE 10 LARGEST TRADE ['LABOR'] UNIONS IN THE USA

| Union | Members |
|---|---|
| 1. International Brotherhood of Teamsters, Chauffeurs, Warehousemen and Helpers of America | 2,000,000 |
| 2. National Education Association | 1,700,000 |
| 3. Food and Commercial Workers' International Union | 1,300,000 |
| 4. International Union of Automobile, Aerospace and Agricultural Implement Workers of America | 1,150,000 |
| 5= International Brotherhood of Electrical Workers | 1,000,000 |
| 5= American Federation of State, County and Municipal Employees | 1,000,000 |
| 7. International Union of Service Employees | 850,000 |
| 8. United Steelworkers of America | 832,748 |
| 9. International Association of Machinists and Aerospace Workers | 800,000 |
| 10. Communications Workers of America | 700,000 |

• • • • • • • • • • • • • • •

# THE 10 COMMONEST CAUSES OF MARITAL DISCORD AND BREAKDOWN

1. Lack of communication
2. Continual arguments
3. Infidelity
4. Sexual problems
5. Physical or verbal abuse
6. Financial problems
7. Work (usually one partner devoting excessive time to work)
8. Children (whether to have them; attitudes towards their upbringing)
9. Addiction (to drinking, gambling, spending, etc.)
10. Step-parenting

Based on information supplied by Relate National Marriage Guidance.

# THE 10 TALLEST GIANTS OF ALL TIME

| Name/date/country | Height | | | |
|---|---|---|---|---|
| | m | cm | ft | in |
| 1. Robert Pershing Wadlow (1918–40) USA | 2 | 72 | 8 | 11.1 |
| 2. John William Rogan (1871–1905) USA | 2 | 64 | 8 | 8 |
| 3. John F. Carroll (1932–69) USA | 2 | 63.5 | 8 | 7.75 |
| 4. Valno Myllyrinne (1909–63) Finland | 2 | 51.4 | 8 | 3 |
| 5= Bernard Coyne (1897–1921) USA | 2 | 48.9 | 8 | 2 |
| 5= Don Koehler (1925–81) USA | 2 | 48.9 | 8 | 2 |
| 7. Patrick Cotter (O'Brien) (c. 1762–1806) Ireland | 2 | 46 | 8 | 1 |
| 8. 'Constantine' (1872–1902) Germany | 2 | 45.8 | 8 | 0.8 |
| 9. Gabriel Estavao Monjane (1944–) Mozambique | 2 | 45.7 | 8 | 0.75 |
| 10. Sulaiman 'Ali Nashnush (1943–) Libya | 2 | 45 | 8 | 0.4 |

*C*otter *claimed a height of
2.63m/8ft 7in, but this was probably an exaggeration
used to attract customers to his personal appearances.
When he stood on the stage at Sadler's Wells Theatre,
London, he was said to have been able to reach into the
boxes, and in the street he amazed onlookers by lighting
his pipe from the gas jets of streetlamps. When he died he
was buried in Bristol – 3.60m/12ft deep and bricked in to
deter body-snatchers.*

*A height of 2.49m/8ft 2in was claimed by Charles
Byrne (1761–83) who, like Cotter, was Irish and similarly
adopted the name O'Brien. Although he asked to be
buried at sea, his skeleton was acquired by Dr William
Hunter and is on display in the Hunterian Museum at the
Royal College of Surgeons, along with his giant gloves
and other personal items.*

Robert Wadlow, pictured with brothers
Eugene, 14, and Harold, 4, shows off all of his
8 feet 11 inches.

# Town & Country

### THE 10 SMALLEST COUNTRIES IN THE WORLD

| | Country | Area sq km | sq miles | Population |
|---|---|---|---|---|
| 1. | Vatican City | 0.4 | 0.15 | 750 |
| 2. | Monaco | 1.5 | 0.58 | 30,000 |
| 3. | Gibraltar | 6 | 2 | 29,692 |
| 4. | Macau | 16 | 6 | 430,000 |
| 5. | Nauru | 21 | 8 | 8,000 |
| 6. | Tuvalu | 26 | 10 | 8,229 |
| 7. | Bermuda | 53 | 20 | 60,000 |
| 8. | San Marino | 62 | 24 | 22,361 |
| 9. | Liechtenstein | 157 | 61 | 27,714 |
| 10. | Antigua | 279 | 108 | 80,000 |

Strolling through the corridors of power in the Vatican – while the world looks on.

# THE 10 LARGEST COUNTRIES IN THE WORLD

| | Country | Area | |
| | | sq km | sq miles |
|---|---|---|---|
| 1. | USSR | 22,402,000 | 8,649,461 |
| 2. | Canada | 9,970,537 | 3,849,646 |
| 3. | China | 9,596,961 | 3,705,408 |
| 4. | United States | 9,372,614 | 3,618,787 |
| 5. | Brazil | 8,511,965 | 3,286,488 |
| 6. | Australia | 7,686,848 | 2,967,909 |
| 7. | India | 3,287,590 | 1,269,346 |
| 8. | Argentina | 2,766,889 | 1,068,302 |
| 9. | Sudan | 2,505,813 | 967,500 |
| 10. | Algeria | 2,381,741 | 919,595 |
| 75. | *United Kingdom* | *244,046* | *94,227* |
| | World total | 136,000,000 | 52,509,600 |

*T*he ten largest countries comprise some 57.7% of the total Earth's surface. The USSR alone occupies approximately 16.5% and has an area 92 times greater than the United Kingdom.

• • • • • • • • • • • • • • • •

# THE 10 LARGEST COUNTRIES IN EUROPE

| | Country | Area | |
| | | sq km | sq miles |
|---|---|---|---|
| 1. | USSR (in Europe) | 5,571,000 | 2,150,975 |
| 2. | France | 547,026 | 211,208 |
| 3. | Spain | 504,782 | 194,897 |
| 4. | Sweden | 449,964 | 173,732 |
| 5. | Finland | 337,032 | 130,129 |
| 6. | Norway | 324,219 | 125,182 |
| 7. | Poland | 312,677 | 120,725 |
| 8. | Italy | 301,225 | 116,304 |
| 9. | Yugoslavia | 255,804 | 98,766 |
| 10. | West Germany | 248,577 | 95,976 |
| 11. | *United Kingdom* | *244,046* | *94,227* |

The Amazonian forest in Brazil, South America's largest country.

# THE 10 LARGEST COUNTRIES IN SOUTH AMERICA

| | Country | Area | |
| | | sq km | sq miles |
|---|---|---|---|
| 1. | Brazil | 8,511,965 | 3,286,488 |
| 2. | Argentina | 2,766,889 | 1,068,302 |
| 3. | Peru | 1,285,216 | 496,225 |
| 4. | Colombia | 1,138,914 | 439,737 |
| 5. | Bolivia | 1,098,581 | 424,165 |
| 6. | Venezuela | 912,050 | 352,144 |
| 7. | Chile | 756,945 | 292,258 |
| 8. | Paraguay | 406,752 | 157,048 |
| 9. | Ecuador | 283,561 | 109,484 |
| 10. | Guyana | 214,969 | 83,000 |

*T*he sizes of these countries vary enormously; Brazil is the 5th largest in the world, while Guyana is smaller than the United Kingdom.

## TOWN & COUNTRY

# THE 10 LARGEST COUNTRIES IN ASIA

| | Country | Area | |
| --- | --- | --- | --- |
| | | sq km | sq miles |
| 1. | USSR (in Asia) | 16,831,000 | 6,498,486 |
| 2. | China | 9,596,961 | 3,705,408 |
| 3. | India | 3,287,590 | 1,269,346 |
| 4. | Saudi Arabia | 2,149,640 | 830,000 |
| 5. | Indonesia | 1,904,569 | 735,358 |
| 6. | Iran | 1,648,000 | 636,296 |
| 7. | Mongolia | 1,565,000 | 604,250 |
| 8. | Pakistan | 803,936 | 310,401 |
| 9. | Turkey (in Asia) | 756,953 | 292,261 |
| 10. | Burma | 676,552 | 261,218 |

Alice Springs: a mere few hundred of the almost eight million square kilometres of Australia.

# THE 10 LARGEST COUNTRIES IN AFRICA

| | Country | Area | |
| --- | --- | --- | --- |
| | | sq km | sq miles |
| 1. | Sudan | 2,505,813 | 967,500 |
| 2. | Algeria | 2,381,741 | 919,595 |
| 3. | Zaire | 2,345,409 | 905,567 |
| 4. | Libya | 1,759,540 | 679,362 |
| 5. | Chad | 1,284,000 | 495,755 |
| 6. | Niger | 1,267,080 | 489,191 |
| 7. | Angola | 1,246,700 | 481,354 |
| 8. | Mali | 1,240,000 | 478,791 |
| 9. | Ethiopia | 1,221,900 | 471,778 |
| 10. | South Africa | 1,221,031 | 471,445 |

# THE 10 LARGEST COUNTRIES IN OCEANIA

| | Country | Area | |
| --- | --- | --- | --- |
| | | sq km | sq miles |
| 1. | Australia | 7,686,848 | 2,967,909 |
| 2. | Papua New Guinea | 461,691 | 178,260 |
| 3. | New Zealand | 268,676 | 103,736 |
| 4. | Solomon Islands | 28,446 | 10,983 |
| 5. | New Caledonia | 19,058 | 7,358 |
| 6. | Fiji | 18,274 | 7,055 |
| 7. | Vanuatu | 14,763 | 5,700 |
| 8. | French Polynesia | 4,000 | 1,544 |
| 9. | Samoa | 3,039 | 1,173 |
| 10. | Kiribati | 728 | 281 |

*S*udan, the largest country in Africa, has an area ten times larger than the United Kingdom.

A Nilotic village in the Sudan, Africa's largest country.

*A*ustralia is over nine times larger than the rest of the Top 10 Oceanian countries put together.

The virtually uninhabited Ross Dependency, which comes under New Zealand's control, is actually larger than New Zealand itself (750,310 sq km/286,696 sq miles, including the permanent ice shelf).

# THE 10 COUNTRIES WITH THE LONGEST COASTLINES

| Country | Coastline length km | miles |
|---|---|---|
| 1. Canada | 90,908 | 56,488 |
| 2. Indonesia | 54,718 | 34,000 |
| 3. USSR | 46,671 | 29,000 |
| 4. Greenland | 44,087 | 27,394 |
| 5. Australia | 25,760 | 16,007 |
| 6. Philippines | 22,540 | 14,006 |
| 7. United States | 19,924 | 12,380 |
| 8. Norway | 16,093 | 10,000 |
| 9. New Zealand | 15,134 | 9,404 |
| 10. China | 14,500 | 9,010 |
| 12. *United Kingdom* | *12,429* | *7,723* |

*T*he coastline of Canada is more than twice as long as the circumference of Earth (40,076 km/24,901.8 miles at the Equator); even the coastline of Great Britain is approximately equivalent to the distance from London to Honolulu. In case you are wondering, number 11 is Greece (13,676 km/8,498 miles).

# THE 10 LARGEST STATES IN THE USA

| State | Area sq km | sq miles |
|---|---|---|
| 1. Alaska | 1,478,425 | 570,823 |
| 2. Texas | 678,924 | 262,134 |
| 3. California | 404,973 | 156,361 |
| 4. Montana | 377,069 | 145,587 |
| 5. New Mexico | 314,456 | 121,412 |
| 6. Arizona | 293,749 | 113,417 |
| 7. Nevada | 284,611 | 109,889 |
| 8. Colorado | 268,753 | 103,766 |
| 9. Wyoming | 251,288 | 97,023 |
| 10. Oregon | 249,115 | 96,184 |
| *United Kingdom* | *240,882* | *93,005* |

*A*laska, the largest state, has the second lowest population (525,000–1987 estimate; Wyoming's 490,000 is the lowest), equivalent to one person per square mile. The smallest US state is Rhode Island (2,717 sq km/1,049 sq miles); the District of Columbia covers 174 sq km/67 sq miles.

The area of England (130,440 sq km/50,363 sq miles), is slightly smaller than Alabama (131,333 sq km/50,708 sq miles).

# THE 10 LONGEST FRONTIERS IN THE WORLD

| Country | Frontiers km | miles |
|---|---|---|
| 1. China | 24,000 | 14,913 |
| 2. USSR | 20,619 | 12,812 |
| 3. Brazil | 13,076 | 8,125 |
| 4. India | 12,700 | 7,891 |
| 5. United States | 12,002 | 7,458 |
| 6. Zaire | 9,902 | 6,153 |
| 7. Argentina | 9,414 | 5,850 |
| 8. Canada | 9,010 | 5,599 |
| 9. Mongolia | 8,000 | 4,971 |
| 10. Sudan | 7,805 | 4,850 |

A long job: guards patrolling a section of the immense border between the USSR and China.

*T*his list represents the total length of frontiers, compiled by adding together the lengths of individual borders. The 12,002 km/7,458 miles of United States' frontiers include the one shared by Alaska with Canada, the Mexican border, and the main US frontier with Canada, at 6,416 km/3,987 miles the longest continuous frontier in the world.

## TOWN & COUNTRY

# **T**HE 10 COUNTRIES WITH THE HIGHEST POPULATION

| | Country | Population |
|---|---|---|
| 1. | China | 1,088,570,000 |
| 2. | India | 800,326,000 |
| 3. | USSR | 283,100,000 |
| 4. | United States | 243,830,000 |
| 5. | Indonesia | 180,368,000 |
| 6. | Brazil | 147,095,000 |
| 7. | Japan | 122,090,000 |
| 8. | Bangladesh | 107,088,000 |
| 9. | Pakistan | 104,601,000 |
| 10. | Nigeria | 101,910,000 |
| *16.* | *United Kingdom* | *56,973,000* |

*T*he staggering population of China is more than 19 times that of the UK and represents some 22% of the total population of the world (more than 5,000,000,000), proving the commonly-stated statistic that 'one person in five is Chinese'.

Some of the teeming millions of India.

## TOWN & COUNTRY

Despite efforts to reverse the trend, China's population will top
1¼ billion by the year 2000.

Men comprise the majority of the population of Bahrain.

# THE 10 COUNTRIES WITH THE HIGHEST ESTIMATED POPULATION IN THE YEAR 2000

| | Country | Population |
|---|---|---|
| 1. | China | 1,255,656,000 |
| 2. | India | 961,531,000 |
| 3. | USSR | 314,818,000 |
| 4. | United States | 268,079,000 |
| 5. | Indonesia | 204,486,000 |
| 6. | Brazil | 179,487,000 |
| 7. | Nigeria | 161,930,000 |
| 8. | Bangladesh | 145,800,000 |
| 9. | Pakistan | 142,554,000 |
| 10. | Japan | 127,683,000 |
| | *United Kingdom* | *56,235,000* |

*T*he estimates for the
population of the Top 10 countries assume increases,
while that of the United Kingdom predicts a decrease as
a result of the trend towards smaller families.

# THE TOP 10 COUNTRIES WHERE MEN OUTNUMBER WOMEN

| | Country | % of population Men | Women |
|---|---|---|---|
| 1. | Bahrain | 60.0 | 40.0 |
| 2. | United Arab Emirates | 59.5 | 40.5 |
| 3. | Kuwait | 57.2 | 42.8 |
| 4. | Guam | 55.8 | 44.2 |
| 5. | Maldives | 53.1 | 46.9 |
| 6. | Pakistan | 53.0 | 47.0 |
| 7. | Jordan | 52.3 | 47.7 |
| 8= | Hong Kong | 52.2 | 47.8 |
| 8= | Solomon Islands | 52.2 | 47.8 |
| 8= | Taiwan | 52.2 | 47.8 |

*T*he male/female ratio of the
world is virtually balanced 50:50, but there are certain
countries where one sex dominates.

TOWN & COUNTRY

# THE TOP 10 COUNTRIES WHERE SHEEP OUTNUMBER PEOPLE

| | Country | Sheep | Human population | Sheep per person (approx.) |
|---|---|---|---|---|
| 1. | Falkland Islands | 705,000 | 1,916 | 368 |
| 2. | New Zealand | 66,400,000 | 3,564,000 | 20 |
| 3. | Australia | 159,177,000 | 16,263,000 | 10 |
| 4. | Mongolia | 13,194,000 | 1,900,000 | 7 |
| 5. | Uruguay | 25,560,000 | 3,060,000 | 8 |
| 6. | Namibia | 6,300,000 | 1,184,000 | 5 |
| 7. | Iceland | 770,000 | 247,000 | 3 |
| 8. | Mauritania | 3,950,000 | 1,888,000 | 2 |
| 9. | Somalia | 11,500,000 | 5,800,000 | 2 |
| 10. | Libya | 5,700,000 | 3,809,000 | 1.5 |

Australian sheep, outnumbering their human compatriots ten to one.

*T*he estimated total world sheep population *(second only to that of cattle) is 1,157,643,000 – an average of more than one sheep for every four people.*

LEFT Women outnumber men in such countries as Grenada.

# THE TOP 10 COUNTRIES WHERE WOMEN OUTNUMBER MEN

| | Country | % of population Women | Men |
|---|---|---|---|
| 1. | Botswana | 54.3 | 45.7 |
| 2. | Grenada | 53.6 | 46.4 |
| 3= | USSR | 53.2 | 46.8 |
| 3= | East Germany | 53.2 | 46.8 |
| 5. | Malta | 53.2 | 47.2 |
| 6= | Portugal | 52.6 | 47.4 |
| 6= | Gabon | 52.6 | 47.4 |
| 6= | Austria | 52.6 | 47.4 |
| 9= | West Germany | 52.4 | 47.6 |
| 9= | Burundi | 52.4 | 47.6 |
| | *United Kingdom* | *51.3* | *48.7* |

# THE 10 LEADING COUNTRIES OF ORIGIN OF IMMIGRANTS TO THE USA, 1820–1987

| | Country | Number |
|---|---|---|
| 1. | Germany | 7,051,000 |
| 2. | Italy | 5,343,000 |
| 3. | Great Britain | 5,082,000 |
| 4. | Ireland | 4,702,000 |
| 5. | Austria/Hungry | 4,329,000 |
| 6. | Canada | 4,237,000 |
| 7. | Russia/USSR | 3,423,000 |
| 8. | Mexico | 2,710,000 |
| 9. | West Indies | 1,172,000 |
| 10. | Sweden | 1,129,000 |

'*Give me your tired, your poor/Your huddled masses yearning to breathe free...*' So started Emma Lazarus's poem, The New Colossus, which is inscribed on the Statue of Liberty. For many years the United States was the magnet that attracted vast numbers of immigrants; in 1903–15, for example, an average of 982,655 arrived every year.

# THE 10 MOST HIGHLY POPULATED STATES IN THE USA

| | State | Population 1900 | 1987 |
|---|---|---|---|
| 1. | California | 1,485,053 | 27,663,000 |
| 2. | New York | 17,825,000 | 17,825,000 |
| 3. | Texas | 3,048,710 | 16,789,000 |
| 4. | Pennsylvania | 6,302,115 | 12,023,000 |
| 5. | Florida | 528,542 | 11,936,000 |
| 6. | Illinois | 4,821,550 | 11,582,000 |
| 7. | Ohio | 4,157,545 | 10,784,000 |
| 8. | Michigan | 2,420,982 | 9,200,000 |
| 9. | New Jersey | 1,883,669 | 7,627,000 |
| 10. | North Carolina | 1,893,810 | 6,413,000 |

*The total population of the United States in 1900 was 76,212,168 – just over 31% of its present population of 243,770,000. In 1790 it was 3,929,214.*

ABOVE German migrants heading for the United States, 1872.

INSET Italian arrivals in New York, 1905.

# THE 10 MOST DENSELY-POPULATED COUNTRIES AND COLONIES IN THE WORLD

| | Country/Colony | Area sq km | Area sq miles | Population | Population per sq mile |
|---|---|---|---|---|---|
| 1. | Macau | 16.06 | 6.2 | 422,000 | 68,065 |
| 2. | Monaco | 1.81 | 0.7 | 29,000 | 41,429 |
| 3. | Hong Kong | 1037.29 | 400.5 | 5,592,000 | 13,963 |
| 4. | Gibraltar | 6.47 | 2.5 | 29,000 | 11,600 |
| 5. | Singapore | 619.01 | 239.0 | 2,616,000 | 10,946 |
| 6. | Vatican City | 0.44 | 0.17 | 1,000 | 5,882 |
| 7. | Malta | 313.39 | 121.0 | 367,000 | 3,033 |
| 8. | Bermuda | 53.35 | 20.6 | 58,000 | 2,816 |
| 9. | Bangladesh | 143,998.15 | 55,598.0 | 107,088,000 | 1,926 |
| 10. | Bahrain | 675.99 | 261.0 | 464,000 | 1,778 |
| | *United States* | *9,372,614.90* | *3,618,787.0* | *243,830,000* | *67* |
| | *United Kingdom* | *244,046.79* | *94,227.0* | *56,973,000* | *605* |
| | *World average* | *135,597,670.00* | *52,509,600.0* | *5,054,798,000* | *96* |

The world's closest neighbours: Macau, the most densely-populated country on earth.

*A*mong the least *densely populated countries in the world are the Falkland Islands – an area of 12,168 sq km/4,698 sq miles with a population of 1,916, or .41 of a person per sq mile, and Greenland – 217,559 sq km/ 840,000 sq miles with a population of 54,000, equivalent to .06 of a person per sq mile.*

# THE 10 MOST HIGHLY POPULATED COUNTRIES IN EUROPE

| | Country | Population |
|---|---|---|
| 1. | USSR (in Europe) | 218,607,000 |
| 2. | West Germany | 60,989,000 |
| 3. | Italy | 57,351,000 |
| 4. | United Kingdom | 56,973,000 |
| 5. | France | 55,630,000 |
| 6. | Spain | 39,001,000 |
| 7. | Poland | 37,727,000 |
| 8. | Yugoslavia | 24,431,000 |
| 9. | Romania | 22,937,000 |
| 10. | East Germany | 16,640,000 |

# THE 10 MOST HIGHLY POPULATED COUNTRIES IN ASIA

| | Country | Population |
|---|---|---|
| 1. | China | 1,088,570,000 |
| 2. | India | 800,326,000 |
| 3. | Indonesia | 180,368,000 |
| 4. | Japan | 122,090,000 |
| 5. | Bangladesh | 107,088,000 |
| 6. | Pakistan | 104,601,000 |
| 7. | USSR (in Asia) | 65,401,000 |
| 8. | Philippines | 61,525,000 |
| 9. | Vietnam | 60,989,000 |
| 10. | Thailand | 53,646,000 |

# THE 10 MOST HIGHLY POPULATED COUNTRIES IN OCEANIA

| | Country | Population |
|---|---|---|
| 1. | Australia | 16,263,000 |
| 2. | Papua New Guinea | 3,564,000 |
| 3. | New Zealand | 3,314,000 |
| 4. | Fiji | 725,000 |
| 5. | Solomon Islands | 285,000 |
| 6. | Samoa (US and Western) | 212,000 |
| 7. | French Polynesia | 186,000 |
| 8. | New Caledonia | 153,000 |
| 9. | Vanuatu | 150,000 |
| 10. | Guam | 127,000 |

· · · · · · · · · · · · · · · ·

# THE 10 MOST HIGHLY POPULATED COUNTRIES IN SOUTH AMERICA

| | Country | Population |
|---|---|---|
| 1. | Brazil | 147,095,000 |
| 2. | Argentina | 31,145,000 |
| 3. | Colombia | 30,661,000 |
| 4. | Peru | 20,739,000 |
| 5. | Venezuela | 18,291,000 |
| 6. | Chile | 12,448,000 |
| 7. | Ecuador | 9,955,000 |
| 8. | Bolivia | 6,800,000 |
| 9. | Paraguay | 4,252,000 |
| 10. | Uruguay | 3,060,000 |

## TOWN & COUNTRY

Edinburgh, one of the United Kingdom's most ancient cities.

# THE 10 OLDEST CITIES IN THE UK

| | City | County | Original charter granted |
|---|---|---|---|
| 1. | Ripon | Yorkshire | 886 |
| 2. | London | Greater London | 1066 |
| 3. | Edinburgh | Lothian | 1124 |
| 4. | Chichester | West Sussex | 1135 |
| 5= | Lincoln | Lincolnshire | 1154 |
| 5= | Oxford | Oxfordshire | 1154 |
| 5= | Derby | Derbyshire | 1154 |
| 8= | Nottingham | Nottinghamshire | 1155 |
| 8= | Winchester | Hampshire | 1155 |
| 10. | Exeter | Devon | 1156 |

# THE WORLD'S 10 HIGHEST CITIES

| | City | Country | Elevation above sea level m | ft |
|---|---|---|---|---|
| 1. | Potosi | Bolivia | 3,976 | 13,045 |
| 2. | Lhasa | Tibet | 3,658 | 12,001 |
| 3. | La Paz | Bolivia | 3,577 | 11,736 |
| 4. | Cuzco | Peru | 3,399 | 11,152 |
| 5. | Quito | Ecuador | 2,819 | 9,249 |
| 6. | Sucre | Bolivia | 2,790 | 9,154 |
| 7. | Toluca | Mexico | 2,680 | 8,793 |
| 8. | Bogotá | Colombia | 2,644 | 8,675 |
| 9. | Cochabamba | Bolivia | 2,558 | 8,392 |
| 10. | Pachuca de Soto | Mexico | 2,426 | 7,959 |

Lhasa, Tibet – 'the roof of the world'.

# THE 10 LARGEST CITIES IN THE UK

| City | Area sq km | Area sq miles | Population density per sq km | Total population |
|---|---|---|---|---|
| 1. Greater London | 1,579 | 609.7 | 4,288 | 6,770,400 |
| 2. Birmingham | 264 | 102.0 | 3,781 | 998,200 |
| 3. Glasgow | 198 | 76.3 | 3,614 | 715,600 |
| 4. Leeds | 562 | 217.0 | 1,262 | 709,000 |
| 5. Sheffield | 368 | 141.9 | 1,446 | 532,300 |
| 6. Liverpool | 113 | 43.6 | 4,212 | 476,000 |
| 7. Bradford | 370 | 142.9 | 1,250 | 462,500 |
| 8. Manchester | 116 | 44.9 | 3,880 | 450,100 |
| 9. Edinburgh | 261 | 100.6 | 1,681 | 438,700 |
| 10. Bristol | 110 | 42.3 | 3,495 | 384,400 |

The West End of London, the United Kingdom's largest city.

# THE 10 LARGEST CITIES IN THE WORLD

| | City | Country | Population |
|---|---|---|---|
| 1. | Tokyo/Yokohama | Japan | 25,434,000 |
| 2. | Mexico City | Mexico | 16,901,000 |
| 3. | São Paulo | Brazil | 14,911,000 |
| 4. | New York | USA | 14,598,000 |
| 5. | Seoul | South Korea | 13,665,000 |
| 6. | Osaka/Kobe/Kyoto | Japan | 13,652,000 |
| 7. | Buenos Aires | Argentina | 10,750,000 |
| 8. | Calcutta | India | 10,462,000 |
| 9. | Bombay | India | 10,137,000 |
| 10. | Rio de Janeiro | Brazil | 10,116,000 |
| *13.* | *London* | *United Kingdom* | *9,442,000* |

*C*alculating the populations of the world's cities is fraught with difficulties, not least that of determining whether the city is defined by its administrative boundaries or by its continuously built-up areas or conurbations. In order to resolve this problem, the US Bureau of the Census has adopted the method of defining cities as population clusters or 'urban agglomerations' with densities of more than 5,000 inhabitants per square mile. This list is based on their figures for 1985. It should be stressed that these totals will differ considerably from those based on other methods.

# THE 10 LARGEST CITIES IN THE USA

| | City | State | Population |
|---|---|---|---|
| 1. | New York | New York | 7,262,700 |
| 2. | Los Angeles | California | 3,259,340 |
| 3. | Chicago | Illinois | 3,009,530 |
| 4. | Houston | Texas | 1,728,910 |
| 5. | Philadelphia | Pennsylvania | 1,642,900 |
| 6. | Detroit | Michigan | 1,086,220 |
| 7. | San Diego | California | 1,015,190 |
| 8. | Dallas | Texas | 1,003,520 |
| 9. | San Antonio | Texas | 914,350 |
| 10. | Phoenix | Arizona | 894,070 |

*T*hese are estimates for central city areas only, not for the total metropolitan areas that surround them, which may be several times as large.

Manhattan, New York, top of the United States' population chart.

## TOWN & COUNTRY

# THE WORLD'S 10 WETTEST CITIES

| | City | Country | Average annual rainfall mm | in |
|---|---|---|---|---|
| 1. | Monrovia | Liberia | 5,131 | 202.01 |
| 2. | Moulmein | Burma | 4,820 | 189.76 |
| 3. | Padang | Sumatra, Indonesia | 4,452 | 175.28 |
| 4. | Conkary | Guinea | 4,341 | 170.91 |
| 5 | Bogor | Java, Indonesia | 4,225 | 166.34 |
| 6. | Douala | Cameroon | 4,109 | 161.77 |
| 7. | Cayenne | French Guiana | 3,744 | 147.40 |
| 8. | Freetown | Sierra Leone | 3,639 | 143.27 |
| 9. | Ambon | Ambon, Indonesia | 3,530 | 138.98 |
| 10. | Mangalore | India | 3,398 | 133.78 |
| | *Manchester* | *England* | *897* | *35.00* |

# THE WORLD'S 10 DRIEST CITIES

| | City | Country | Average annual rainfall mm | in |
|---|---|---|---|---|
| 1. | Antofagasta | Chile | 0.4 | 0.02 |
| 2. | Luxor | Egypt | 0.5 | 0.02 |
| 3. | Aswan | Egypt | 1.0 | 0.04 |
| 4. | Asyut | Egypt | 5.0 | 0.20 |
| 5. | Callao | Peru | 12.0 | 0.47 |
| 6. | Trujillo | Peru | 14.0 | 0.54 |
| 7. | Suez | Egypt | 22.0 | 0.87 |
| 8. | Giza | Egypt | 28.0 | 1.10 |
| 9. | Cairo | Egypt | 29.0 | 1.14 |
| 10. | Zagazig | Egypt | 30.0 | 1.18 |

BELOW Monrovia, Liberia, on one of its rare rain-free days. A typical year's rainfall would cover a double-decker bus.

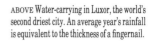

ABOVE Water-carrying in Luxor, the world's second driest city. An average year's rainfall is equivalent to the thickness of a fingernail.

# THE WORLD'S 10 HOTTEST CITIES

| City | Country | Average temperature °C | °F |
|---|---|---|---|
| 1. Djibouti | Djibouti | 30.0 | 86.0 |
| 2= Timbuktu | Mali | 29.3 | 84.7 |
| 2= Tirunelveli | India | 29.3 | 84.7 |
| 2= Tuticorin | India | 29.3 | 84.7 |
| 5= Aden | South Yemen | 28.9 | 84.0 |
| 5= Madurai | India | 28.9 | 84.0 |
| 5= Naimey | Niger | 28.9 | 84.0 |
| 8. Tiruchirapalli | India | 28.8 | 83.8 |
| 9= Khartoum | Sudan | 28.7 | 83.7 |
| 9= Omdurman | Sudan | 28.7 | 83.7 |

# THE WORLD'S 10 COLDEST CITIES

| City | Country | Average temperature °C | °F |
|---|---|---|---|
| 1. Norilsk | USSR | −10.9 | 12.4 |
| 2. Yakutusk | USSR | −10.1 | 13.8 |
| 3. Ulan-Bator | Mongolia | −4.5 | 23.9 |
| 4. Fairbanks | USA | −3.5 | 25.7 |
| 5. Chita | USSR | −2.7 | 27.1 |
| 6. Bratsk | USSR | −2.2 | 28.0 |
| 7. Ulan-Ude | USSR | −1.7 | 28.9 |
| 8. Angarsk | USSR | −1.3 | 29.7 |
| 9. Irkutsk | USSR | −1.1 | 30.0 |
| 10. Komsomolsk-n-Amure | USSR | −0.7 | 30.7 |

LEFT A sun-baked mosque in Timbuktu, one of the world's hottest cities.

BELOW Winter in Norilsk, USSR, the world's coldest city. Temperatures here can fall to minus 10.9°C.

# THE 10 MOST EXPENSIVE CITIES IN THE WORLD

| | City | Country | UN Index |
|---|---|---|---|
| 1. | Tripoli | Libya | 156 |
| 2. | Tokyo | Japan | 150 |
| 3. | Geneva | Switzerland | 140 |
| 4. | N'Djamena | Chad | 126 |
| 5= | Djibouti | Djibouti | 125 |
| 5= | Kampala | Uganda | 125 |
| 7. | Sanaa | Yemen | 124 |
| 8= | Moroni | Comoro Islands | 123 |
| 8= | Helsinki | Finland | 123 |
| 10. | Bangui | Central African Republic | 122 |
| | *London* | *England* | *111* |

*T*wice a year the United Nations produces a retail price index based on the living costs of its officials (including the cost of housing) in the world's major cities. Taking New York as the base (100), it shows, for example, that it costs 50% more to live in Tokyo than in New York. If the cost of housing is excluded, the index for Tripoli goes up to 177. The same data also reveals that Quito, Ecuador (49 on the UN Index), and Warsaw, Poland (50), are the cheapest cities of all.

# THE 10 MOST EXPENSIVE TOWNS IN THE UK

1. Greater London
2. Welwyn Garden City
3. Brighton
4. Hemel Hempstead
5. Berkhamsted
6. Woking
7. Oxford
8. Slough
9. Crawley
10. Bath

*B*ased on the Reward Group's February 1989 survey of the comparative costs of living in 103 towns in the United Kingdom. From an analysis of the major items of expenditure (housing, goods and services, etc.) by families in eight different income groups, towns are ranked according to the income required to maintain their standard of living.

# THE 10 CHEAPEST TOWNS IN THE UK

1. Larne
2. Carrickfergus
3. Ballymena
4. Barnsley
5. Craigavon
6. Thurso
7. Derry
8. Belfast
9. Kirkwall
10. Peterhead

# THE 10 COMMONEST PLACE NAMES IN THE USA

| | Name | No. of occurrences |
|---|---|---|
| 1. | Fairview | 104 |
| 2. | Midway | 90 |
| 3. | Centerville | 72 |
| 4. | Oak Grove | 68 |
| 5. | Riverside | 67 |
| 6. | Five Points | 65 |
| 7. | Mount Pleasant | 56 |
| 8= | Oakland | 54 |
| 8= | Pleasant Hill | 54 |
| 10. | Georgetown | 49 |

# THE 10 COMMONEST STREET NAMES IN THE USA

1. Second Street
2. Park Street
3. Third Street
4. Fourth Street
5. Fifth Street
6. First Street
7. Sixth Street
8. Seventh Street
9. Washington Street
10. Maple Street

*T*he list continues with Oak, Eighth, Elm, Lincoln, Ninth, Pine, Walnut, Tenth and Cedar.

The famous Welsh tongue-twister, now overtaken in the longest-name stakes by publicity-seekers on the Fairbourne Steam Railway (see page 88).

# THE 10 LONGEST PLACE NAMES IN THE UK

1. Gorsafawddachaidraigddanheddogleddollônpenrhyn-areurdraethceredigion (67 letters)
(see page 88, World List, No. 3)

2. Llanfairpwllgwyngyllgogerychwyrndrobwllllanty-siliogogogoch (58 letters)
(see page 88, World List, No. 4)

3. Sutton-under-Whitestonecliffe, North Yorkshire (27)

4. Llanfihangel-yng-Ngwynfa, Powys (22)

5= Llanfihangel-y-Creuddyn, Dyfed (21)

5= Llanfihangel-y-traethau, Gwynedd (21)

7. Cottonshopeburnfoot, Northumberland (19)

8= Blakehopeburnhaugh, Northumberland (18)

8= Coignafeuinternich, Inverness-shire (18)

10. Claddochknockline and Claddochbaleshare, North Uist, Outer Hebrides (both 17)

*These are all single and hyphenated names. The longest multiple name in England is North Leverton with Habblesthorpe, Nottinghamshire (30), followed by Skidbrooke cum Saltfeet Haven, Lincolnshire (26) and Preston upon the Weald Moors, Shropshire (24). In Wales it is Lower Llanfihangel-y-Creuddyn, Dyfed, 26 letters) followed by Llansantffraid Cwmdeuddwr, Powys (24), and in Scotland Huntingtower and Ruthvenfield (27) – although there is also a loch on the island of Lewis called Loch Airidh Mhic Fhionnlaidh Dhuibh (31) (see World List, No. 10). If the parameters are extended to encompass Ireland, the single word Muckanaghederdauhaulia (22) is scooped into the net.*

*The longest parish name in the United Kingdom was for many years Saint Andrew, Holborn above the Bars, with Saint George the Martyr (54) in London, until the formation on 5 April 1971 of Saint Mary le More and All Hallows with Saint Leonard and Saint Peter, Wallingford (68).*

# THE 10 LONGEST PLACE NAMES IN THE WORLD

1. Krung Thep Mahanakhon Bovorn Ratanakosin Mahintharayutthaya Mahadilok pop Noparatratchathani Burirom Udomratchanivetmahasathan Amornpiman Avatarnsathit Sakkathattiyavisnukarmprasit (167 letters)

*When the poetic name of Bangkok, capital of Thailand, is used, it is usually abbreviated to 'Krung Thep' (city of angels).*

2. Taumatawhakatangihangakoauauotamateaturi-pukakapikimaungahoronukupokaiwhenuakitanatahu (85 letters)

*This is the longer version (the other has only 83 letters) of the Maori name of a hill in New Zealand. It translates as, 'The place where Tamatea, the man with the big knees, who slid, climbed and swallowed mountains, known as land-eater, played on the flute to his loved one'.*

3. Gorsafawddachaidraigddanheddogleddollônpenrhyn-areurdraethceredigion (67 letters)

*A name contrived by the Fairbourne Steam Railway, Gwynedd, North Wales, for publicity purposes and in order to out-do number 4.*

4. Llanfairpwllgwyngyllgogerychwyrndrobwllllanty-siliogogogoch (58 letters)

*This is the place in Gwynedd famed especially for the length of its railway tickets. It means, 'St Mary's Church by the pool of the white hazel trees, near the rapid whirlpool, by the red cave of the church of St Tysilio'. Its official name comprises only the first 20 letters.*

5. El Pueblo de Nuestra Señora la Reina de los Angeles de la Porciuncula (57 letters)

*'The town of Our Lady the Queen of the Angels of the Little Portion', the site of a Franciscan missionary and the full Spanish name of Los Angeles. Nowadays it is customarily known by its initial letters, 'LA', making it also one of the shortest-named cities in the world.*

6. Chargoggagoggmanchauggagoggchaubunagungamaugg (45 letters)

*America's longest place name, a lake near Webster, Massachusetts. Its Indian name, loosely translated means, 'You fish on your side, I'll fish on mine, and no one fishes in the middle'. It is pronounced, 'Char-gogg-a-goog (pause) man-chaugg-a-gogg (pause) chau-bun-a-gung-a-maugg'.*

7= Lower North Branch Little Southwest Miramichi (40 letters)

*Canada's longest place name – a short river in New Brunswick.*

7= Villa Real de la Santa Fe de San Francisco de Asis (40 letters)

*The full Spanish name of Santa Fe, New Mexico, translates as 'Royal city of the holy faith of St Francis of Assisi'.*

9. Te Whakatakanga-o-te-ngarehu-o-te-ahi-a-Tamatea (38 letters)

*The Maori name of Hammer Springs, New Zealand; like the second name in this list, it refers to a legend of Tamatea, explaining how the springs were warmed by 'the falling of the cinders of the fire of Tamatea'.*

10. Loch Airidh Mhic Fhionnlaidh Dhuibh (31 letters)

*This is the name of a loch on the island of Lewis, Scotland.*

# Buildings & Structures

· · · · · · · · · · · · · · · · · · · · · · · · · · · ·

## THE WORLD'S 10 TALLEST BUILDINGS BEFORE THE AGE OF SKYSCRAPERS

|    | Building | Location | Year completed | m | ft |
|----|----------|----------|----------------|---|----|
| 1. | Eiffel Tower | Paris, France | 1889 | 300 | 984 |
| 2. | Washington Memorial | Washington, DC, USA | 1885 | 169 | 555 |
| 3. | Ulm Cathedral | Ulm, Germany | 1890 | 161 | 529 |
| 4. | Lincoln Cathedral | Lincoln, England | c.1307 (destroyed 1548) | 160 | 525 |
| 5. | Cologne Cathedral | Cologne, Germany | 1880 | 157 | 515 |
| 6. | Notre-Dame | Rouen, France | 1530 | 156 | 512 |
| 7. | St Pierre Church | Beauvais, France | 1568 | 153 | 502 |
| 8. | St Paul's Cathedral | London, England | 1315 (destroyed 1561) | 149 | 489 |
| 9. | Great Pyramid | Giza, Egypt | c.2580 BC | 146.5 | 480.9 |
| 10. | St Nicholas Church | Hamburg, Germany | 1846–47 | 144 | 475 |

BELOW A musical celebration of the one-time tallest building in the world.

*The first tall office buildings of ten storeys or more were constructed in Chicago and New York in the 1880s, with the Eiffel Tower following at the end of the decade. It was not until 1913 that the first true 'skyscraper' – a secular building exceeding the height of the great medieval cathedrals – was built: the Woolworth Building, New York. At 241m/792ft it remained the tallest habitable building in the world until 1930, when the Chrysler Building (see The World's 10 Tallest Habitable Buildings, page 90) overtook both it and the Eiffel Tower. A year later the Empire State Building topped them all, and remained the world's tallest for 40 years.*

*The height of the Washington Memorial is less than it was when it was erected, as it has steadily sunk into the ground. Lincoln Cathedral was the tallest building in the world for over 200 years, but fell in a storm. St Pierre at Beauvais collapsed in 1573. 'Old St Paul's' was destroyed by lightning on 4 June 1561; the present St Paul's Cathedral is only 112m/366ft high. The Great Pyramid stood as the world's tallest building for nearly 4,000 years, and was numbered among the Seven Wonders of the World. The loss of its topstone reduced its height to 137m/449ft.*

## BUILDINGS & STRUCTURES

# THE WORLD'S 10 TALLEST HABITABLE BUILDINGS

The Sears Tower (far left) in Chicago, currently the tallest habitable building in the world.

| | Building | Location | Year completed | Storeys | m | ft |
|---|---|---|---|---|---|---|
| 1. | Sears Tower | Chicago, USA | 1974 | 110 | 443 | 1,454 |
| 2. | Word Trade Center (twin towers) | New York City, USA | 1972 1973 | 110 110 | 417 415 | 1,388 1,362 |
| 3. | Empire State Building | New York City, USA | 1931 | 102 | 381 | 1,250 |
| 4. | Bank of China | Hong Kong | 1989 | 72 | 368 | 1,209 |
| 5. | Standard Oil Building | Chicago, USA | 1971 | 80 | 346 | 1,136 |
| 6. | John Hancock Center | Chicago, USA | 1967 | 100 | 344 | 1,127 |
| 7. | Chrysler Building | New York City, USA | 1930 | 77 | 319 | 1,046 |
| 8. | Texas Commerce Plaza | Houston, USA | 1981 | 75 | 305 | 1,002 |
| 9. | Allied Bank Plaza | Houston, USA | 1983 | 71 | 300 | 985 |
| 10. | Columbia Center | Seattle, USA | 1985 | 76 | 291 | 954 |

*C*entral Place skyscraper, under construction in Brisbane Australia, at 445m/1,460ft, was planned to become the world's tallest inhabited building, but local objections have halted its construction.

## BUILDINGS & STRUCTURES

# THE 10 TALLEST HABITABLE* BUILDINGS IN THE UK

| | Building | Year completed | Height m | ft |
|---|---|---|---|---|
| 1. | National Westminster Tower, London EC2 | 1979 | 183 | 600 |
| 2. | Post Office Tower, London W1 | 1966 | 177 | 580 |
| 3. | Blackpool Tower | 1894 | 158 | 519 |
| 4. | Shakespeare Tower | 1971 | 128 | 419 |
| | Cromwell Tower | 1973 | 128 | 419 |
| | Lauderdale Tower | 1974 | 128 | 419 |
| | Barbican, London EC2 | | | |
| 5. | Euston Tower, Euston Road, London NW1 | 1969 | 124 | 408 |
| 6. | Cooperative Insurance Society Building, Miller Street, Manchester | 1962 | 122 | 399 |
| 7. | Centrepoint, New Oxford Street, London WC1 | 1966 | 121 | 398 |
| 8. | Britannic House, Moor Lane, London EC2 | 1967 | 120 | 395 |
| 9= | Commercial Union, Undershaft, London EC3 | 1969 | 118 | 387 |
| 9= | Millbank Tower, Millbank, London SW1 | 1963 | 118 | 387 |

*excludes radio masts, chimneys and church spires

*Although the National Westminster Tower is Britain's tallest office building, it does not even rank in the Top 100 in the league table of the world's tallest. The Canary Wharf tower, currently under construction, is planned to attain 243.8m/800ft.*

The 'Nat West' Tower dominates the London skyline.

# THE 10 LARGEST HOTELS IN THE UK

| | Hotel | Number of rooms |
|---|---|---|
| 1. | Regent Palace, London | 1,034 |
| 2= | Forum, London | 907 |
| 2= | Cumberland, London | 907 |
| 4. | Tower, London | 808 |
| 5. | Strand Palace, London | 777 |
| 6. | Metropole, Birmingham | 694 |
| 7. | Post House, Heathrow | 607 |
| 8. | Hilton International, Kensington | 606 |
| 9. | Excelsior, Heathrow | 580 |
| 10. | White House, London | 577 |

# THE 10 TALLEST CHURCHES IN THE WORLD

| | Building | Year completed | m | ft |
|---|---|---|---|---|
| 1. | Chicago Methodist Temple | 1924 | 173 | 568 |
| 2. | Ulm Cathedral | 1890 | 161 | 528 |
| 3. | Cologne Cathedral | 1880 | 156 | 513 |
| 4. | Rouen Cathedral | 1876 | 148 | 485 |
| 5. | St Nicholas, Hamburg | 1847 | 145 | 475 |
| 6. | Notre Dame, Strasbourg | 1439 | 142 | 465 |
| 7. | St Peter's, Rome | 1612 | 140 | 458 |
| 8. | St Stephen's Cathedral, Vienna | 1433 | 136 | 446 |
| 9. | St Joseph's Oratory, Montreal | 1922 | 126 | 412 |
| 10. | Antwerp Cathedral | 1525 | 124 | 406 |
| | *Salisbury Cathedral* | *1375* | *123* | *404* |

## BUILDINGS & STRUCTURES

'Great Paul', the largest bell in the United Kingdom, en route for St Paul's Cathedral.

# THE 10 LARGEST BELLS IN THE UK

| Bell/Location | Year cast | Weight tonnes |
|---|---|---|
| 1. 'Great Paul', St Paul's Cathedral, London | 1882 | 16.97 |
| 2. 'Great George', Liverpool Cathedral | 1942 | 14.99 |
| 3. 'Big Ben', Houses of Parliament, London | 1858 | 13.77 |
| 4. 'Great Peter', York Minster | 1927 | 11.02 |
| 5. The Hour Bell, 'Little John', Nottingham Exchange Building | 1928 | 10.57 |
| 6. 'Great George', Bristol University | 1925 | 9.75 |
| 7. The Hour Bell, 'Great Abel', Manchester Town Hall | 1883 | 8.28 |
| 8. Bourdon Bell, 'Hosannah', Buckfast Abbey | 1936 | 7.57 |
| 9. Bourdon Bell, Great Bell or 'Great John', Beverley Minster | 1901 | 7.16 |
| 10. 'Great Tom of Oxford', Christ Church College, Oxford (re-cast later in the 17th century) | 1680 | 6.35 |

*A*ll these large bells, except 'Great Tom of Oxford' and 'Big Ben', were cast by Taylors of Loughborough. An earlier 'Big Ben' was cast in Stockton-on-Tees and transported to London by sea and river, but cracked during testing. The metal was re-used in casting the new bell by the Whitechapel Bell Foundry (which also cast the Liberty Bell, Philadelphia, and the Bicentennial Bell presented to the United States by HM The Queen). 'Big Ben' is the most heard bell in the world, since its chimes are broadcast every weekday at the opening of ITV's News At Ten and to introduce BBC radio news programmes. 'Great Paul' has a diameter of 2.90 m/9 ft 6½ in.

Britain's tallest chimney (no. 7 in the world) at Drax power station.

# THE 10 LARGEST BELLS IN THE WESTERN WORLD

| | Bell/Location | Year cast | Weight tonnes |
|---|---|---|---|
| 1. | Tsar Kolokol, Moscow, USSR | 1733 | 196.09 |
| 2= | 'Kaiserglocke', Cologne Cathedral, West Germany | 1925 | 25.40 |
| 2= | Lisbon Cathedral, Portugal | post-1344 | 25.40 |
| 4. | St Stephen's Cathedral, Vienna, Austria | 1957 | 21.39 |
| 5. | 'Savoyarde', Sacré-Coeur Basilica, Paris, France | 1895 | 19.71 |
| 6. | Riverside Church, New York, USA | 1931 | 18.54 |
| 7. | Olmütz, Czechoslovakia | 1931 | 18.19 |
| 8. | Campagna Gorda, Toledo Cathedral, Spain | 1753 | 17.27 |
| 9. | Great Paul, St Paul's Cathedral, London, England | 1882 | 16.97 |
| 10. | Montreal Cathedral, Canada | 1847 | 11.25 |

*T*he largest bell in the world is the 5.91-m/19 ft 4.5-in diameter Tsar Kolokol, cast in Moscow for the Kremlin. It cracked before its installation, so has remained outside the Kremlin, unrung, ever since. The Cologne Cathedral bell is the heaviest suspended bell in use in the world. The bell of the Riverside Church, New York (the largest ever cast in England), is the bourdon (the lowest-sounding note) of the Laura Spelman Rockefeller Memorial carillon. It weighs 18.54 tonnes with a diameter of 3.10 m/10 ft 2in. It is only one of the 74-bell carillon, the world's largest, the total weight of which is 103.64 tonnes. Outside the West, the Mingoon bell in Mandalay, Burma, cast in 1780, weighs approximately 88 tonnes, but was designed to be struck with a beam, not rung with a clapper like Western bells. There are also large oriental-style bells in Chonan, Japan (75 tonnes) and Peking (54 tonnes).

Tsar Kolokol, Moscow, the world's most gigantic bell, showing the doorway-sized crack that caused it to remain silent.

# THE 10 TALLEST CHIMNEYS IN THE WORLD

| | Chimney/location | Height m | ft |
|---|---|---|---|
| 1. | International Nickel Company, Copper Hill, Sudbury, Ontario, Canada | 380 | 1,246 |
| 2. | Pennsylvania Electric Company and New York State Electric & Gas Corporation, Homer City, Pennsylvania, USA | 369 | 1,210 |
| 3. | Ohio Power Company, Mitchell power plant, Cresap, West Virginia, USA | 368 | 1,206 |
| 4. | Kennecott Copper Corporation, Magna, Utah, USA | 366 | 1,200 |
| 5. | Zasavje power station Trboulje, Yugoslavia | 360 | 1,181 |
| 6. | Empresa Nacional de Electricidad SA, Puentes de García Rodriguez, Spain | 350 | 1,148 |
| 7. | Drax power station, Yorkshire, England | 259 | 850 |
| 8. | Kashira power station, USSR | 250 | 820 |
| 9. | Grain power station, Isle of Grain, Kent | 244 | 800 |
| 10. | Ohio Electric Corporation, Clifty Creek, Madison, Indiana (3 chimneys) | 215 | 707 |

*N*umbers 1–4 and 6 were all built by M.W. Kellogg, an American engineering company. The largest internal volume is number 6, which is 1,897,239 cu m/ 6,700,000 cu ft. The outside diameter of number 4 is the largest in the world – 38m/124ft at the base, tapering to 12m/40ft at the top.

# THE 10 LARGEST REFLECTING TELESCOPES IN THE WORLD

| | Telescope | Location | Year opened | Aperture cm |
|---|---|---|---|---|
| 1. | Mauna Kea | Hawaii | 1989 | 1,000 |
| 2. | Mount Semirodrik | USSR | 1976 | 600 |
| 3. | Mount Palomar | California | 1948 | 508 |
| 4. | La Palma | Canaries | 1987 | 420 |
| 5= | Cerro Torro | Chile | 1970 | 401 |
| 5= | Kitt Peak | Arizona | 1970 | 401 |
| 7. | Siding Spring (Anglo-Australian) | Australia | 1974 | 389 |
| 8= | Mount Stromlo | Australia | 1972 | 381 |
| 8= | La Cilla | Chile | 1975 | 381 |
| 10. | Mauna Kea (Canadian-French-Hawaiian) | Hawaii | 1970 | 366 |

The giant telescope in California's Mount Palomar Observatory.

# THE 10 OLDEST CLOCKS IN GREAT BRITAIN

1. Salisbury Cathedral, *c*.1386
   A faceless clock, and probably the oldest working timepiece in the world, it was restored in 1956.

2. Wells Cathedral, *c*.1392
   Now in the Science Museum, London.

3. Ottery St Mary, late 14th century
   Much altered from its original construction.

4. Hexagonal Burgundian clock, *c*.1450
   From the Victoria & Albert Museum collection, now on permanent loan to the British Museum.

5. St Mary's Church, Launceston, *c*.1480
   A clock with a 24-hour stone face.

6. Cothele House, Cornwall, *c*.1495
   Mostly original.

7. Exeter Cathedral, late 15th century
   With an astronomical dial; the striking train probably dates from the 16th century.

8. Durham Cathedral, *c*.1500
   In an elaborately carved case with dials.

9. Domestic clock, early 15th century
   A clock with a castellated dial, now in the British Museum.

10. St Augustine of Canterbury Church, East Hendred, Berkshire, 1535
    A clock with three trains made by John Seymour of Wantage, Berkshire.

Wells Cathedral's medieval clock; the original mechanism survives in the Science Museum, London.

# BUILDINGS & STRUCTURES

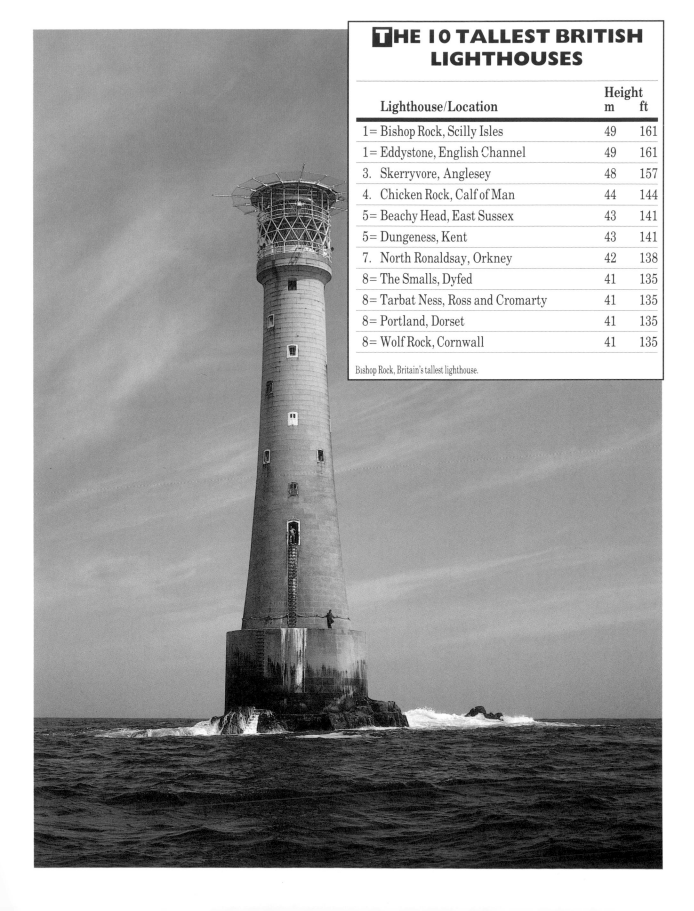

## THE 10 TALLEST BRITISH LIGHTHOUSES

| Lighthouse/Location | Height m | ft |
|---|---|---|
| 1= Bishop Rock, Scilly Isles | 49 | 161 |
| 1= Eddystone, English Channel | 49 | 161 |
| 3. Skerryvore, Anglesey | 48 | 157 |
| 4. Chicken Rock, Calf of Man | 44 | 144 |
| 5= Beachy Head, East Sussex | 43 | 141 |
| 5= Dungeness, Kent | 43 | 141 |
| 7. North Ronaldsay, Orkney | 42 | 138 |
| 8= The Smalls, Dyfed | 41 | 135 |
| 8= Tarbat Ness, Ross and Cromarty | 41 | 135 |
| 8= Portland, Dorset | 41 | 135 |
| 8= Wolf Rock, Cornwall | 41 | 135 |

Bishop Rock, Britain's tallest lighthouse.

## BUILDINGS & STRUCTURES

### THE 10 OLDEST PILLAR BOXES IN DAILY USE IN THE UK

| | |
|---|---|
| 1= | Union Street, St Peter Port, Guernsey (1853) |
| 1= | Barnes Cross, Bishops Caundle, Dorset (1853) |
| 3= | Mount Pleasant/College Road, Framlingham, Suffolk (1856) |
| 3= | Double Street, Framlingham, Suffolk (1856) |
| 3= | Market Place, Banbury, Oxfordshire (1856) |
| 3= | Mudeford Green, Christchurch, Dorset (1856) |
| 3= | Cornwallis/Victoria Road, Milford-on-Sea, Hampshire (1856) |
| 3= | Eastgate, Warwick (1856) |
| 3= | Westgate, Warwick (1856) |
| 3= | High Street, Eton, Berkshire (1856) |

*T*he Penny Post was introduced in 1840, and soon afterwards the public pressed for roadside posting boxes, which already existed in Belgium and France. In 1851 Anthony Trollope (best known as the author of The Barchester Chronicles, but at this time a Post Office Surveyor's Clerk) first suggested their use in St Helier, Jersey. They were set up in four locations there on 23 November 1852. No trace of them survives, but it is known that they were painted dark red. The following year, on 8 February 1853, one was erected in St Peter Port, Guernsey – the oldest still in use in the United Kingdom – to be followed by others, of which those in this list are the earliest survivors. A later model, the hexagonal 'Penfold' pillar-box dating from 1859–66, is still found in surprising numbers; over 40 are in daily use in London alone.

RIGHT The pillar-box in Union Street, St Peter Port, dates from 1853.

### THE 10 MOST POPULAR HOME IMPROVE-MENTS

1. Double glazing
2. House extensions
3. Fitted kitchens
4. Central heating
5. New bathroom suites
6. Roof repairs
7. Conservatory or porch
8. Landscaping
9. New garages
10. Fitted bedroom furniture

Based on a survey conducted by the Halifax Building Society.

*T*here are certain regional variations in home improvements. Double glazing, for example, is in greater demand in the West Country and North of England, central heating is the most common improvement in the northwest, while house extensions and landscaping are more popular in the south, where higher property prices prevail.

### THE 10 COMMONEST HOUSE NAMES IN THE UK

1. The Bungalow
2. The Cottage
3. Rose Cottage
4. The School House
5. The White House
6. Hillcrest
7. The Lodge
8. Woodlands
9. The Coach House
10. Hillside

### CROWN BERGER'S 10 BESTSELLING PAINT COLOURS

1. Brilliant White
2. Magnolia
3. Pale Grey
4. Pale Pink
5. Pale Peach
6. Pale Beige
7. Warm Pink
8. Peach
9. Pale Cream
10. Pale Blue

# Art

· · · · · · · · · · · · · · · · · · · · · · · · · ·

## THE 10 MOST EXPENSIVE PAINTINGS EVER SOLD AT AUCTION

1.  Vincent van Gogh, *Irises* $53,900,000/£30,187,623
    Sotheby's, New York, 11 November 1987

*The world record for any work of art, the identity of its purchaser remains a mystery: speculation has pointed towards the Australian businessman Alan Bond.*

2.  Pablo Picasso, *Self-portrait* $45,865,500/£28,147,000
    Sotheby's, New York, May 1989

*The world record for a 20th-century painting, it had been sold in 1970 for $352,200/£147,000. Its new price thus represents an increase of over 19,000%.*

3.  Jacopo da Carucci (Pontormo), *Portrait of Cosimo di Medici* $35,200,000/£22,003,000
    Christie's, New York, 31 May 1989

*The world record price for an Old Master, it was bought by the J. Paul Getty Museum, Malibu. The previous record for an Old Master – and at that time for any work of art – was held by Andrea Mantegna's Adoration of the Magi, sold at Christie's, London, on 18 April 1985 for £8,100,000.*

4.  Vincent van Gogh, *Sunflowers* £24,750,000/$39,400,000
    Christie's, London, 30 March 1987

*Bought by the Yasuda Fire and Marine Insurance Company of Tokyo, Japan.*

5.  Pablo Picasso, *Acrobate et Jeune Arlequin* £20,900,000/$37,808,000
    Christie's, London, 28 November 1988

*Bought by Mitsukoshi, a Japanese department store.*

6.  Claude Monet, *Dans la Prairie* £14,300,000/$26,026,000
    Sotheby's, London, 28 June 1988

7.  Pablo Picasso, *Maternité* $24,750,000/£13,674,033
    Christie's, New York, 14 June 1988

*Bought by an unnamed Latin-American collector, the painting was formerly owned by William Goetz, producer of such films as The Glenn Miller Story, and his wife Edith, the daughter of Hollywood producer Louis B. Mayer.*

8.  Vincent van Gogh, *Le Pont de Trinquetaille* £12,650,000/$20,610,000
    Christie's, London, 29 June 1987

9.  Pierre-Auguste Renoir, *La Promenade* £10,340,000/$17,600,000
    Sotheby's, London, 4 April 1989

*Sold on behalf of the British Rail Pension Fund, which in 1976 had paid £682,000 for it, thereby making a 1,500% profit on their investment. Bought by the J. Paul Getty Museum, Malibu, California.*

10. Jasper Johns, *False Start* $17,050,000/£9,406,896
    Sotheby's, New York, 10 November 1988

*The world record for a painting by a living artist. In 1960, the same painting had been sold for $3,150/£1,120 – it has thus increased in value by over 500,000%*

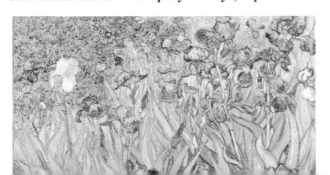

*Irises* (1889) by Vincent Van Gogh celebrated its centenary by maintaining its record as the world's most expensive painting.

# ART

# THE TOP 10 PRICES PAID FOR MODERN SCULPTURE

1. Edgar Degas, *Petite danseuse de quatorze ans*
   $9,250,000/£5,138,889
   Christie's, New York, 1 November 1988

2. Edgar Degas, *Petite danseuse de quatorze ans*
   $9,200,000/£4,893,617
   Sotheby's, New York, 10 May 1988

3. Alberto Giacometti, *L'Homme qui marche I*
   $6,222,000/£3,400,000
   Christie's, London, 28 November 1988

4. Alberto Giacometti, *Trois hommes qui marchent*
   $3,500,000/£1,861,702
   Christie's, New York, 11 May 1988

5. Alberto Giacometti, *Grande femme debout II*
   $3,300,000/£2,000,000
   Christie's, New York, 12 May 1987

6. Alberto Giacometti, *Grande femme debout I*
   $2,800,000/£1,696,970
   Christie's, New York, 12 May 1987

7. Alberto Giacometti, *Grande femme debout III*
   $2,300,000/£1,393,939
   Christie's, New York, 12 May 1987

8. Alberto Giacometti, *La clairière*
   $2,065,000/£1,134,216
   Drouot, Paris, 22 June 1988

9. Alberto Giacometti, *Homme qui marche sous la pluie*
   $1,800,000/£1,000,000
   Christie's, New York, 15 November 1988

10. Henri Matisse, *Nu couché I (Aurore)*
    $1,300,000/£915,493
    Christie's, New York, 14 November 1986

*converted at rate prevailing at time of sale

# THE 10 LARGEST MUSEUMS IN THE UK

(A) Based on total site area used by the museum, but excluding adjoining gardens

| Museum | Site area hectares | acres |
|---|---|---|
| 1= Washington F Pit Museum, Tyne & Wear | 243 | 600 |
| 1= Ancient Iron Mines Museum, Clearwell, Gloucestershire | 243 | 600 |
| 3. Science Museum at Wroughton, Wiltshire | 202 | 500 |
| 4. Stockton Borough Council Museums, Cleveland | 194 | 480 |
| 5. Transport Museum, Belfast | 162 | 400 |
| 6. Beverley Art Gallery & Museum, Yorkshire | 158 | 390 |
| 7. Imperial War Museum, London SE1, with Duxford Airfield, Cambridgeshire | 121 | 300 |
| 8. Derby Museums & Art Galleries, Derbyshire | 108 | 267 |
| 9. North of England Open Air Museum Beamish, Co. Durham | 105 | 260 |
| 10. Woodhorn Colliery Museum, Ashington, Northumberland | 61 | 150 |

*Nu couché I* by Henri Matisse – just within the Top Ten, though sold for less than a fifth of the price of the world's most valuable sculpture.

**ART**

# THE 10 LARGEST MUSEUMS IN THE UK

(B) Based on floor area of buildings occupied by the museums

| Museum | Floor area sq m | sq ft |
|---|---|---|
| 1. British Museum (Natural History), London | 87,000 | 936,459 |
| 2. British Museum, London | 80,000 | 861,112 |
| 3. Science Museum, London | 42,873 | 461,481 |
| 4. Doncaster Museum and Art Gallery | 36,000 | 387,500 |
| 5. Harewood House, Leeds | 35,000 | 376,737 |
| 6. Black Country Museum, Dudley | 32,000 | 344,445 |
| 7. David Livingstone Centre, Blantyre, Strathclyde | 31,972 | 344,145 |
| 8= Ulster Folk and Transport Museum, Holywood, County Down | 25,000 | 269,098 |
| 8= National Railway Museum, York | 25,000 | 269,098 |
| 10. Grosvenor Museum, Chester | 18,395 | 198,002 |

*The floor area of the British Museum (Natural History) is equivalent to 12 football pitches.*

The cathedral-like British Museum (Natural History), opened in 1881 and expanded in recent years, making it the largest museum in the United Kingdom.

# THE 10 BEST-ATTENDED POST-WAR ART EXHIBITIONS IN THE UK

| Subject | Location | Date | Total attendance |
|---|---|---|---|
| 1. Treasures of Tutankhamun | BM | 1972 | 1,694,117 |
| 2. Britain Can Make It | V&A | 1947 | 1,500,000 |
| 3. Chinese | RA | 1974 | 771,466 |
| 4. Post-Impressionism | RA | 1980 | 648,281 |
| 5. Pompeii | RA | 1977 | 633,347 |
| 6. Great Japan | RA | 1982 | 523,005 |
| 7. The Vikings | BM | 1980 | 465,000 |
| 8. Genius of Venice | RA | 1983 | 452,885 |
| 9. Turner | RA | 1975 | 424,629 |
| 10. Renoir | HG | 1985 | 365,000 |

BM – British Museum; HG – Hayward Gallery; RA – Royal Academy; V&A – Victoria & Albert Museum

*Although the Treasures of Tutankhamun remains the best-attended art exhibition of all time, many exhibitions during the 19th century attracted enormous numbers of visitors, among them the 1881 Spanish Art Treasures exhibition at the Victoria & Albert Museum, which was seen by 1,220,000 people, The more general exhibitions, in which art shows were only a part of the extravaganza, were often visited by staggering numbers; more than 6,000,000 saw the 1851 Great Exhibition, while 8,500,000 attended the 1951 Festival of Britain.*

## ART

## THE 10 BEST-ATTENDED EXHIBITIONS AT THE ROYAL ACADEMY*

| | Subject | Date | Total attendance |
|---|---|---|---|
| 1. | Chinese | 1974 | 771,466 |
| 2. | Post-Impressionism | 1980 | 648,281 |
| 3. | Pompeii | 1977 | 633,347 |
| 4. | Great Japan | 1982 | 523,005 |
| 5. | Genius of Venice | 1983 | 452,885 |
| 6. | Turner | 1975 | 424,629 |
| 7. | El Dorado | 1979 | 344,033 |
| 8. | Age of Chivalry | 1987/88 | 340,150 |
| 9. | Chagall | 1985 | 282,851 |
| 10. | 20th-Century British Art | 1987 | 211,972 |

*during the past 20 years, the only period for which detailed comparative figures exist

## THE 10 BEST-ATTENDED EXHIBITIONS AT THE TATE GALLERY

| | Subject | Date | Total attendance |
|---|---|---|---|
| 1. | John Constable | 1976 | 313,615 |
| 2. | Salvador Dali – A Retrospective | 1980 | 236,615 |
| 3. | The Pre-Raphaelites | 1984 | 224,659 |
| 4. | David Hockney – A Retrospective | 1988/9 | 173,334 |
| 5. | Late Picasso, 1953–72 | 1988 | 139,457 |
| 6. | The Essential Cubism | 1983 | 122,246 |
| 7. | Thomas Gainsborough | 1980/1 | 112,517 |
| 8. | Francis Bacon | 1985 | 109,732 |
| 9. | William Blake | 1978 | 106,229 |
| 10. | George Stubbs | 1984/5 | 97,852 |

*A*lthough the Top 10 exhibitions are ranked according to total attendance, the figures are affected by the duration of a show, which may be open for a few weeks to three months. Dali comes out on top of the highest attendance per day chart, with an average of 3,943 over the 61 days the exhibition was open. Exhibitions devoted to such artists as Peter Blake and Andy Warhol would appear in a Top 10 based on average daily attendance.

One of the Flying Horses of Kansu, a major attraction in the Royal Academy Chinese exhibition in 1974. The bronze horses date from the seventh-century Eastern Han dynasty, and were excavated in 1969 at the Wu-Wie tomb in Kansu.

RIGHT *Yarmouth Jetty* by John Constable, in the Tate Gallery's collection. One of three versions of the same scene, the painting dates from 1823.

**ART**

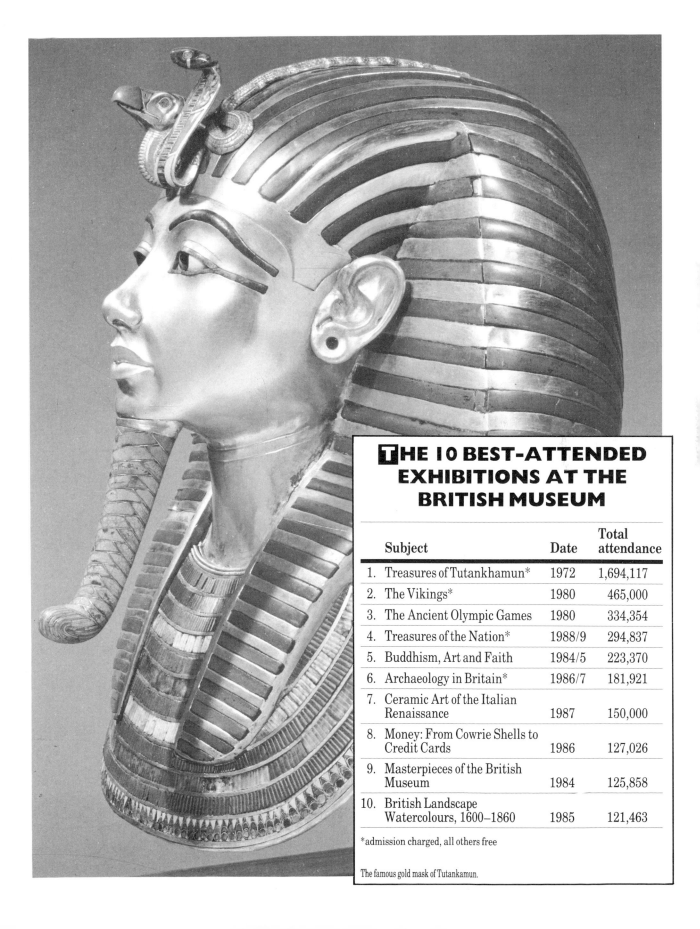

## THE 10 BEST-ATTENDED EXHIBITIONS AT THE BRITISH MUSEUM

| | Subject | Date | Total attendance |
|---|---|---|---|
| 1. | Treasures of Tutankhamun* | 1972 | 1,694,117 |
| 2. | The Vikings* | 1980 | 465,000 |
| 3. | The Ancient Olympic Games | 1980 | 334,354 |
| 4. | Treasures of the Nation* | 1988/9 | 294,837 |
| 5. | Buddhism, Art and Faith | 1984/5 | 223,370 |
| 6. | Archaeology in Britain* | 1986/7 | 181,921 |
| 7. | Ceramic Art of the Italian Renaissance | 1987 | 150,000 |
| 8. | Money: From Cowrie Shells to Credit Cards | 1986 | 127,026 |
| 9. | Masterpieces of the British Museum | 1984 | 125,858 |
| 10. | British Landscape Watercolours, 1600–1860 | 1985 | 121,463 |

*admission charged, all others free

The famous gold mask of Tutankamun.

# ART

## THE 10 BESTSELLING POSTCARDS IN THE BRITISH LIBRARY

1. View of the British Library Reading Room
2. Opening page of the *Lindisfarne Gospels*, 698AD
3. The '42-line Bible' (the first printed Bible) probably by Gutenberg, Fust & Schoeffer, 1453–55
4. Page showing the 'Queen of Hearts' from *Alice's Adventures Under Ground*, 1864, Lewis Carroll's autograph manuscript of the book that became *Alice in Wonderland*
5. Noah's Ark from the *Bedford Book of Hours*, 1423
6. Indian rhinoceros, an 18th-century painting by an unknown Indian artist
7. Robert Dighton's 'Caricature Map of England and Wales', 1795
8. Detail of a page from a concerto by George Frederick Handel
9. Lithograph by V. Burlink from a Russian Futurist book, 1914
10. Illustration from an advertisement for a Daimler sports saloon, 1935

*T*he British Library's *bestselling postcards show something of the enormous diversity of its collections, which range across the books, manuscripts and music, maps and ephemera represented here to stamps, newspapers and sound recordings.*

Popular postcards: *The Seine at Asnières* (top), *Carnation, Lily, Lily, Rose* (above right) and the *Lindisfarne Gospels*' opening page.

## THE 10 BESTSELLING POSTCARDS IN THE NATIONAL GALLERY

| | Artist | Painting |
|---|---|---|
| 1. | Pierre-Auguste Renoir | *The Seine at Asnières* |
| 2. | Vincent van Gogh | *Sunflowers* |
| 3. | Vincent van Gogh | *A Cornfield with Cypresses* |
| 4. | Claude Monet | *The Water-lily Pond* |
| 5. | Claude Monet | *The Thames Below Westminster* |
| 6. | Pierre-Auguste Renoir | *The Umbrellas* |
| 7. | Pierre-Auguste Renoir | *Première Sortie* |
| 8. | John Constable | *The Haywain* |
| 9. | Jean-Baptiste Perroneau | *A Girl with a Kitten* |
| 10. | J.M.W. Turner | *Rain, Steam, and Speed* |

*T*he first seven are all *Impressionists or Post-Impressionists. Only numbers 8 and 10 are English.*

## THE 10 BESTSELLING POSTCARDS IN THE TATE GALLERY

| | Artist | Painting |
|---|---|---|
| 1. | John Singer Sargent | *Carnation, Lily, Lily, Rose* |
| 2. | David Hockney | *A Bigger Splash* |
| 3. | J.M.W. Turner | *Norham Castle* |
| 4. | John Everett Millais | *Ophelia* |
| 5. | Auguste Rodin | *The Kiss* |
| 6. | Francis Bacon | *Study of William Blake* |
| 7. | Wassily Kandinsky | *Swinging* |
| 8. | Henri Matisse | *Snail* |
| 9. | Salvador Dali | *Metamorphosis of Narcissus* |
| 10. | Arthur Hughes | *April Love* |

*T*wo Pre-Raphaelites (4 and *10), two contemporary painters (2 and 6), a sculptor (5), a Surrealist (9), an American (1), two French (5 and 8), one Russian (7) and five British artists represent in miniature the wealth of the Tate's collections – and something of the taste of the postcard-buying public.*

# Language, Literature & Education

## ▆HE 10 LARGEST LIBRARIES IN THE WORLD

| | Library | Location | Founded | Books |
|---|---|---|---|---|
| 1. | Library of Congress | Washington, DC, USA | 1800 | 22,000,000 |
| 2. | British Library | London, England | 1753/1973* | 18,000,000 |
| 3. | Stave V.I. Lenin Library of the USSR | Moscow, USSR | 1862 | 11,750,000 |
| 4. | Harvard University Library | Cambridge, Mass., USA | 1638 | 10,929,899 |
| 5. | Biblioteca Academiei Republicii Socialiste Romania | Bucharest, Romania | 1867 | 9,100,000 |
| 6= | New York Public Library | New York City, USA | 1848 | 9,000,000 |
| 6= | Bibliothèque National | Paris, France | 1480 | 9,000,000 |
| 8. | Yale University Library | New Haven, Conn., USA | 1701 | 8,821,105 |
| 9. | State M.E. Saltykov-Shchedrin State Public Library | Leningrad, USSR | 1795 | 8,000,000 |
| 10. | National Diet Library | Tokyo, Japan | 1948 | 6,560,000 |

*Founded as part of the British Museum in 1753; became independent body in 1973.

The Library of Congress in Washington, still the largest library in the world despite rival claims.

*Rivalries between libraries in the Iron Curtain and the West seem to have been responsible for the hugely inflated figures claimed for the State M.E. Saltykov-Shchedrin Library (21,500,000) and for the State V.I. Lenin Library (28,216,000). As these appear to include individual copies of newspapers and periodicals, they cannot be compared with the holdings of bound books in Western libraries. It is also known that a very large number of books were recently destroyed in a disastrous fire at the Saltykov-Shchedrin.*

# LANGUAGE, LITERATURE & EDUCATION

## THE 10 LARGEST LIBRARIES IN THE UK

| | Library | Location | Founded | Books |
|---|---|---|---|---|
| 1. | British Library | London | 1753/1973 | 18,000,000 |
| 2= | Bodleian Library | Oxford | 1602 | 5,000,000 |
| 2= | National Library of Scotland | Edinburgh | 1682 | 5,000,000 |
| 4. | University of Cambridge | Cambridge | *c.*1400 | 4,200,000 |
| 5. | Hampshire County Library | Winchester | 1925 | 3,500,000 |
| 6. | Lancashire County Library | Preston | 1924 | 3,452,895 |
| 7. | John Rylands Library* | Manchester | 1851 | 3,350,000 |
| 8. | Kent County Library | Maidstone | 1921 | 3,300,000 |
| 9. | Birmingham Public Lilbrary | Birmingham | 1861 | 2,562,000 |
| 10. | National Library of Wales | Aberystwyth | 1907 | 2,500,000 |

*In 1972 the John Rylands Library (founded 1900) was amalgamated with Manchester University Library (1851).

Oxford's famous Bodleian Library.

# THE 10 AUTHORS WITH THE MOST BORROWED BOOKS IN THE UK TOP 100

| Author | Titles |
| --- | --- |
| 1. Catherine Cookson | 35 |
| 2. Dick Francis | 12 |
| 3= Jeffrey Archer | 6 |
| 3= Jack Higgins | 6 |
| 3= Wilbur Smith | 6 |
| 6. Danielle Steel | 5 |
| 7= Barbara Taylor Bradford | 3 |
| 7= Alistair MacLean | 3 |
| 9= Desmond Bagley | 2 |
| 9= Len Deighton | 2 |
| 9= Frederick Forsyth | 2 |
| 9= Susan Howatch | 2 |
| 9= Lena Kennedy | 2 |
| 9= Sidney Sheldon | 2 |

*The Public Lending Rights Office monitors library lendings in order to allocate fees to registered authors in proportion to the number of borrowings of their books (although its data also includes lendings of unregistered authors). It is thus able to issue a list of the 100 most-borrowed library books.*

The prolific novelist Catherine Cookson, Britain's most borrowed author.

Asterix by Goscinny, Britain's most borrowed children's author.

# THE 10 MOST PUBLISHED TYPES OF BOOK IN THE UK

| Type | Total published |
| --- | --- |
| 1. Fiction | 6,496 |
| 2. Children's books | 5,063 |
| 3. Political science and economics | 4,307 |
| 4. Medical science | 3,423 |
| 5. History | 2,153 |
| 6. Biography | 2,131 |
| 7. Religion and theology | 2,047 |
| 8. Commerce | 2,033 |
| 9. School textbooks | 2,007 |
| 10. Law and public administration | 1,932 |

*In 1988 some 56,514 new books, reprints and new editions of books were published in the United Kingdom. With slight annual fluctuations, the total figure has been progressively increasing: 40 years ago, fewer than 15,000 new books were published; 20 years ago it exceeded 30,000 for the first time.*

# THE 10 CHILDREN'S AUTHORS WITH THE MOST BORROWED BOOKS IN THE UK TOP 100

| Author | Titles |
| --- | --- |
| 1. Goscinny (Asterix books) | 15 |
| 2. Shirley Hughes | 12 |
| 3. Allan Ahlberg | 10 |
| 4. Eric Hill | 7 |
| 5. Roald Dahl | 6 |
| 6. Val Biro | 5 |
| 7= Judy Blume | 4 |
| 7= Pat Hutchins | 4 |
| 9= Judith Kerr | 3 |
| 9= Jill Murphy | 3 |
| 9= Helen Nicoll & Jan Pienkowski | 3 |

# LANGUAGE, LITERATURE & EDUCATION

*It* is extremely difficult to establish precise sales even of contemporary books, and virtually impossible to do so with books published long ago. The publication of variant editions, unrecorded foreign versions and pirated copies all affect the global picture, and few publishers or authors are willing to expose their royalty statements to public scrutiny. As a result, this Top 10 list offers no more than the 'best guess' at the great bestsellers of the past, and it may well be that there are other books with a valid claim to place on it.

If *Old Moore's Almanac* were classed as a book rather than a periodical or a pamphlet, it would appear high on the list. Having been published annually since 1697, its total sales to date are believed to be well over 100,000,000. Numerous translations of books by Marx, Lenin and Stalin have probably sold more than 20,000,000 copies. Among runners-up that are known to have sold in excess of 10,000,000 copies are the *Better Homes and Gardens Cook Book* (first published in 1930), *Webster's New World Dictionary of the American Language*, *Betty Crocker's Cookbook* (1950), Mario Puzo's *The Godfather (1969)*, William Blatty's *The Exorcist* (1971), Harper Lee's *To Kill a Mockingbird* (1960), *The Pocket Atlas* (1917), and Grace Metalious's *Peyton Place* (1956).

Over 97,000,000 copies of the Jehovah's Witness tract, *The Truth That Leads to Eternal Life*, first published in 1968, are believed to have been distributed, but as they were not sold, it does not technically rank as a bestseller.

## THE 10 BESTSELLING BOOKS OF ALL TIME

1. *The Bible*     3,000,000,000

*No* one really knows how many copies of the Bible have been printed, sold or distributed. The Bible Society's attempt to calculate the number printed between 1816 and 1975 produced the figure of 2,458,000,000. It is now thought to be closer to 3,000,000,000. Whatever the precise figure, it is by far the bestselling book of all time.

2. *Quotations from the Works of Mao Tse-Tung*     800,000,000

*C*hairman Mao's 'Little Red Book' could scarcely fail to become a bestseller: between the years 1966–71, it was compulsory for every Chinese adult to own a copy.

3. *American Spelling Book* by Noah Webster     100,000,000

*F*irst published in 1783, this reference book by American man of letters Noah Webster (1758–1843) – of Webster's Dictionary *fame* – remained a bestseller throughout the 19th century.

4. *The Guinness Book of Records*     60,000,000+

*F*irst published in 1955, the Guinness Book of Records *stands out as the greatest contemporary publishing achievement. In the United Kingdom there have been 31 annual editions; there have also been numerous foreign language editions.*

5. *The McGuffey Readers* by William Holmes McGuffey     60,000,000

*P*ublished in numerous editions from 1853, some authorities have put the sales of these educational textbooks by American anthologist William Holmes McGuffey (1800–73) as high as 122,000,000.

6. *A Message to Garcia* by Elbert Hubbard     40–50,000,000

*H*ubbard's polemic on the subject of labour relations was published in 1899 and within a few years had achieved these phenomenal sales largely because many American employers purchased

ABOVE The Gutenberg Bible, the first printed edition of the world's bestselling book.

LEFT Chairman Mao surrounded by a handful of the 800,000,000 owners of his 'Little Red Book'.

## LANGUAGE, LITERATURE & EDUCATION

*bulk supplies to distribute to their employees. The literary career of Elbert Hubbard (1856–1915) was cut short when he went down with the* Lusitania, *but even in death he was a record-breaker: his posthumous* My Philosophy *(1916) was published in the largest-ever 'limited edition' of 9,983 copies!*

| 7. World Almanac | 36,000,000+ |
|---|---|

*This has been published annually since 1868, hence its status as a long-term bestseller.*

| 8. In His Steps: 'What Would Jesus Do?' by Rev. Charles Monroe Sheldon | 28,500,000 |
|---|---|

*Though virtually unknown today, Charles Sheldon (1857–1946) achieved fame and fortune with this 1896 religious treatise.*

| 9. Valley of the Dolls by Jacqueline Susann | 28,712,000+ |
|---|---|

*This racy tale of sex, violence and drugs by Jacqueline Susann (1921–74), first published in 1966, is, perhaps surprisingly, the world's bestselling novel.*

| 10. The Commonsense Book of Baby and Child Care by Benjamin Spock | 24,000,000+ |
|---|---|

*Dr Spock's 1946 manual became a bible of infant care for subsequent generations of parents.*

# THE FIRST 10 PUBLICATIONS PRINTED IN ENGLAND

1. *Propositio ad Carolum Ducem Burgundiae*
2. Cato, *Disticha de Morbidus*
3. Geoffrey Chaucer, *The Canterbury Tales*
4. *Ordinale Seu Pica ad Usem Sarum* ('Sarum Pie')
5. John Lydgate, *The Temple of Glass*
6. John Lydgate, *Stans Puer Mensam*
7. John Lydgate, *The Horse, the Sheep and the Goose*
8. John Lydgate, *The Churl and the Bird*
9. *Infanta Salvatoris*
10. William Caxton, Advertisement for 'Sarum Pie'

*All the first known publications in England were printed by William Caxton at Westminster. He had previously printed books in Bruges, where in c.1474 he printed the first book in English,* Recuyell of the Historyes of Troye, *followed by* The Game and Playe of the Chesse. *He then moved to England where* Propositio ad Carolum Ducem Burgundiae *was printed some time before September 1476; the others were all printed at unknown dates in either 1476 or 1477. It is probable that Chaucer's* Canterbury Tales *was the first book in English printed in England.*

Some of Caxton's work, now stored in the Bodleian Library, Oxford,

# THE 10 LONGEST ENGLISH WORDS

1. Acetylseryltyrosylserylisoleucylthreonylserylprolyl-
serylglutaminylphenylalanylvalylphenylalanyll-
eucylserylserylvalyltryptophylalanylaspartylprolyl-
isoleucylglutamylleucylleucylasparaginylvalylcyste-
inylthreonylserylserylleucylglycllasparaginylglut-
aminylphenylalanylglutaminylthreonylglutaminyl-
glutaminylalanylarginylthreonylthreonylglut-
aminylvalylglutaminylglutaminylphenylalanylseryl-
glutaminylvalyltryptophyllysylprolylphenylalanyl-
prolylglutaminylserylthreonylvalylarginylphenyl-
alanylprolylglycylaspartylvalyltyrosyllsyslvalyl-
tyrosylarginyltyrosylasparaginylalanylvalylleucyl-
aspartylprolylleucylisoleucylthreonylalanylleucyl-
leucylglycylthreonylphenylalanylaspartylthreonyl-
arginylasparaginylarginylisoleucylisoleucylglut-
amylvalylglutamylasparaginylglutaminylglut-
aminylserylprolylthreonylthreonylalanylglutamyl-
threonylleucylaspartylalanylthreonylarginylarg-
inylvalylaspartylaspartylalanylthreonylvalylalanyl-
isoleucylarginylserylalanylasparaginylisoleucyl-
asparaginylleucylvallasparaginylglutamylleucyl-
valylarginylglycylthreonylglycylleucyltyrosylaspara-
ginylglutaminylasparaginylthreonylphenylalanyl-
glutamylserylmethionylserylglycylleucylvalyltrypto-
phylthreonylserylalanylprolylalanylserine (1,185
letters)

*The word for the Tobacco
Mosaic Virus, Dahlemense Strain, qualifies as the
longest word in English because it has actually been
used in print (in the American Chemical Society's
Chemical Abstracts), whereas certain even longer words
for chemical compounds, which have been cited in such
sources as the Guinness Book of Records, are bogus in
the sense that they have never been used by scientists or
appeared in print. Long words for chemical compounds
may be regarded by purists as cheating, since such
words as trinitrophenylmethylnitramine (29 letters) – a
type of explosive – can be created by linking together the
scientific names of their components. Other words that
are also discounted are those that have been invented
with the sole intention of being long words, such as
James Joyce's 100-letter examples in Finnegan's Wake.*

2. Lopadotenachoselachogaleokranioleipsanodrimhipo-
trimmatosilphioparaomelitokatakechymenokichlepi-
kossyphophattoperisteralektryonoptekephalliokig-
klopeleiolagoiosiraiobaphetraganopterygon
(182 letters)

*The English translation of a
170-letter Greek word that appears in The Ecclesiazusae
(a comedy on government by women) by the Greek
playwright, Aristophanes (c.448–380 BC). It is used as a
description of a 17-ingredient dish.*

3. Aequeosalinocalcalinosetaceoaluminosocupreovitriolic
(52 letters)

*Invented by a medical writer,
Dr Edward Strother (1675–1737), to describe the spa
waters at Bath.*

4. Osseocarnisanguineoviscericartilaginonervomedullary
(51 letters).

*Coined by writer and East
India Company official Thomas Love Peacock
(1785–1866), and used in his satire, Headlong Hall (1816),
as a description of the structure of the human body.*

5. Pneumonoultramicroscopicsilicovolcanoconiosises (47
letters)

*The plural of
'pneumonoultramicroscopicsilicovolcanoconiosis',
which first appeared in print (though ending in
'-koniosis') in F. Scully's Bedside Manna [sic] (1936), it
then found its way into Webster's Dictionary and is now
in the Oxford English Dictionary – but with the note that
it occurs 'chiefly as an instance of a very long word'. It is
said to mean a lung disease caused by breathing fine
dust.*

6. Hepaticocholangiocholecystenterostomies (39 letters)

*A surgical operation to
create channels of communication between gall-
bladders and hepatic ducts or intestines.*

7. Pseudoantidisestablishmentarianism (34 letters)

*A word meaning 'false
opposition to the withdrawal of state support from a
church', derived from that perennial favourite long
word, antidisestablishmentarianism (a mere 28 letters).
Another composite made from it (though usually
hyphenated) is ultra-antidisestablishmentarianism,
which means 'extreme opposition to the withdrawal of
state support from a church' (33 letters).*

8. Supercalifragilisticexpialidocious (34 letters)

*An invented word, but
perhaps now eligible since it has appeared in the Oxford
English Dictionary. It was popularized by the song of
this title in the film, Mary Poppins (1964), where it was
used to mean 'wonderful', but it was originally written in
1949 by Parker & Young, who spelt it
'supercalafajalistickespialadojus' (32 letters).*

# LANGUAGE, LITERATURE & EDUCATION

9. Encephalomyeloradiculoneuritis (30 letters)

*A syndrome caused by a virus associated with encephalitis.*

10. Hippopotomonstrosesquipedalian (30 letters)

*Appropriately, the word that means 'pertaining to an extremely long word'.*

*If the rules are changed and number 1 is disqualified as a compound chemical name, and number 2 because it is a transliteration from Greek, the next two longest words, both with respectable literary pedigrees are:*

Floccinaucinihilipilification (29 letters)

*The action of estimating as worthless – until supercalifragilisticexpialidocious, floccinaucinihilipilification was the longest word in the Oxford English Dictionary.*

Honorificabilitudinitatibus (27 letters)

*Invented by Shakespeare to mean 'with honourableness', it appears in* Love's Labour's Lost *(Act V, Scene I).*

· · · · · · · · · · · · · · ·

## THE 10 COMMONEST WORDS IN WRITTEN ENGLISH

1. the
2. of
3. and
4. a
5. to
6. in
7. is
8. you
9. that
10. it

荷塘月色

朱自清

这几天心里颇不宁静。今晚在院子里坐着乘凉，忽然想起日日走过的荷塘，在这满月的光里，总该另有一番样子吧。月亮渐渐地升高了，墙外马路上孩子们的欢笑，已经听不见了；妻在屋里拍着闰儿，迷迷糊糊地哼着眠歌。我悄悄地披了大衫，带上门出去。

沿着荷塘，是一条曲折的小煤屑路。这是一条幽僻的路；白天也少人走，夜晚更加寂寞。荷塘四面，长着许多树，蓊蓊郁郁的。路的一旁，是些杨柳，和一些不知道名字的树。没有月光的晚上，这路上阴森森的，有些怕人。今晚却很好，虽然月光也还是淡淡的。

Mandarin, the language understood by one person in six in the world.

## THE 10 MOST WIDELY-SPOKEN LANGUAGES IN THE WORLD

| Language | Where spoken* | Number of speakers |
|---|---|---|
| 1. Mandarin | North and east-central China | 825,000,000 |
| 2. English | British Isles, North America, Australia, New Zealand and former British colonies | 431,000,000 |
| 3. Hindi | India | 325,000,000 |
| 4. Spanish | Spain; South America | 320,000,000 |
| 5. Russian | USSR | 289,000,000 |
| 6. Arabic | Middle East and North Africa | 187,000,000 |
| 7. Bengali | India and Bangladesh | 178,000,000 |
| 8. Portuguese | Portugal, former Portuguese colonies, Brazil | 169,000,000 |
| 9. Malay-Indonesian | Malaya, Indonesia | 135,000,000 |
| 10. Japanese | Japan | 124,000,000 |

*i.e. adopted as national language

## LANGUAGE, LITERATURE & EDUCATION

# THE 10 BESTSELLING WOMEN'S MAGAZINES IN BRITAIN

| Magazine | Average sales |
|---|---|
| 1. *Woman's Weekly* | 1,240,009 W |
| 2. *Bella* | 1,100,000 W |
| 3. *Woman's Own* | 1,024,852 W |
| 4. *Best* | 987,160 W |
| 5. *Woman* | 985,565 W |
| 6. *Essentials* | 851,565 M |
| 7. *Family Circle* | 602,865 M |
| 8. *Woman and Home* | 600,120 M |
| 9. *Woman's Realm* | 597,515 W |
| 10. *People's Friend* | 566,658 M |

W – Weekly;   M – Monthly

*B*ased on average sales January–June 1988. The highest circulation general-interest magazine during the same period was Reader's Digest *with average sales of 1,633,097.*

# THE 10 OLDEST NEWSPAPERS IN THE UK

1.  *London Gazette* 16 November 1665

*O*riginally published in Oxford as the Oxford Gazette, *while the royal court resided there during an outbreak of the plague. After 23 issues, it moved to London with the court and changed its name.*

2.  *Berrow's Worcester Journal* c. 1709

*B*ritain's oldest surviving provincial newspaper (the Norwich Post *was founded in 1701, but is defunct), it first appeared as the* Worcester Post-Man *and changed its name to Berrow's Worcester* Journal *in 1808. Its claim to have started as early as 1690 has never been substantiated.*

3.  *Lincoln, Rutland and Stamford Mercury* c. 1710

*O*riginally published as the Stamford Mercury *c. 1710 (allegedly 1695, and possibly in 1712), it later became the* Lincoln, Rutland and Stamford Mercury.

4.  *Lloyds List* 1726

*P*roviding shipping news, originally on a weekly basis, but since 1734 Britain's oldest daily.

5.  *News Letter* (Belfast) 6 March 1738

*P*ublished daily since 1855.

6.  *The Times* 1 January 1785

*F*irst published as the Daily Universal Register, *it changed its name to* The Times *on 1 March 1788.*

7.  *Observer* 4 December 1791

*B*ritain's oldest Sunday newspaper.

8.  *Morning Advertiser* 1794

*B*ritain's oldest trade newspaper (a daily established by the Licensed Victuallers' Association in order to earn income for their asylum), it is now called the Morning Advertiser and Licensed Restaurateur.

9.  *Sunday Times* February 1821

*I*ssued as the New Observer *until March 1821, the* Independent Observer *from April 1821 until October 1822, and the* Sunday Times *ever since. On 4 February 1962 it became the first British newspaper to issue a colour supplement.*

10.  *Guardian* May 1821

*P*ublished as the Manchester Guardian *until August 1959, when 'Manchester' was dropped.*

*An early edition of the* London Gazette.

The London Gazette.

## LANGUAGE, LITERATURE & EDUCATION

# THE TOP 10 DAILY NEWSPAPER PUBLISHERS

| | Country | No. of daily newspapers | Average daily circulation |
|---|---|---|---|
| 1. | USSR | 2,495 | 257,705,000 |
| 2. | Japan | 125 | 67,380,000 |
| 3. | United States | 1,687 | 63,263,000 |
| 4. | China | 60 | 30,000,000 |
| 5. | Great Britain | 108 | 23,206,000 |
| 6. | West Germany | 380 | 21,362,000 |
| 7. | India | 1,334 | 14,847,000 |
| 8. | France | 101 | 11,598,000 |
| 9. | Mexico | 312 | 9,252,000 |
| 10. | East Germany | 39 | 9,199,000 |

The composing room at *Pravda*, best-known of the Soviet Union's 2,495 daily newspapers.

# THE TOP 10 NATIONAL NEWSPAPERS IN BRITAIN

| | Newspaper | Average daily sale |
|---|---|---|
| 1. | *Sun* | 4,195,056 |
| 2. | *Daily Mirror* | 3,131,879 |
| 3. | *Daily Mail* | 1,786,303 |
| 4. | *Daily Express* | 1,676,786 |
| 5. | *Daily Telegraph* | 1,128,588 |
| 6. | *Daily Star* | 1,006,416 |
| 7. | *Daily Record* (*Daily Mirror* in Scotland) | 773,627 |
| 8. | *Today* | 501,920 |
| 9. | *Guardian* | 447,565 |
| 10. | *Times* | 440,979 |

Based on average sales July–December 1988. The 11th bestselling newspaper is the relative newcomer, the *Independent*, with daily sales of 378,454.

# THE 10 MOST POPULAR IMPORTED AMERICAN COMICS

| | Comic | Publisher |
|---|---|---|
| 1. | *X-Men* | Marvel Comics |
| 2. | *Excalibur* | Marvel Comics |
| 3. | *X-Factor* | Marvel Comics |
| 4. | *Detective Comics* | DC Comics |
| 5. | *Batman* | DC Comics |
| 6. | *She-Hulk* | Marvel Comics |
| 7. | *Hellblazer* | DC Comics |
| 8. | *Wolverine* | Marvel Comics |
| 9. | *West Coast Avengers* | Marvel Comics |
| 10. | *Justice League Europe* | DC Comics |

RIGHT X-men, outstripping even Batman in the US-import stakes.

## LANGUAGE, LITERATURE & EDUCATION

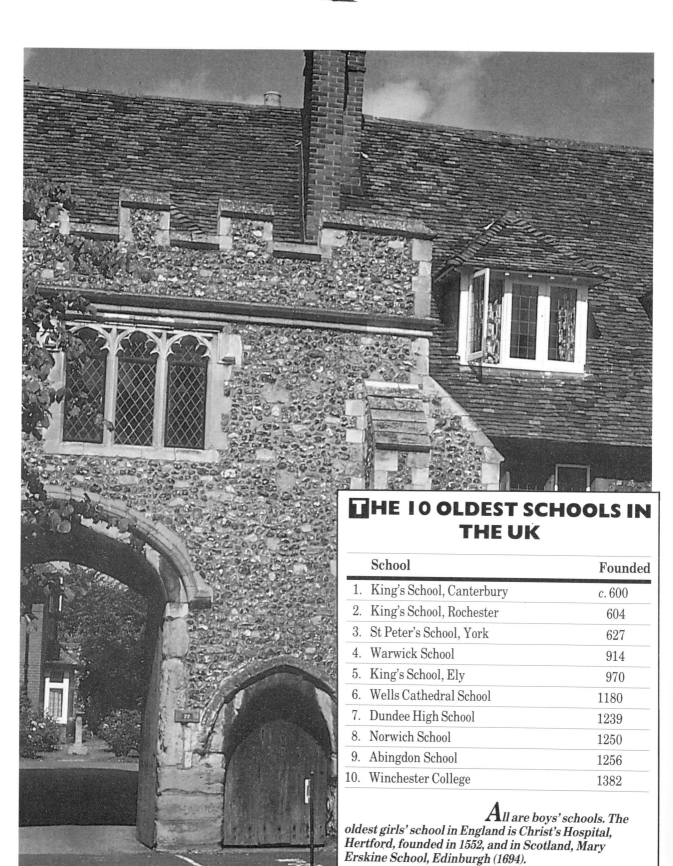

### THE 10 OLDEST SCHOOLS IN THE UK

| | School | Founded |
|---|---|---|
| 1. | King's School, Canterbury | *c.* 600 |
| 2. | King's School, Rochester | 604 |
| 3. | St Peter's School, York | 627 |
| 4. | Warwick School | 914 |
| 5. | King's School, Ely | 970 |
| 6. | Wells Cathedral School | 1180 |
| 7. | Dundee High School | 1239 |
| 8. | Norwich School | 1250 |
| 9. | Abingdon School | 1256 |
| 10. | Winchester College | 1382 |

*A*ll are boys' schools. The oldest girls' school in England is Christ's Hospital, Hertford, founded in 1552, and in Scotland, Mary Erskine School, Edinburgh (1694).

King's School, Canterbury.

## LANGUAGE, LITERATURE & EDUCATION

Harrow, Britain's most expensive Public School.

# THE 10 MOST EXPENSIVE PUBLIC SCHOOLS IN GREAT BRITAIN

| School | Boarding fees per year £ |
|---|---|
| 1.  Harrow School, Middlesex | 8,175 |
| 2= Stowe School, Buckinghamshire | 7,800 |
| 2= Winchester College, Hampshire | 7,800 |
| 4.  Charterhouse, Surrey | 7,755 |
| 5.  Bryanston School, Dorset | 7,728 |
| 6.  Cranleigh School, Surrey | 7,635 |
| 7.  Rugby School, Warwickshire | 7,575 |
| 8.  Clifton College, Bristol | 7,560 |
| 9.  Canford School, Dorset | 7,510 |
| 10. Marlborough College, Wiltshire | 7,500 |

*E*ton College appears lower on the list, with annual fees of £6,450. There are no girls' schools in the Top 10.

# THE 10 LARGEST STATE SECONDARY SCHOOLS IN ENGLAND

1.  Exmouth Community College, Devon
2.  Wolfreton School, Humberside
3.  Great Barr School, Birmingham
4.  Crown Woods School, Inner London
5.  De Ferrers High School, Staffordshire
6.  Wantage School, Oxfordshire
7.  Lord Williams School, Oxfordshire
8.  Bexleyheath School, Kent
9.  John Cleveland School, Leicestershire
10. The Plume School, Essex

*T*he number of pupils varies from year to year, but at its peak the largest of these schools had over 2,600.

Two thousand-plus pupils of Exmouth College assemble on the school playing-field.

# THE 10 OLDEST UNIVERSITIES IN GREAT BRITAIN

| University | Founded |
|---|---|
| 1. Oxford | 1249 |
| 2. Cambridge | 1284 |
| 3. St Andrews | 1411 |
| 4. Glasgow | 1451 |
| 5. Aberdeen | 1495 |
| 6. Edinburgh | 1583 |
| 7. Durham | 1832 |
| 8. London | 1836 |
| 9. Manchester | 1851 |
| 10. Newcastle | 1852 |

*Newcastle was a college of Durham University until 1963.*

A nineteenth-century impression of Queens' College, Oxford, seen from the High Street.

# THE 10 OLDEST OXFORD COLLEGES

| College | Founded |
|---|---|
| 1. University | 1249 |
| 2. Balliol | 1263 |
| 3. Merton | 1264 |
| 4. St Edmund Hall | 1278 |
| 5. Exeter | 1314 |
| 6. Oriel | 1326 |
| 7. Queen's | 1340 |
| 8. New | 1379 |
| 9. Lincoln | 1427 |
| 10. All Souls | 1438 |

# THE 10 OLDEST CAMBRIDGE COLLEGES

| College | Founded |
|---|---|
| 1. Peterhouse | 1284 |
| 2. Clare | 1326 |
| 3. Pembroke | 1347 |
| 4. Gonville and Caius | 1348 |
| 5. Trinity Hall | 1350 |
| 6. Corpus Christi | 1352 |
| 7. King's | 1441 |
| 8. Queens' | 1448 |
| 9. St Catharine's | 1473 |
| 10. Jesus | 1496 |

One of Cambridge University's many quadrangles – at Clare Hall.

# Music

The success of Band Aid's *Do They Know it's Christmas?* unleashed a flood of fund-raising hit singles. *We are the World,, You'll Never Walk Alone* (above), *Let It Be* and *Ferry 'Cross the Mersey* all reached No. 1 in the UK singles chart.

## THE 10 ALL-TIME BESTSELLING SINGLES IN THE UK

| | Song | Artist |
|---|---|---|
| 1. | *Do They Know it's Christmas?* | Band Aid |
| 2. | *Mull of Kintyre* | Wings |
| 3. | *Rivers of Babylon/Brown Girl in the Ring* | Boney M |
| 4. | *You're the One that I Want* | John Travolta and Olivia Newton-John |
| 5. | *She Loves You* | The Beatles |
| 6. | *A Hard Day's Night* | The Beatles |
| 7. | *I Want to Hold Your Hand* | The Beatles |
| 8. | *Mary's Boy Child/Oh, My Lord* | Boney M |
| 9. | *Relax!* | Frankie Goes to Hollywood |
| 10. | *Tears* | Ken Dodd |

*Sales of Band Aid's number 1 in the United Kingdom to date are almost 4,000,000, and over 8,000,000 globally. Profits from sales of the record went to the Ethiopian Famine Relief Fund.*

## THE 10 SINGLES THAT STAYED LONGEST IN THE BRITISH CHARTS

| | Song | Artist | Weeks in charts |
|---|---|---|---|
| 1. | *My Way* | Frank Sinatra | 122 |
| 2. | *Amazing Grace* | Judy Collins | 67 |
| 3. | *Rock Around the Clock* | Bill Haley and The Comets | 57 |
| 4. | *Release Me* | Englebert Humperdinck | 56 |
| 5. | *Stranger on the Shore* | Acker Bilk | 55 |
| 6. | *Relax!* | Frankie Goes to Hollywood | 52 |
| 7. | *Blue Monday* | New Order | 49 |
| 8. | *I Love You Because* | Jim Reeves | 47 |
| 9. | *Let's Twist Again* | Chubby Checker | 44 |
| 10. | *White Lines (Don't Do It)* | Grandmaster Flash/Melle Mel | 43 |

# THE 10 ALL-TIME BESTSELLING SINGLES IN THE WORLD

| Song | Artist | Sales exceed |
| --- | --- | --- |
| 1. *White Christmas* | Bing Crosby | 30,000,000 |
| 2. *Rock Around the Clock* | Bill Haley & his Comets | 17,000,000 |
| 3. *I Want to Hold Your Hand* | The Beatles | 12,000,000 |
| 4. *It's Now or Never* | Elvis Presley | 10,000,000 |
| 5= *Hound Dog/Don't Be Cruel* | Elvis Presley | 9,000,000 |
| 5= *Diana* | Paul Anka | 9,000,000 |
| 7= *Hey Jude* | The Beatles | 8,000,000 |
| 7= *I'm a Believer* | The Monkees | 8,000,000 |
| 9= *We Are the World* | USA for Africa | 7,000,000 |
| 9= *Can't Buy Me Love* | The Beatles | 7,000,000 |

A scene from the 1954 film, *White Christmas*. Bing Crosby smiles at the thought of his future royalties on the song of the same name.

*G*lobal sales are notoriously difficult to calculate, particularly in countries outside the UK and USA and especially in the Far East. 'Worldwide' is thus usually taken to mean the known minimum 'Western World' sales. Bing Crosby's 1942 record, 'White Christmas', is indisputably the all-time bestselling single, and the song, recorded by others and sold as sheet music, has also achieved such enormous sales that it would additionally appear in the number 1 position in any list of bestselling songs.

# THE 10 BESTSELLING ALBUMS OF ALL TIME IN THE UK

| Album | Artist |
| --- | --- |
| 1. *Brothers in Arms* | Dire Straits |
| 2. *Thriller* | Michael Jackson |
| 3. *Bad* | Michael Jackson |
| 4. *Sgt Pepper's Lonely Hearts Club Band* | The Beatles |
| 5. *Greatest Hits Vol. 1* | Abba |
| 6. *Bridge Over Troubled Water* | Simon and Garfunkel |
| 7. *Dark Side of the Moon* | Pink Floyd |
| 8. *Rumours* | Fleetwood Mac |
| 9. *Greatest Hits* | Queen |
| 10. *Tubular Bells* | Mike Oldfield |

*S*ales of **Brothers in Arms** in the UK alone exceed 3,000,000.

# THE 10 BESTSELLING ALBUMS OF ALL TIME WORLDWIDE

| Album | Artist |
| --- | --- |
| 1. *Thriller* | Michael Jackson |
| 2. *Saturday Night Fever* | Various |
| 3. *Grease* Soundtrack | Various |
| 4. *Sgt Pepper's Lonely Hearts Club Band* | The Beatles |
| 5. *Bridge Over Troubled Water* | Simon and Garfunkel |
| 6. *Born in the USA* | Bruce Springsteen |
| 7. *The Sound of Music* Soundtrack | Various |
| 8. *Abbey Road* | The Beatles |
| 9. *Rumours* | Fleetwood Mac |
| 10. *South Pacific* Soundtrack | Various |

*G*lobal sales of **Thriller** have now topped 40,000,000.

## MUSIC

# THE 10 BRITISH CHART SINGLES WITH THE LONGEST TITLES

| Title | Artist | Highest chart position | Year | No. of letters |
|---|---|---|---|---|
| 1. *I'm in Love With the Girl on a Certain Manchester Megastore Checkout Desk* | Freshies | 54 | 1981 | 60 |
| 2. *If I Said You Had a Beautiful Body Would You Hold it Against Me?* | Bellamy Brothers | 3 | 1979 | 50 |
| 3. *Gilly Gilly Ossenfeffer Katzenallen Bogen by the Sea* | Max Bygraves | 7 | 1954 | 45 |
| 4= *There's a Guy Works Down the Chipshop Swears He's Elvis* | Kirsty MacColl | 14 | 1981 | 44 |
| 4= *Have You Seen Your Mother Baby, Standing in the Shadow?* | Rolling Stones | 5 | 1966 | 44 |
| 6. *When the Girl in Your Arms Is the Girl in Your Heart* | Cliff Richard | 3 | 1961 | 41 |
| 7. *I'm Gonna Sit Right Down and Write Myself a Letter* | Billy Williams | 22 | 1957 | 40 |
| | Barry Manilow | 36 | 1982 | 40 |
| 8= *Loving You's a Dirty Job but Someone's Got to Do it* | Bonnie Tyler | 73 | 1985 | 39 |
| 8= *Itsy Bitsy Teeny Weeny Yellow Polka Dot Bikini* | Bryan Hyland | 8 | 1960 | 39 |
| 8= *You Don't Have to Be in the Army to Fight in the War* | Mungo Jerry | 13 | 1971 | 39 |
| 8= *Two Pints of Lager and a Packet of Crisps Please* | Splodgeness-abounds | 7 | 1980 | 39 |

*T*his list includes only titles that do not contain words or phrases in brackets. It also includes only chart hits, and thus does not contain such gems as *Fairport Convention's* album track, Sir B. McKenzie's Daughter's Lament for the 77th Mounted Lancers' Retreat from the Straits of Loch Knombe in the Year of Our Lord 1717, on the Occasion of the Announcement of her Marriage to the Laird of Kinleakie. *The shortest title of a chart record is Shirley Bassey's* I.

# THE 10 MOST SUCCESSFUL ORIGINAL SOUNDTRACK ALBUMS IN THE UK

1. *Saturday Night Fever*
2. *Grease*
3. *The Sound of Music*
4. *Fame*
5. *That'll Be the Day*
6. *A Star Is Born*
7. *South Pacific*
8. *West Side Story*
9. *Who's That Girl?*
10. *Flashdance*

Madonna belts it out.

Connie Francis, hit-maker of the late '50s and early '60s.

# THE 10 FEMALE SINGERS WITH THE MOST TOP 20 HITS IN THE UK

| Singer | Hits |
| --- | --- |
| 1. Madonna | 19 |
| 2= Diana Ross (including one duet with Marvin Gaye, and one with Lionel Richie) | 17 |
| 2= Petula Clark (excluding the reissue of *Downtown*) | 17 |
| 2= Connie Francis | 17 |
| 5. Donna Summer (including one duet with Barbra Streisand) | 15 |
| 6. Dusty Springfield (including one duet with The Pet Shop Boys) | 14 |
| 6= Cilla Black | 14 |
| 6= Winifred Atwell | 14 |
| 9= Shirley Bassey | 12 |
| 9= Brenda Lee | 12 |

*R*unners-up include Kate Bush (11, including one duet with Peter Gabriel), Olivia Newton-John (10, including two duets with John Travolta, one with ELO, and one with Cliff Richard), and Doris Day (10, including two duets with Johnnie Ray and one with Frankie Lane).

# THE 10 FEMALE SINGERS WITH THE MOST TOP 20 HITS IN THE USA AND UK

| Singer | Hits |
| --- | --- |
| 1= Connie Francis | 28 |
| 1= Aretha Franklin (including one duet with George Michael) | 28 |
| 1= Diana Ross (including three duets with Marvin Gaye, one with Lionel Richie and one with Julio Iglesias) | 28 |
| 4. Olivia Newton-John (including two duets with John Travolta and one each with Andy Gibb, Cliff Richard and ELO) | 26 |
| 5. Brenda Lee | 24 |
| 6= Donna Summer (including one duet with Barbra Streisand) | 21 |
| 6= Petula Clark | 21 |
| 8= Dionne Warwick (including one duet with the Detroit Spinners and one with 'Friends': Stevie Wonder, Gladys Knight and Elton John) | 19 |
| 8= Madonna | 19 |
| 10. Dusty Springfield (including one duet with The Pet Shop Boys) | 16 |

*T*his covers USA and/or UK Top 20 hits, including the listed duets with other acts, but not those achieved as a member of a group; Diana Ross's successes with The Supremes are therefore not counted.

MUSIC

Diana Ross in glittering form.

## THE 10 FEMALE SINGERS WITH THE MOST TOP 50 HITS* IN THE UK

| | Singer | Hits |
|---|---|---|
| 1. | Diana Ross | 39 |
| 2. | Donna Summer | 30 |
| 3. | Petula Clark | 27 |
| 4. | Shirley Bassey | 26 |
| 5. | Connie Francis | 23 |
| 6. | Brenda Lee | 19 |
| 7= | Cilla Black | 19 |
| 7= | Madonna | 19 |
| 7= | Sandie Shaw | 19 |
| 7= | Dusty Springfield | 19 |
| 10= | Alma Cogan | 18 |
| 10= | Aretha Franklin | 18 |
| 10= | Kim Wilde | 18 |

*including duets

Shirley Bassey, a record-holder with her total of 313 weeks in the singles charts.

## THE 10 FEMALE SINGERS WHO HAVE STAYED LONGEST IN THE TOP 50 BRITISH SINGLES CHARTS

| | Singer | Total weeks in charts |
|---|---|---|
| 1. | Shirley Bassey | 313 |
| 2. | Diana Ross | 297 |
| 3. | Petula Clark | 247 |
| 4. | Connie Francis | 241 |
| 5. | Donna Summer | 234 |
| 6. | Madonna | 219 |
| 7. | Brenda Lee | 210 |
| 8. | Cilla Black | 192 |
| 9. | Dusty Springfield | 173 |
| 10. | Sandie Shaw | 163 |

# BBC RADIO 1 LISTENERS' 10 FAVOURITE SINGLES

| Song | Artist |
| --- | --- |
| 1. *I Owe You Nothing* | Bros |
| 2. *Bohemian Rhapsody* | Queen |
| 3. *Careless Whisper* | George Michael |
| 4. *Stairway to Heaven* | Led Zeppelin |
| 5. *Nothing's Gonna Change My Love for You* | Glenn Medeiros |
| 6. *Drop the Boy* | Bros |
| 7. *Angel Eyes* | Wet Wet Wet |
| 8. *Bad* | Michael Jackson |
| 9. *Tainted Love* | Soft Cell |
| 10. *Thriller* | Michael Jackson |

*A poll of 20,000 BBC Radio 1 listeners completed in August 1988 established this list of 'all-time' Top 10 favourite singles – but as it includes several relative newcomers, the next poll is almost certain to contain some entirely different 'all-time' favourites.*

# THE TOP 10 EUROVISION SONG CONTEST-WINNERS

| Country | Wins |
| --- | --- |
| 1= France | 5 |
| 1= Luxembourg | 5 |
| 3= United Kingdom | 4 |
| 3= Netherlands | 4 |
| 5. Ireland | 3 |
| 6= Switzerland | 2 |
| 6= Sweden | 2 |
| 6= Spain | 2 |
| 6= Israel | 2 |
| 10= Denmark, Italy, Austria, Monaco, West Germany, Norway, Belgium | 1 |

*This is a list in which almost every country that has entered appears. Britain's four winners were in 1967 (Sandie Shaw, Puppet on a String), 1969 (Lulu, Boom Bang-a-Bang – joint winner with Spain, The Netherlands and France), 1976 (Brotherhood of Man, Save Your Kisses for Me) and 1981 (Bucks Fizz, Making Your Mind Up). The Eurovision Song Contest has been held annually since 1956 and launched the international careers of such performers as the Swedish group, Abba, who won in 1974 with Waterloo.*

'I Owe You Nothing?' Craig (left) claimed he was owed plenty – and got it – after his departure from Bros.

Swedish 'Supergroup' Abba, who shot to stardom after their Eurovision Song Contest win.

## MUSIC

# THE 10 MOST SUCCESSFUL BEATLES SINGLES

| | Song | Year |
|---|---|---|
| 1. | *She Loves You* | 1963 |
| 2. | *I Want to Hold Your Hand* | 1963 |
| 3. | *Can't Buy Me Love* | 1964 |
| 4. | *Hey Jude* | 1968 |
| 5. | *Get Back* | 1969 |
| 6. | *Help!* | 1965 |
| 7. | *Ticket to Ride* | 1965 |
| 8. | *I Feel Fine* | 1964 |
| 9. | *Hello Goodbye* | 1967 |
| 10. | *The Ballad of John and Yoko* | 1969 |

The Beatles, one of Britain's leading export industries during the 1960s.

*A*ll of these singles were number 1 hits in the UK.

• • • • • • • • • • • • • • • • • • • • • • • • • • • •

# THE 10 MOST SUCCESSFUL ROLLING STONES SINGLES

| | Song | Year |
|---|---|---|
| 1. | *Honky Tonk Women* | 1969 |
| 2. | *The Last Time* | 1965 |
| 3. | *It's All Over Now* | 1964 |
| 4. | *(I Can't Get No) Satisfaction* | 1965 |
| 5. | *Get Off of My Cloud* | 1965 |
| 6. | *Paint it Black* | 1966 |
| 7. | *Jumpin' Jack Flash* | 1968 |
| 8. | *Miss You* | 1978 |
| 9. | *Little Red Rooster* | 1964 |
| 10. | *Brown Sugar* | 1971 |

*A*ll of these were number 1 hits, except **Miss You** (highest position 3) and **Brown Sugar** (2).

Mick Jagger: the mouth behind The Stones' success.

# CAPITAL RADIO'S 1988 'HALL OF FAME' TOP 10

| | Song | Artist |
|---|---|---|
| 1. | *Careless Whisper* | George Michael |
| 2. | *Stairway to Heaven* | Led Zeppelin |
| 3. | *Against All Odds* | Phil Collins |
| 4. | *I Owe You Nothing* | Bros |
| 5. | *Bohemian Rhapsody* | Queen |
| 6. | *Romeo and Juliet* | Dire Straits |
| 7. | *Sexual Healing* | Marvin Gaye |
| 8. | *Bad* | Michael Jackson |
| 9. | *Dock of the Bay* | Otis Redding |
| 10. | *Crazy for You* | Madonna |

*C*apital Radio, an independent London radio station, conducted its poll of listeners' 500 favourites throughout the year from thousands of calls to disc jockey John Sachs. The artist who appears most in the Capital Radio 'Hall of Fame' Top 500 is Michael Jackson, with a total of 19 entries, as a soloist and with the Jackson Five, Jacksons, Paul McCartney and Seidah Garrett.

**MUSIC**

# BRITISH STUDENTS' 10 FAVOURITE ALBUMS

| Album | Artist |
|---|---|
| 1. *The Wall* | Pink Floyd |
| 2. *The Joshua Tree* | U2 |
| 3. *Brothers in Arms* | Dire Straits |
| 4. *Bat Out of Hell* | Meatloaf |
| 5. *The Queen Is Dead* | The Smiths |
| 6. *Love Over Gold* | Dire Straits |
| 7. *Graceland* | Paul Simon |
| 8. *Steve McQueen* | Prefab Sprout |
| 9. *Sgt Pepper's Lonely Hearts Club Band* | The Beatles |
| 10. *Dream of the Blue Turtles* | Sting |

*The various 'Students' Favourites' in the Music and Film sections are based on an exhaustive poll conducted in 1988 by Nescafé and University Radio, York. Questionnaires were sent to 24,000 students throughout the country via student radio stations.*

# BRITISH STUDENTS' 10 ALL-TIME FAVOURITE SINGLES

| Song | Artist |
|---|---|
| 1. *Bohemian Rhapsody* | Queen |
| 2. *Stairway to Heaven* | Led Zeppelin |
| 3. *Vienna* | Ultravox |
| 4. *Blue Monday* | New Order |
| 5. *Baker Street* | Gerry Rafferty |
| 6. *Don't You Forget About Me* | Simple Minds |
| 7. *Romeo and Juliet* | Dire Straits |
| 8. *Wuthering Heights* | Kate Bush |
| 9. *How Soon Is Now?* | The Smiths |
| 10. *Will You?* | Hazel O'Connor |

*The Top 50 contains four singles by Dire Straits, three by U2 and Peter Gabriel and two each by Eric Clapton, Phil Collins, The Police and The Beatles. Queen are in the unusual position of holding the number 1 spot, but not having any other single in the Top 50. Perhaps surprisingly, Bruce Springsteen has only one entry (Born to Run at number 33). Another oddity is the presence (at number 48) of the Canadian group, Martha and the Muffins, whose song Echo Beach was the only chart hit they ever had in Great Britain.*

LEFT A frame from Pink Floyd's film, *The Wall*, the album of which is still rated No 1 by British students.

BELOW LEFT *Brothers in Arms*, the bestselling album of all time in the UK, but No 3 in the British students' poll.

BELOW A classic in the making: setting up Peter Blake's album cover for The Beatles' *Sgt Pepper*.

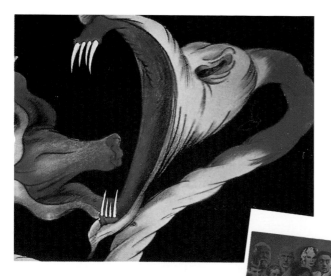

MUSIC

## BRITISH STUDENTS' 10 ALL-TIME FAVOURITE LIVE ACTS

1. Queen
2. U2
3. Genesis
4. Bruce Springsteen
5. Dire Straits
6. Peter Gabriel
7. Marillion
8. Rush
9. The Pogues
10. Simple Minds

## BRITISH STUDENTS' 10 ALL-TIME FAVOURITE GROUPS

1. Genesis
2. The Beatles
3. Queen
4. The Smiths
5. Dire Straits
6. U2
7. Pink Floyd
8. Marillion
9. The Police
10. The Rolling Stones

## BRITISH STUDENTS' 10 ALL-TIME FAVOURITE MALE SINGERS

1. Phil Collins
2. Peter Gabriel
3. David Bowie
4. Sting
5. Morrisey
6. Bruce Springsteen
7. Chris De Burgh
8. Elvis Costello
9. Michael Jackson
10. Elton John

## BRITISH STUDENTS' 10 ALL-TIME FAVOURITE FEMALE SINGERS

1. Kate Bush
2. Annie Lennox
3. Whitney Houston
4. Aretha Franklin
5. Suzanne Vega
6. Alison Moyet
7. Debbie Harry
8. Stevie Nicks
9. Tina Turner
10. Siouxsie Sioux

British students' No 1 favourite male singer, Phil Collins.

ABOVE Queen Rules! Freddie Mercury's dynamic stage performance accompanied by three virtuoso musicians led to the group's being voted the favourite live act of British students.

**MUSIC**

# THE 10 MOST EXPENSIVE ITEMS OF POP MEMORABILIA

1. John Lennon's 1965 Rolls-Royce Phantom V touring limousine, finished in psychedelic paintwork. Sold by Sotheby's, New York, 29 June 1985 – $2,299,000/£1,768,462.

2. Elvis Presley's 1963 Rolls-Royce Phantom V touring limousine. Sold by Sotheby's, London, 28 August 1986 – £110,000.

3. Elvis Presley's one-piece 'Shooting Star' stage outfit, 1972. Sold by Phillips, London, 24 August 1988 – £28,000.

4. An unreleased 8mm film of The Beatles in America, 1965. Sold (with copyright) by Christie's, London, 29 August 1986 – £24,000.

5. Tape-recorded interview with John Lennon, 1968. Sold (with copyright) by Sotheby's, London, 5 August 1987 – £23,650.

6. Biographical booklet annotated by John Lennon. Sold by Sotheby's, London, 28 August 1986 – £20,900.

7= Original unpublished manuscript for a book by John Lennon. Sold by Sotheby's, London, 31 August 1984 – £17,600.

7= Elton John's Wurlitzer Model 750 juke box, c. 1940. Sold by Sotheby's London, 6 September 1988 – £17,600.

9. John Entwistle's Peter Cook-customized Fender electric bass guitar (one of the few that survived a Who stage performance). Sold by Sotheby's, London, 7 April 1988 – £16,500.

10. Handwritten letter from Paul McCartney concerning the possible re-formation of The Beatles, August 1970. Sold by Sotheby's, London, 29 August 1985 – £11,000.

*P*ioneered particularly by Sotheby's in London, pop memorabilia has become big business – especially if it involves personal association with mega-stars such as The Beatles. In addition to the Top 10, high prices have also been paid for a guitar belonging to Jimmy Hendrix and pianos that were once owned by Paul McCartney and John Lennon.

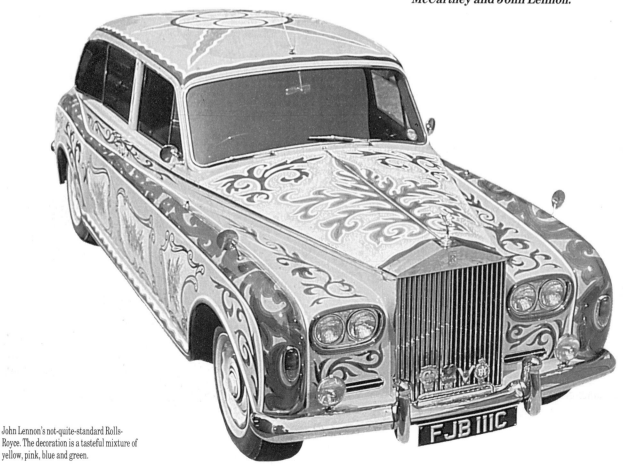

John Lennon's not-quite-standard Rolls-Royce. The decoration is a tasteful mixture of yellow, pink, blue and green.

**MUSIC**

# THE 10 MOST-PERFORMED OPERAS AT THE ROYAL OPERA HOUSE, COVENT GARDEN

| | Opera | Composer | Première at Covent Garden | Performances |
|---|---|---|---|---|
| 1. | *Carmen* | Bizet | 27 May 1882 | 468 |
| 2. | *La Bohème* | Puccini | 2 October 1897 | 462 |
| 3. | *Aïda* | Verdi | 22 June 1876 | 446 |
| 4. | *Faust* | Gounod | 18 July 1863 | 428 |
| 5. | *Rigoletto* | Verdi | 14 May 1853 | 402 |
| 6. | *Don Giovanni* | Mozart | 17 April 1834 | 365 |
| 7. | *Norma* | Bellini | 12 July 1833 | 353 |
| 8. | *La Traviata* | Verdi | 25 May 1858 | 339 |
| 9. | *Tosca* | Puccini | 12 July 1900 | 331 |
| 10. | *Madama Butterfly* | Puccini | 10 July 1905 | 325 |

One of many Carmens at the Royal Opera House: Zélie de Lussan during the 1902 season.

*The total number of performances is up to 31 July 1989. The records are complete back to 1847, but for the two operas premièred earlier, the figure is based on the best available evidence.*

• • • • • • • • • • • • • • • • • • • • • • • • • • • • •

# THE 10 LONGEST OPERAS PERFORMED AT THE ROYAL OPERA HOUSE, COVENT GARDEN

| | Opera | Composer | Running time* hr | min |
|---|---|---|---|---|
| 1. | *Götterdämmerung* | Wagner | 6 | |
| 2. | *Die Meistersinger von Nürnberg* | Wagner | 5 | 40 |
| 3. | *Siegfried* | Wagner | 5 | 25 |
| 4. | *Tristan und Isolde* | Wagner | 5 | 19 |
| 5. | *Die Walküre* | Wagner | 5 | 15 |
| 6. | *Parsifal* | Wagner | 5 | 9 |
| 7. | *Donnerstag aus Licht* | Stockhausen | 4 | 42 |
| 8. | *Lohengrin* | Wagner | 4 | 26 |
| 9. | *Der Rosenkavalier* | Strauss | 4 | 25 |
| 10. | *Don Carlo* | Verdi | 4 | 19 |

*including intervals

The 1932 production of *Die Meistersinger*.

# Theatre

· · · · · · · · · · · · · · · · · · · · · · · · · · · · ·

## SHAKESPEARE'S 10 LONGEST PLAYS

| Play | Lines |
|---|---|
| 1. *Hamlet* | 3,901 |
| 2. *Richard III* | 3,886 |
| 3. *Coriolanus* | 3,820 |
| 4. *Cymbeline* | 3,813 |
| 5. *Othello* | 3,672 |
| 6. *Antony and Cleopatra* | 3,630 |
| 7. *Troilus and Cressida* | 3,576 |
| 8. *Henry VIII* | 3,450 |
| 9. *Henry V* | 3,368 |
| 10. *The Winter's Tale* | 3,354 |

ABOVE Sir John Falstaff (right), Shakespeare's most garrulous character.

RIGHT John Kemble takes the role of Hamlet in an 1833 production.

## SHAKESPEARE'S 10 MOST DEMANDING ROLES

| Role | Play | Lines |
|---|---|---|
| 1. Hamlet | *Hamlet* | 1,422 |
| 2. Falstaff | *Henry IV, Parts I and II* | 1,178 |
| 3. Richard III | *Richard III* | 1,124 |
| 4. Iago | *Othello* | 1,097 |
| 5. Henry V | *Henry V* | 1,025 |
| 6. Othello | *Othello* | 860 |
| 7. Vincentio | *Measure for Measure* | 820 |
| 8. Coriolanus | *Coriolanus* | 809 |
| 9. Timon | *Timon of Athens* | 795 |
| 10. Antony | *Antony and Cleopatra* | 766 |

***H**amlet's role comprises 11,610 words – over 36% of the total number of lines spoken in the play, but he is beaten by Falstaff who, apart from appearing in* Henry IV, Parts I and II, *also appears in* The Merry Wives of Windsor *where he has 436 lines. His total of 1,614 lines thus makes him the most talkative of all Shakespeare's characters.*

## THEATRE

# THE TEN LONGEST-RUNNING SHOWS OF ALL TIME IN THE UK

| Show | Performances |
| --- | --- |
| 1. *The Mousetrap* | 15,129* |
| 2. *No Sex, Please – We're British* | 6,761 |
| 3. *The Black and White Minstrel Show* | 6,464 |
| 4. *Oh! Calcutta!* | 3,918 |
| 5. *Me and My Girl* | 3,368* |
| 6. *Jesus Christ, Superstar* | 3,357 |
| 7. *Cats* | 3,310* |
| 8. *Life with Father* | 3,213 |
| 9. *Evita* | 2,900 |
| 10. *Oliver* | 2,618 |

*still running; total at 31 March 1989

# THE 10 LONGEST-RUNNING MUSICALS OF ALL TIME IN THE UK

| Show | Performances |
| --- | --- |
| 1. *The Black and White Minstrel Show* | 6,464 |
| 2. *Me and My Girl* | 3,368* |
| 3. *Jesus Christ, Superstar* | 3,357 |
| 4. *Cats* | 3,310* |
| 5. *Evita* | 2,900 |
| 6. *Oliver* | 2,618 |
| 7. *The Sound of Music* | 2,386 |
| 8. *Salad Days* | 2,283 |
| 9. *My Fair Lady* | 2,281 |
| 10. *Chu Chin Chow* | 2,238 |

*still running; total at 31 March 1989

*A*ll the longest-running shows in the United Kingdom have been London productions. The Mousetrap opened on 25 November 1952 at the Ambassador's Theatre. After 8,862 performances it transferred to St Martin's Theatre where it re-opened on 25 March 1974. It is not the only play in the world to have run continuously since the 1950s; Eugene Ionesco's The Bald Prima Donna has been on in Paris since 1953.

The Black and White Minstrel Show total includes both the original ten-year run (1962–72) and the 1973 revival.

Me and My Girl's figure up to 1982 was 1,646. The revival opened on 12 February 1985 and had clocked up 1,722 performances to 31 March 1989. Total performances are listed.

ABOVE Teddy St Denis as Sally and Lupino Lane as Bill in the original production of *Me and My Girl* at the Victoria Theatre.

LEFT Born 1952 and still going strong: *The Mousetrap*, a record-breaker in its 13th year and now into its 37th.

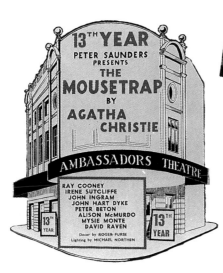

The London Coliseum, London's largest theatre.

## THE 10 LONGEST-RUNNING NON-MUSICALS OF ALL TIME IN THE UK

| | Show | Performances |
|---|---|---|
| 1. | *The Mousetrap* | 15,129* |
| 2. | *No Sex, Please – We're British* | 6,761 |
| 3. | *Oh! Calcutta!* | 3,918 |
| 4. | *Life with Father* | 3,213 |
| 5. | *There's a Girl in My Soup* | 2,547 |
| 6. | *Pyjama Tops* | 2,498 |
| 7. | *Sleuth* | 2,359 |
| 8. | *Run for Your Wife* | 2,220* |
| 9. | *Boeing Boeing* | 2,035 |
| 10. | *Blithe Spirit* | 1,997 |

*still running; total at 31 March 1989

**O**h! Calcutta! *is included here as it is regarded as a review with music, rather than a musical.*

## THE 10 LARGEST THEATRES IN LONDON

| | Theatre | Seats |
|---|---|---|
| 1. | London Coliseum | 2,358 |
| 2. | London Palladium | 2,317 |
| 3. | Theatre Royal, Drury Lane | 2,283 |
| 4. | Royal Opera House | 2,095 |
| 5. | Dominion | 2,007 |
| 6. | Prince Edward Theatre | 1,666 |
| 7. | Victoria Palace | 1,565 |
| 8. | Apollo Victoria | 1,564 |
| 9. | Sadler's Wells | 1,499 |
| 10. | Royal Adelphi Theatre | 1,481 |

**T**he Hammersmith Odeon *has 3,483 seats, but is used for rock concerts and other non-theatrical events. Neither of London's newest theatres, the Olivier at the National Theatre (1,228 seats) and the Barbican (1,162 seats) rank in the Top 10. London also boasts several large concert halls, including the Royal Festival Hall (3,111 seats), Barbican Hall (2,047 seats) and the Royal Albert Hall, which can hold up to 7,000. The newly-opened London Arena is the largest, seating 12,500.*

# Film

## THE 10 COUNTRIES WITH THE MOST CINEMAS

| | Country | Cinemas |
|---|---|---|
| 1. | USSR | 176,991 |
| 2. | United States | 16,032 |
| 3. | India | 8,070 |
| 4. | France | 5,190 |
| 5. | Italy | 4,885 |
| 6. | West Germany | 3,418 |
| 7. | Spain | 3,109 |
| 8. | Bulgaria | 3,052 |
| 9. | Czechoslovakia | 3,006 |
| 10. | Mexico | 2,172 |

## THE 10 LEADING FILM-GOING COUNTRIES

| | Country | Annual cinema visits |
|---|---|---|
| 1. | USSR | 5,042,500,000 |
| 2. | India | 4,920,000,000 |
| 3. | United States | 1,053,300,000 |
| 4. | Vietnam | 343,800,000 |
| 5. | Romania | 188,200,000 |
| 6. | France | 172,200,000 |
| 7. | Japan | 155,100,000 |
| 8. | Italy | 122,300,000 |
| 9. | West Germany | 104,200,000 |
| 10. | Spain | 101,100,000 |

*T*his list is based on UNESCO's figures for indoor cinemas equipped to show 35mm films – the format used for most feature films. In addition, France has 1,949 and Bulgaria 222 cinemas showing 16mm film, and the United States has a further 2,852 drive-in cinemas. The total for the USSR seems almost incredible, but UNESCO has been reporting similarly huge figures for many years, a reflection of the value placed on film in the Soviet Union as a medium of entertainment and political ideology.

Indian cinemas attract almost 5 billion customers a year.

**FILM**

# TOP 10 FILM LISTS

'Most successful' is based on the total rental fees paid by United States and Canadian cinemas to distributors, which is regarded as a reasonable guide to what a film has earned. It is not the same as 'box-office gross', which is another commonly used way of comparing the success of films. While the latter method is certainly valid over a short period – for example, to compare films released in the same year – it indicates more what individual cinemas earned than the films themselves, and, of course, varies according to ticket price.

Inflation is a key factor in calculating 'success', whichever method of assessment is used: as cinema ticket prices go up, so do box office income *and* the rental fees charged by distributors. This means that the biggest earners tend to be among the most recent releases. If inflation is taken into account, the most successful film ever would be *Gone With the Wind*; while it has earned *actual* rental fees of $78,000,000, inflation since the film's release in 1939 makes this the equivalent of about $500,000,000 in today's money.

Worthy attempts have been made to compile comparative lists by building in factors for increases in ticket prices and inflation, but with such changes taking place so frequently in recent years, and with a total lack of uniformity in box-office prices even in one country, it is virtually impossible to achieve consistent or meaningful results.

Where the system breaks down is with older films that may still be doing steady business in cinemas around the world, but which within a few years of their release were dropped from the distributor's calculations. Only the Disney Studio, which continues actively to re-release and publicize films (such as *Snow White and the Seven Dwarfs*, first released over 50 years ago), makes any attempt to keep its figures up to date.

It must not be forgotten that over recent years additional income has been derived by distributors from sales of video recordings and TV broadcasting rights; this is not generally included in rental fees.

As a very rough rule of thumb – and one used by the film industry itself – doubling the 'domestic' (USA and Canada) rental receipts gives a very approximate world total.

Figures have been rounded off throughout to the nearest $500,000. Where two films appear to have earned exactly the same rentals but are given successive positions in the list, the first of the two was marginally ahead of the other before this rounding-off. If two films are given equal ranking, that is because their distributors reported identical figures. Conversions to £ sterling have been given at the rate prevailing in April 1989.

# THE 10 MOST EXPENSIVE FILMS EVER MADE

| | Film | Year | Production cost $ | Production cost £ |
|---|---|---|---|---|
| 1. | *Rambo III* | 1988 | 58,000,000 | 34,250,000 |
| 2. | *Superman* | 1978 | 55,000,000 | 32,500,000 |
| 3. | *Superman II* | 1981 | 54,000,000 | 32,000,000 |
| 4. | *Who Framed Roger Rabbit?* | 1988 | 53,000,000 | 31,250,000 |
| 5. | *The Adventures of Baron Munchausen* | 1989 | 52,000,000 | 30,750,000 |
| 6. | *Ishtar* | 1987 | 45,000,000 | 26,750,000 |
| 7. | *Heaven's Gate* | 1980 | 44,000,000 | 26,000,000 |
| 8. | *Cleopatra* | 1963 | 44,000,000 | 26,000,000 |
| 9. | *The Cotton Club* | 1984 | 40,000,000 | 23,750,000 |
| 10. | *Greystoke: The Legend of Tarzan* | 1984 | 40,000,000 | 23,750,000 |

*P*ublished reports that *Rambo III cost as much at $70,000,000/£41,500,000 and Superman II $60,000,000/£35,500,000 have been refuted as exaggerations, but whis does not alter the fact that both were extremely expensive.*

Sylvester Stallone in *Rambo III*, the most expensive film ever made.

# THE 10 MOST SUCCESSFUL MUSICAL FILMS OF ALL TIME

| | Film | Total rentals $ | £ |
|---|---|---|---|
| 1. | *Grease* (1978) | 96,500,000 | 57,101,000 |
| 2. | *The Sound of Music* (1965) | 80,000,000 | 47,337,000 |
| 3. | *Mary Poppins* (1964) | 45,000,000 | 26,627,000 |
| 4. | *Fiddler on the Roof* (1971) | 38,500,000 | 22,781,000 |
| 5. | *Annie* (1982) | 37,500,000 | 22,189,000 |
| 6. | *A Star Is Born* (1976) | 37,000,000 | 21,893,000 |
| 7. | *Coal Miner's Daughter* (1980) | 35,000,000 | 20,710,000 |
| 8= | *The Blues Brothers* (1980) | 32,000,000 | 18,935,000 |
| 8= | *The Muppet Movie* (1979) | 32,000,000 | 18,935,000 |
| 10. | *Purple Rain* (1984) | 31,500,000 | 18,639,000 |

TOP A scene from *Grease*, the most successful musical film of all time.

RIGHT 'The Hills are Alive …' – Maria and the Trapp family in *The Sound of Music*.

# THE 10 LONGEST FILMS EVER SCREENED

| | Film | Duration hr | min |
|---|---|---|---|
| 1. | *The Longest and Most Meaningless Movie in the World* (GB, 1970) | 48 | |
| 2. | *The Burning of the Red Lotus Temple* (China, 1928–31) | 27 | |
| 3. | **** (US, 1967) | 25 | |
| 4. | *Heimat* (West Germany, 1984) | 15 | 40 |
| 5. | *Berlin Alexanderplatz* (West Germany/ Italy, 1980) | 15 | 21 |
| 6. | *The Old Testament* (Italy, 1922) | 13 | |
| 7. | *Comment Yukong déplace les montagnes* (France, 1976) | 12 | 43 |
| 8. | *Out 1: Noli me Tangere* (France, 1971) | 12 | 40 |
| 9. | *Ningen No Joken* (The Human Condition) (Japan, 1958–60) | 9 | 29 |
| 10= | *Wagner* (GB/Hungary/Austria, 1983) | 9 | |
| 10= | *Napoleon* (France, 1927) | 9 | |
| 10= | *Greed* (US, 1924) | 9 | |

The Longest and Most Meaningless Movie in the World *was later cut to a more manageable 1 hr 30 min, but remained just as meaningless. Abel Gance's* Napoleon *has not been shown at its full length since it was first released, but as new segments of it have been discovered, it has been meticulously reassembled to a length approaching that of the original version.*

**FILM**

# THE 10 BIGGEST FILM FLOPS OF ALL TIME

| | Film | Year | Loss $ | Loss £ |
|---|---|---|---|---|
| 1. | *Heaven's Gate* | 1980 | 42,000,000 | 24,852,071 |
| 2. | *Ishtar* | 1987 | 37,500,000 | 22,189,349 |
| 3. | *Pirates* | 1986 | 30,000,000 | 17,751,479 |
| 4. | *Rambo III* | 1988 | 30,000,000 | 17,751,479 |
| 5. | *Raise the Titanic* | 1980 | 29,000,000 | 17,159,763 |
| 6. | *Once Upon a Time in America* | 1984 | 27,500,000 | 16,272,189 |
| 7. | *Empire of the Sun* | 1987 | 27,500,000 | 16,272,189 |
| 8. | *Superman IV* | 1987 | 27,000,000 | 15,976,331 |
| 9. | *Return to Oz* | 1985 | 25,000,000 | 14,792,899 |
| 10. | *Howard the Duck* | 1986 | 24,000,000 | 14,201,183 |

*B*ased on North American (USA + Canada) receipts balanced against production cost. Where two films have incurred similar losses, the losses on the lower-placed one on the list are still being mitigated by on-going income from world-wide distribution, video and television showings. From such sources, the overall losses on several of these films may in time be reduced.

Numbers 1, 2 and 4 also appear in the '10 Most Expensive Films' list. It is also rumoured that Inchon (1981) failed to recover a fraction of its $35,000,000/£21,500,000 production costs. Financed by the Moonies religious sect, it features Laurence Olivier as General MacArthur receiving divine guidance during the Korean War. It was described by Jack Kroll of Newsweek as 'The worst film ever made, a turkey the size of Godzilla'.

# THE 10 ALL-TIME FILM RENTAL BLOCKBUSTERS

| | Film | Total rental $ | Total rental £ |
|---|---|---|---|
| 1. | *E.T.* (1982) | 228,500,000 | 135,000,000 |
| 2. | *Star Wars* (1977) | 193,500,000 | 114,500,000 |
| 3. | *The Return of the Jedi* (1983) | 168,000,000 | 99,500,000 |
| 4. | *The Empire Strikes Back* (1980) | 141,500,000 | 84,000,000 |
| 5. | *Ghostbusters* (1984) | 130,000,000 | 77,000,000 |
| 6. | *Jaws* (1975) | 129,500,000 | 76,500,000 |
| 7. | *Raiders of the Lost Ark* (1981) | 115,500,000 | 68,500,000 |
| 8. | *Indiana Jones and the Temple of Doom* (1984) | 109,000,000 | 64,500,000 |
| 9. | *Beverly Hills Cop* (1984) | 108,000,000 | 64,000,000 |
| 10. | *Back to the Future* (1985) | 104,500,000 | 62,000,000 |

*S*tephen Spielberg directed numbers 1, 6, 7 and 8, and produced number 10; George Lucas directed number 2 and produced numbers 3, 4, 7 and 8.

E.T. – out-of-this-world star of the biggest film hit of all time.

ABOVE Glenn Close and Michael Douglas, co-stars of *Fatal Attraction*, the highest-grossing film of 1988.

## THE 10 HIGHEST-GROSSING FILMS IN GREAT BRITAIN IN 1988

| | Film | Box-office gross £ |
|---|---|---|
| 1. | *Fatal Attraction* | 15,441,584 |
| 2. | *Crocodile Dundee II* | 13,324,673 |
| 3. | *Three Men and a Baby* | 9,662,992 |
| 4. | *A Fish Called Wanda* | 7,399,743 |
| 5. | *Coming to America* | 5,808,136 |
| 6. | *Good Morning Vietnam* | 5,049,480 |
| 7. | *The Last Emperor* | 4,070,826 |
| 8. | *The Jungle Book* | 3,944,843 |
| 9. | *Buster* | 3,689,268 |
| 10. | *Beetlejuice* | 3,604,282 |

*O*nly one film, Buster, *was actually British-made, although* A Fish Called Wanda *was a joint British/US production, and* The Last Emperor *a British/Italian/Chinese co-production.*

## THE 10 MOST SUCCESSFUL ANIMATED FILMS OF ALL TIME

| | Film | $ | Total rental £ |
|---|---|---|---|
| 1. | *Who Framed Roger Rabbit?* (1988) | 78,000,000 | 46,000,000 |
| 2. | *Snow White and the Seven Dwarfs* (1937) | 62,000,000 | 36,750,000 |
| 3. | *Bambi* (1942) | 47,500,000 | 28,000,000 |
| 4. | *Cinderella* (1949) | 41,000,000 | 24,250,000 |
| 5. | *The Lady and the Tramp* (1955) | 40,000,000 | 23,750,000 |
| 6. | *The Jungle Book* (1967) | 39,500,000 | 23,250,000 |
| 7. | *101 Dalmatians* (1961) | 38,500,000 | 22,750,000 |
| 8. | *Pinocchio* (1940) | 33,000,000 | 19,500,000 |
| 9. | *Song of the South* (1946) | 29,000,000 | 17,250,000 |
| 10. | *Fantasia* (1940) | 28,500,000 | 16,750,000 |

*A*ll except number 1 were *made by the Disney Studio. Numbers 1 and 9 are part animation, part live action.*

Bob Hoskins and friend in *Who Framed Roger Rabbit?*

FILM

# THE 10 MOST SUCCESSFUL WAR FILMS OF ALL TIME

| Film | Total rental $ | £ |
|---|---|---|
| 1. *Platoon* (1986) | 69,500,000 | 41,000,000 |
| 2. *Good Morning, Vietnam* (1987) | 58,000,000 | 34,500,000 |
| 3. *Apocalypse Now* (1979) | 38,000,000 | 22,500,000 |
| 4. *M\*A\*S\*H* (1970) | 36,500,000 | 21,500,000 |
| 5. *Patton* (1970) | 28,000,000 | 16,500,000 |
| 6. *The Deer Hunter* (1978) | 27,500,000 | 16,250,000 |
| 7. *Full Metal Jacket* | 22,500,000 | 13,250,000 |
| 8. *Midway* (1976) | 21,500,000 | 12,750,000 |
| 9. *The Dirty Dozen* (1967) | 20,500,000 | 12,000,000 |
| 10. *A Bridge Too Far* (1977) | 20,500,000 | 12,000,000 |

# THE 10 MOST SUCCESSFUL PRE-WAR FILMS

| Film | Total rental $ | £ |
|---|---|---|
| 1. *Gone With the Wind* (1939) | 77,500,000 | 46,000,000 |
| 2. *Snow White and the Seven Dwarfs* (1937) | 62,000,000 | 36,500,000 |
| 3. *The Birth of a Nation* (1915) | 10,000,000 | 6,000,000 |
| 4. *The Big Parade* (1925) | 5,500,000 | 3,250,000 |
| 5. *King Kong* (1933) | 5,000,000 | 3,000,000 |
| 6. *Ben Hur* (1926) | 4,500,000 | 2,750,000 |
| 7. *The Wizard of Oz* (1939) | 4,500,000 | 2,750,000 |
| 8. *San Francisco* (1936) | 4,000,000 | 2,250,000 |
| 9. *The Singing Fool* (1928) | 4,000,000 | 2,250,000 |
| 10= *Cavalcade* (1933) | 3,500,000 | 2,000,000 |
| 10= *The Jazz Singer* (1927) | 3,500,000 | 2,000,000 |

*N*umbers 1, 2 and 7 were filmed in Technicolor; number 6, despite its early date, contains a colour sequence. Numbers 3, 4 and 6 are silent films, and **The Jazz Singer** *is hailed as the first talkie.*

RIGHT The greatest tear-jerker of all: *Gone With the Wind.*

Butch Cassidy and the Sundance Kid, the classic western.

# THE 10 MOST SUCCESSFUL WESTERNS OF ALL TIME

| Film | Total rental $ | £* |
|---|---|---|
| 1. *Butch Cassidy and the Sundance Kid* (1969) | 46,000,000 | 27,250,000 |
| 2. *Jeremiah Johnson* (1972) | 22,000,000 | 13,000,000 |
| 3. *How the West Was Won* (1962) | 21,000,000 | 12,500,000 |
| 4. *Young Guns* (1988) | 19,500,000 | 11,500,000 |
| 5= *Little Big Man* (1970) | 15,000,000 | 8,750,000 |
| 5= *Bronco Billy* (1980) | 15,000,000 | 8,750,000 |
| 7. *True Grit* (1969) | 14,500,000 | 8,500,000 |
| 8. *The Outlaw Josey Wales* (1976) | 13,500,000 | 8,000,000 |
| 9. *Duel in the Sun* (1946) | 11,500,000 | 6,750,000 |
| 10. *Cat Ballou* (1965) | 9,500,000 | 5,500,000 |

# THE 10 MOST SUCCESSFUL COMEDY FILMS OF ALL TIME

|  | Film | Total rental $ | £ |
|---|---|---|---|
| 1. | *Beverly Hills Cop* (1984) | 108,000,000 | 64,000,000 |
| 2. | *Tootsie* (1982) | 96,500,000 | 57,000,000 |
| 3. | *Three Men and a Baby* (1987) | 81,500,000 | 48,000,000 |
| 4. | *Beverly Hills Cop II* | 81,000,000 | 47,750,000 |
| 5. | *The Sting* (1973) | 78,000,000 | 46,000,000 |
| 6. | *National Lampoon's Animal House* (1978) | 71,000,000 | 42,000,000 |
| 7. | *Crocodile Dundee* (1986) | 70,000,000 | 41,500,000 |
| 8. | *Coming to America* | 65,000,000 | 38,500,000 |
| 9. | *Nine to Five* (1980) | 59,000,000 | 35,000,000 |
| 10. | *Smokey and the Bandit* (1977) | 59,000,000 | 35,000,000 |

**C**rocodile Dundee II *(1988) is gaining ground fast; within the year of its release it had already earned $57,500,000/£34,000,000 in rental fees and was set to overtake* Stir Crazy *(1980), which has earned $58,500,000/£34,500,000, and make its mark in the Top 10.*

# BRITISH STUDENTS' 10 ALL-TIME FAVOURITE MUSIC FILMS

1. *The Blues Brothers* (1980)
2. *The Wall* – Pink Floyd (1982)
3. *Grease* (1978)
4. *The Rocky Horror Picture Show* (1975)
5. *Tommy* – The Who (1975)
6. *Stop Making Sense* – Talking Heads (1987)
7. *The Sound of Music* (1965)
8. *Little Shop of Horrors* (1986)
9. *Woodstock* (1970)
10. *Highlander* (1986)

Based on a 1988 poll conducted by Nescafé and University Radio, York.

RIGHT John Belushi and Dan Ackroyd in *The Blues Brothers*, rated by students as their all-time favourite musical film.

# THE 10 MOST SUCCESSFUL SCIENCE-FICTION FILMS OF ALL TIME

|  | Film | Total rental $ | £ |
|---|---|---|---|
| 1. | *E.T.* (1982) | 228,500,000 | 135,000,000 |
| 2. | *Star Wars* (1977) | 193,500,000 | 114,500,000 |
| 3. | *Return of the Jedi* (1983) | 168,000,000 | 99,500,000 |
| 4. | *The Empire Strikes Back* (1980) | 141,500,000 | 84,000,000 |
| 5. | *Back to the Future* (1985) | 104,500,000 | 62,000,000 |
| 6. | *Close Encounters of the Third Kind* (1977/1980) | 83,000,000 | 49,000,000 |
| 7. | *Superman* (1978) | 83,000,000 | 49,000,000 |
| 8. | *Gremlins* (1984) | 79,500,000 | 47,000,000 |
| 9. | *Superman II* (1983) | 65,000,000 | 38,500,000 |
| 10. | *Star Trek IV: The Voyage Home* (1986) | 57,000,000 | 33,750,000 |

**R**eflecting our taste for *escapist fantasy adventures, the first five in this list also appear in the 10 All-Time Blockbusters list.*

*Although sequels are seldom as successful as the films they follow,* Star Trek IV *has out-performed the original* Star Trek *(1979), which has earned $56,000,000/£33,000,000 and would be in 11th place. If the list is extended further, it reveals that* Aliens *(1986), in 12th position with rentals totalling $44,000,000/£26,000,000, has similarly beaten its precursor,* Alien *(1979), which has earned $40,500,000/£24,000,000.*

**FILM**

# THE 10 MOST SUCCESSFUL JAMES BOND FILMS

| Film | Total rental $ | £ |
|---|---|---|
| 1. *Octopussy* (1983) | 34,000,000 | 20,000,000 |
| 2. *Moonraker* (1979) | 34,000,000 | 20,000,000 |
| 3. *Thunderball* (1965) | 29,000,000 | 17,000,000 |
| 4. *Never Say Never Again* (1983) | 28,000,000 | 16,500,000 |
| 5. *The Living Daylights* (1987) | 28,000,000 | 16,500,000 |
| 6. *A View To A Kill* (1985) | 25,500,000 | 15,000,000 |
| 7. *The Spy Who Loved Me* (1977) | 24,500,000 | 14,500,000 |
| 8. *Goldfinger* (1964) | 23,000,000 | 13,500,000 |
| 9. *Diamonds Are Forever* (1967) | 20,000,000 | 11,750,000 |
| 10. *You Only Live Twice* (1967) | 19,500,000 | 11,500,000 |

# THE 10 MOST POPULAR WOODY ALLEN FILMS

| Film | Total rental $ | £ |
|---|---|---|
| 1. *Annie Hall* (1977) | 19,000,000 | 11,250,000 |
| 2. *Hannah and Her Sisters* (1986) | 18,000,000 | 10,750,000 |
| 3. *Manhattan* (1979) | 17,500,000 | 10,250,000 |
| 4. *Casino Royale* (1967) | 10,000,000 | 6,000,000 |
| 5. *Everything You Ever Wanted to Know About Sex, But Were Afraid to Ask* (1972) | 9,000,000 | 5,250,000 |
| 6. *What's New Pussycat?* (1965) | 8,500,000 | 5,000,000 |
| 7. *Sleeper* (1973) | 8,500,000 | 5,000,000 |
| 8. *Love and Death* (1975) | 7,500,000 | 4,500,000 |
| 9. *Zelig* (1983) | 7,000,000 | 4,250,000 |
| 10. *Radio Days* (1987) | 6,500,000 | 3,750,000 |

*A*s he is so extraordinarily versatile, the list includes films which Woody Allen has either written, starred in or directed.

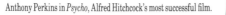

# THE 10 MOST SUCCESSFUL ALFRED HITCHCOCK FILMS

| Film | Total rental $ | £ |
|---|---|---|
| 1. *Psycho* (1960) | 11,000,000 | 6,500,000 |
| 2. *Rear Window* (1954) | 10,000,000 | 6,000,000 |
| 3. *North by Northwest* (1959) | 6,500,000 | 3,750,000 |
| 4. *Family Plot* (1976) | 6,500,000 | 3,750,000 |
| 5. *Torn Curtain* (1966) | 6,500,000 | 3,750,000 |
| 6. *Frenzy* (1972) | 6,500,000 | 3,750,000 |
| 7. *Vertigo* (1958) | 5,500,000 | 3,250,000 |
| 8. *The Birds* (1963) | 5,000,000 | 3,000,000 |
| 9. *Spellbound* (1945) | 5,000,000 | 3,000,000 |
| 10. *Notorious* (1946) | 5,000,000 | 3,000,000 |

Anthony Perkins in *Psycho*, Alfred Hitchcock's most successful film.

# Radio, TV & Video

## THE TOP 10 TELEVISION-OWNING COUNTRIES

| Country | TV sets per 1,000 population |
|---|---|
| 1. United States | 813 |
| 2. Monaco | 741 |
| 3. Oman | 734 |
| 4. Guam | 709 |
| 5= St Pierre and Miquelon | 617 |
| 5= Bermuda | 617 |
| 7. Japan | 585 |
| 8. US Virgin Islands | 566 |
| 9. Canada | 546 |
| 10. United Kingdom | 534 |

## THE TOP 10 RADIO-OWNING COUNTRIES

| Country | Radio sets per 1,000 population |
|---|---|
| 1. United States | 2,030 |
| 2. Australia | 1,300 |
| 3. American Samoa | 1,260 |
| 4. Bermuda | 1,218 |
| 5. Guam | 1,200 |
| 6. Gibraltar | 1,170 |
| 7. Christmas Island | 1,100 |
| 8. United Kingdom | 993 |
| 9. Finland | 987 |
| 10. Norfolk Island | 900 |

*These very high densities in the most affluent countries contrast sharply with the position in most parts of the Third World. In Ethiopia, for example, there is the equivalent of 1.7 television sets per 1,000 population, and in Mali, where there are only 1,000 television sets in the entire country, the figure is close to 0.1 per 1,000.*

Streamlined hi-fi, fifties-style: the 'Ideal Home' wireless set.

# THE 10 BIGGEST EVER TV AUDIENCES IN THE USA

| | Programme | Date | Households viewing |
|---|---|---|---|
| 1. | M*A*S*H Special | 28 Feb 83 | 50,150,000 |
| 2. | Super Bowl XX | 26 Jan 86 | 41,490,000 |
| 3. | Dallas | 21 Nov 80 | 41,470,000 |
| 4. | Super Bowl XVII | 30 Jan 83 | 40,480,000 |
| 5. | Super Bowl XXI | 25 Jan 87 | 40,030,000 |
| 6. | Super Bowl XVI | 24 Jan 82 | 40,020,000 |
| 7. | Super Bowl XIX | 20 Jan 85 | 39,390,000 |
| 8. | Super Bowl XXIII | 22 Jan 89 | 39,320,000 |
| 9. | Super Bowl XVIII | 22 Jan 84 | 38,800,000 |
| 10. | The Day After (ABC Theater) | 20 Nov 83 | 38,850,000 |

*The episode of* M*A*S*H *was the last to be screened. The episode of* Dallas *was the one that revealed who shot J.R. In addition to these programmes and other Super Bowl games, very high (30,000,000+) audiences have been achieved by the series* Roots *(1977),* The Thorn Birds *(1983) and by the film* Gone With the Wind, *screened in two parts on 7 and 8 November 1976.*

The cast of M*A*S*H, the last screening of which attracted America's largest ever TV audience.

## RADIO, TV & VIDEO

# THE 10 BIGGEST EVER TV AUDIENCES IN THE UK

| | Programme | Date | Audience |
|---|---|---|---|
| 1. | Royal Wedding of HRH Prince Charles to Lady Diana Spencer | 29 Jul 81 | 39,000,000 |
| 2. | Brazil v England 1970 World Cup | 10 Jun 70 | 32,500,000 |
| 3= | Chelsea v Leeds Cup Final Replay | 28 Apr 70 | 32,000,000 |
| 3= | England v West Germany 1966 World Cup Final | 30 Jul 66 | 32,000,000 |
| 5= | *EastEnders* Christmas Episode | 26 Dec 87 | 30,000,000 |
| 6= | *Morecambe & Wise Christmas Show* | 25 Dec 77 | 28,000,000 |
| 7= | *Dallas* | 22 Nov 80 | 27,000,000 |
| 7= | World Heavyweight Boxing Championship, Joe Frazier v Cassius Clay | 8 Mar 71 | 27,000,000 |
| 9. | *To the Manor Born* (last episode) | 11 Nov 79 | 24,000,000 |
| 10. | *Live and Let Die* (James Bond film) | 20 Jan 80 | 23,500,000 |

*T*he episode of **Dallas** revealing who shot J.R. is the only programme in the Top 10 on both sides of the Atlantic. It was shown one day later in the United Kingdom. Had it been shown on the same day, in view of the time difference between the USA and UK, the British audience would have seen it first and could thus telephone their friends in the States and spoil it for them; instead, it worked the other way round . . .

# THE 10 LONGEST-RUNNING PROGRAMMES ON BBC TELEVISION

| | Programme | First shown |
|---|---|---|
| 1. | *Come Dancing* | 29 September 1950 |
| 2. | *Panorama* | 11 November 1953 |
| 3. | *The Sky at Night* | 24 April 1957 |
| 4. | *Grandstand* | 11 October 1958 |
| 5. | *Songs of Praise* | 1 October 1961 |
| 6. | *Dr Who* | 23 November 1963 |
| 7. | *Top of the Pops* | 1 January 1964 |
| 8. | *Horizon* | 2 May 1964 |
| 9. | *Match of the Day* | 22 August 1964 |
| 10. | *Call My Bluff* | 17 October 1965 |

*O*nly current programmes are listed. Several other long-running BBC series, such as **The Good Old Days** *(1953–83)*, are now defunct.

ABOVE The Royal Wedding, watched by 39,000,000 British viewers – as well as millions more around the world.

RIGHT BBC Television's *Come Dancing* has been on the air since 1950.

## THE TOP 10 BBC 2 AUDIENCES, 1988

| Programme | Date | Audience |
|---|---|---|
| 1. *Clarence* | 4 January | 10,500,000 |
| 2. *Christabel* | 7/10 December | 8,700,000 |
| 3. *Yes, Prime Minister* | 7 January | 8,100,000 |
| 4. *40 Minutes* | 20/23 October | 7,950,000 |
| 5. *The Boy Who Had Everything* | 28 November | 7,750,000 |
| 6. *International Snooker* | 1 May | 7,600,000 |
| 7. *Moonlighting* | 4 January | 7,500,000 |
| 8. *Wimbledon: Men's Singles Final* | 4 July | 7,400,000 |
| 9. *Buddies* | 24 October | 7,200,000 |
| 10. *The Temptation of Eileen Hughes* | 3 April | 7,150,000 |

## THE TOP 10 CHANNEL 4 AUDIENCES, 1988

| Programme | Date | Audience |
|---|---|---|
| 1. *Treasure Hunt* | 17 March | 7,850,000 |
| 2. *Brookside* | 14/19 November | 7,700,000 |
| 3. *Echoes* | 25/26 May | 6,350,000 |
| 4. *In the Realm of the Shark* | 4 February | 6,250,000 |
| 5. *Comeback* | 16 February | 6,050,000 |
| 6. *Dance With a Stranger* | 3 March | 6,000,000 |
| 7. *Nurse* | 1 March | 5,950,000 |
| 8. *The Cosby Show* | 1 April | 5,800,000 |
| 9. *Heavenly Pursuits* | 17 March | 5,550,000 |
| 10= *Single Bars, Single Women* | 23 February | 5,350,000 |
| 10= *A Private Function* | 10 March | 5,350,000 |
| 10= *Gregory's Girl* | 3 April | 5,350,000 |

## THE TOP 10 BBC 1 AUDIENCES, 1988

| Programme | Date | Audience |
|---|---|---|
| 1. *EastEnders* | 19/24 January | 24,950,000 |
| 2. *Bread* | 11 December | 20,950,000 |
| 3. *Neighbours* | 23 December | 20,550,000 |
| 4. *Royal Variety Performance* | 26 November | 18,150,000 |
| 5. *News, Sport and Weather* | 26 November | 17,300,000 |
| 6. *Last of the Summer Wine* | 24 December | 17,100,000 |
| 7. *'Allo 'Allo* | 24 December | 17,050,000 |
| 8= *The Queen's Christmas Broadcast* | 25 December | 16,600,000 |
| 8= *Only Fools and Horses* | 25 December | 16,600,000 |
| 10. *Comic Relief: Question of Sport Meets Spitting Image* | 5 February | 16,400,000 |

'The Street' – the set of ITV's long-running *Coronation Street*.

## THE TOP 10 ITV AUDIENCES, 1988

| Programme | Date | Audience |
|---|---|---|
| 1. *Coronation Street* | 4 January | 18,150,000 |
| 2. *For Your Eyes Only* | 4 April | 17,800,000 |
| 3. *Octopussy* | 30 January | 15,900,000 |
| 4. *The Man With the Golden Gun* | 6 February | 15,350,000 |
| 5. *This Is Your Life* | 2 November | 15,500,000 |
| 6. *Blind Date* | 19 November | 14,900,000 |
| 7. *News at Ten* | 30 May | 14,700,000 |
| 8. *Wish You Were Here . . .?* | 18 January | 14,650,000 |
| 9. *Moonraker* | 13 February | 14,500,000 |
| 10. *Jack the Ripper* | 18 October | 14,100,000 |

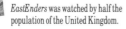

*EastEnders* was watched by half the population of the United Kingdom.

## RADIO, TV & VIDEO

Video rental, the boom business of the 1980s.

## THE 10 MOST RENTED VIDEOS OF 1988 IN THE UK

1. *Lethal Weapon*
2. *Dirty Dancing*
3. *Platoon*
4. *Beverly Hills Cop II*
5. *Crocodile Dundee*
6. *The Fly*
7. *Full Metal Jacket*
8. *Innerspace*
9. *The Witches of Eastwick*
10. *Raw Deal*

## THE 10 MOST-RENTED VIDEOS OF ALL TIME IN THE UK

1. *Crocodile Dundee*
2. *ET*
3. *Back to the Future*
4. *Police Academy*
5. *Beverly Hills Cop*
6. *Raiders of the Lost Ark*
7. *Ghostbusters*
8. *Dirty Dancing*
9. *Top Gun*
10. *Aliens*

*It* has been estimated that more than 10,000,000 people have watched the top five of these titles on video. The top two titles are also responsible for the largest ever 'ship-outs' (numbers of copies distributed to the rental trade) in UK video history – over 60,000 copies of each.

# Industry, Commerce & Communications

## THE 10 OLDEST-ESTABLISHED BRITISH INSURANCE COMPANIES

| Company | Established |
|---------|-----------|
| 1. Sun | 1710 |
| 2. Union Assurance | 1714 |
| 3. Westminster Fire | 1717 |
| 4= London Assurance | 1720 |
| 4= Royal Exchange | 1720 |
| 6. Equitable Life | 1762 |
| 7. Phoenix | 1782 |
| 8. Norwich Union | 1797 |
| 9. Essex & Suffolk | 1802 |
| 10= Law Union & Rock | 1806 |
| 10= London Life | 1806 |

ABOVE and RIGHT Early cast-iron firemarks for the Union, Phoenix and Sun insurance companies.

In the days of timber-framed buildings and primitive standards of safety, fire was one of the most serious hazards in Britain's cities. The insurance of ships and life has existed since the Middle Ages, or even earlier, but it was not until the devastating Great Fire of London in 1666 that the demand for fire insurance led to the establishment of the first company by Dr Nicholas Barbon, an enterprising businessman. Barbon, whose original name was the extraordinary Unless-Christ-had-died-for-thee-thou-hadst-been-damned Barebones, the son of Praise-God Barebones(!), first realized the opportunities offered by fire insurance and set up a business which later became known as 'The Fire Office'. It was soon followed by rivals, among them the first on this list, the Sun Fire Office, whose original deed dates from 7 April 1710. To protect the buildings they covered, fire insurance offices often employed their own fire brigades, and in order to identify properties that they insured, brightly coloured 'firemarks' were fixed to the walls, and can still be seen occasionally on old buildings. Few of the earliest firms survived, but those in the Top Ten, after 200 or more years and numerous acquisitions and mergers, continue to flourish among Britain's leading insurance companies.

# OFFICE RENTAL: THE WORLD'S 10 MOST EXPENSIVE CITIES

| | City | Country | Rent per sq foot £ |
|---|---|---|---|
| 1. | Tokyo | Japan | 89 |
| 2. | London | England | 69 |
| 3. | Hong Kong | Hong Kong | 51 |
| 4. | Zurich | Switzerland | 46 |
| 5. | Geneva | Switzerland | 41 |
| 6= | Paris | France | 31 |
| 6= | Sydney | Australia | 31 |
| 7. | Stockholm | Sweden | 26 |
| 8. | Madrid | Spain | 25 |
| 10. | Milan | Italy | 24 |

*R*ent is the average cost per annum for a first-class suite of 465 sq m/5,000 sq ft in a prime city location. Exceptional properties in outstanding locations may cost even more. At the opposite end of the scale from Tokyo, office rents in, say, Antwerp, Belgium, may cost as little as £5 per sq ft. Perhaps surprisingly, in 1989 New York (£23 per sq ft) dropped out of the Top 10, partly a reflection of the rate of exchange against sterling, and partly because other cities' rents have streaked ahead.

Office blocks in Tokyo are the world's most expensive.

# THE 10 LEADING GOVERNMENT EMPLOYERS

| | Department | Employees |
|---|---|---|
| 1. | Ministry of Defence | 143,400 |
| 2. | Department of Health and Social Security | 102,300 |
| 3. | Inland Revenue | 66,600 |
| 4. | Department of Employment | 58,300 |
| 5. | Home Office | 39,200 |
| 6. | Department of the Environment | 33,000 |
| 7. | Customs and Excise | 26,300 |
| 8. | Department of Trade and Industry | 14,600 |
| 9. | Department of Transport | 14,100 |
| 10. | Scottish Office | 13,000 |

*T*he total number of Civil Service jobs in 1988 was 579,600, a reduction of 156,100 in the ten years since 1978.

The British Army – just one of the responsibilities of the MoD's 143,400 employees.

## INDUSTRY, COMMERCE & COMMUNICATIONS

Dangerous jobs: steeplejacks (above) and asbestos worker (bottom left).

# THE TOP 10 SELF-EMPLOYMENT TRADES

## (A) NFSE and SB STATISTICS

1. Building
2. Artists/Authors
3. General retailing
4. Business services (secretarial bureaux, etc.)
5. Beauty/Hairdressing
6. Farming/Floristry
7. Car repair
8. Clothes shops
9. Office- and window-cleaning services
10. Cafés and snack bars

Based on a 1988 survey of members of the National Federation of Self-Employed and Small Businesses Limited (NFSE AND SB).

## (B) GOVERNMENT STATISTICS

| Occupation | Total no. |
|---|---|
| 1. Construction | 487,000 |
| 2. 'Other services' | 454,000 |
| 3. Retailing | 429,000 |
| 4. Agriculture, forestry and fishing | 248,000 |
| 5. Business services | 234,000 |
| 6. Hotels and catering | 191,000 |
| 7. Repairs | 162,000 |
| 8. 'Other production industries' | 147,000 |
| 9. Transport and communication | 111,000 |
| 10. Metal goods, engineering and vehicles | 62,000 |

# THE 10 MOST STRESSFUL JOBS IN THE USA

1. Firefighter
2. Racing car driver
3. Astronaut
4. Surgeon
5. National Football League player
6. Police officer
7. Osteopath
8. State police officer
9. Air traffic controller
10. Mayor

# THE 10 MOST DANGEROUS JOBS

1. Asbestos worker
2. Crews of boats, ships, railway trains and aircraft
3. Demolition contractor
4. Diver
5. Firefighter
6. Miner
7. Oil/gas-rig worker
8. Steeplejack
9. Tunneller
10. Steel erector

*L*ife assurance companies carefully base their premiums on actuarial statistics that take into account the likelihood of people in each job being involved in an accident that injures or kills them at work, or as a result of their contact with dangerous substances. This does not mean that assurance companies will not provide cover for such professions, but the more risky the job, the higher the premium.

*A*ccording to government statistics, in 1986 there were 2,567,000 self-employed people in Great Britain (1,935,000 men and 631,000 women). Of them, a total of 209,000 were in manufacturing industries and 1,622,000 in service industries. 'Other services' includes a number of groups that are listed separately in the NFSE and SB survey, such as hairdresssers, cleaners, writers and artists, 'Other production industries' are those that are not included with 'Metal goods, etc'.

Men at work: the building industry is the principal trade of the self-employed.

# INDUSTRY, COMMERCE & COMMUNICATIONS

A BP oil platform near Shetland – just part of the mega-company's interests.

## THE 10 REGIONS WITH THE MOST SELF-EMPLOYED PEOPLE

| | Area | Total no. |
|---|---|---|
| 1. | Southeast | 904,000 |
| 2. | Northwest | 267,000 |
| 3. | Southwest | 256,000 |
| 4. | Yorkshire and Humberside | 216,000 |
| 5. | Scotland | 205,000 |
| 6. | West Midlands | 187,000 |
| 7. | East Midlands | 167,000 |
| 8. | Wales | 154,000 |
| 9= | East Anglia | 105,000 |
| 9= | North | 105,000 |

## BRITAIN'S TOP 10 COMPANIES

| | Company | Sales £ |
|---|---|---|
| 1. | British Petroleum (petroleum products, oil and gas exploration) | 27,578,032,000 |
| 2. | Electricity Council (electricity) | 11,335,445,000 |
| 3. | ICI (chemicals, plastics, paints) | 11,123,012,000 |
| 4. | British Telecom (telecommunications) | 10,157,185,000 |
| 5. | BAT Industries (tobacco, financial services, paper & pulp, retailing) | 7,522,009,000 |
| 6. | British Gas (gas) | 7,343,889,000 |
| 7. | Hanson (financial conglomerate) | 6,682,008,000 |
| 8. | Grand Metropolitan (hotels, food, drinks, leisure) | 5,705,501,000 |
| 9. | General Electric Company (engineering) | 5,537,331,000 |
| 10. | Uniliver (consumer products, food) | 5,428,007,000 |

Figures up to 1988

# THE 10 LEADING ADVERTISERS IN THE UK

1. Unilever
2. HM Government
3. Procter & Gamble
4. Mars
3. Nestlé
6. F. W. Woolworth
7. Kellogg's
8. Electricity Council
9. Allied-Lyons
10. Dixons Group

Saatchi (left) & Saatchi (right), eponymous heads of the world's largest advertising agency.

*B*ritain's Top 10 advertisers are all companies or organizations spending in excess of £25,000,000 a year, and Unilever, at number 1, spends over £100,000,000. The Top 10 advertisers spend a total of over £500,000,000, equivalent to 14.4% of the UK total national advertising expenditure.

# THE 10 LEADING ADVERTISERS IN THE WORLD

| | Advertiser | Estimated annual spending | |
|---|---|---|---|
| | | $ | £* |
| 1. | Procter & Gamble | 2,100,000,000 | 1,250,000,000 |
| 2. | Philip Morris | 1,700,000,000 | 1,006,000,000 |
| 3. | Unilever | 1,300,000,000 | 769,000,000 |
| 4. | General Motors | 1,200,000,000 | 710,000,000 |
| 5. | RJR/Nabisco | 1,000,000,000 | 592,000,000 |
| 6= | Ford | 900,000,000 | 532,500,000 |
| 6= | Sears, Roebuck | 900,000,000 | 532,500,000 |
| 8= | PepsiCo | 800,000,000 | 473,500,000 |
| 8= | Nestlé | 800,000,000 | 473,500,000 |
| 8= | Eastman/Kodak | 800,000,000 | 473,500,000 |

*calculated at rate prevailing in April 1989

# THE 10 LARGEST ADVERTISING AGENCIES IN THE WORLD

| | Agency | Country | Billings $ | £* |
|---|---|---|---|---|
| 1. | Saatchi & Saatchi | UK | 11,360,000,000 | 6,722,000,000 |
| 2. | Dentsu | Japan | 6,780,000,000 | 4,012,000,000 |
| 3. | Interpublic Group | USA | 6,620,000,000 | 3,917,000,000 |
| 4. | Omnicom Group | USA | 6,270,000,000 | 3,710,000,000 |
| 5. | WPP Group | UK | 5,950,000,000 | 3,521,000,000 |
| 6. | Ogilvy Group | USA | 5,040,000,000 | 2,982,000,000 |
| 7. | Young & Rubicam | USA | 4,910,000,000 | 2,905,000,000 |
| 8. | Hakuhodo International | Japan | 2,900,000,000 | 1,716,000,000 |
| 9. | Eurocom | France | 2,760,000,000 | 1,601,000,000 |
| 10. | D'Arcy Massius B & B | USA | 2,490,000,000 | 1,473,000,000 |

*calculated at rate prevailing in April 1989

The striking logo of Procter & Gamble, the world's leading advertisers.

# THE 10 BIGGEST BANKS IN THE WORLD

## (A) RANKED BY SHAREHOLDERS' EQUITY

| | Bank | Country | Shareholders' Equity $ | £* |
|---|---|---|---|---|
| 1. | National Westminster | UK | 9,165,260,000 | 5,423,230,000 |
| 2. | Citicorp | USA | 8,810,000,000 | 5,213,018,000 |
| 3. | Caisse Nationale du Crédit Agricole | France | 8,741,160,000 | 5,172,284,000 |
| 4. | Barclays | UK | 7,707,280,000 | 4,560,521,000 |
| 5. | Union Bank of Switzerland | Switzerland | 7,626,190,000 | 4,512,538,000 |
| 6. | Deutsche Bank | West Germany | 7,111,660,000 | 4,208,083,000 |
| 7. | Swiss Bank Corporation | Switzerland | 6,855,090,000 | 4,056,266,000 |
| 8. | Banque Nationale de Paris | France | 5,379,400,000 | 3,183,077,000 |
| 9. | Sumimoto Bank | Japan | 5,262,850,000 | 3,114,112,000 |
| 10. | Crédit Suisse | Switzerland | 5,174,340,000 | 3,061,740,000 |

*calculated at rate prevailing in April 1989

## (B) RANKED BY TOTAL ASSETS

| | Bank | Country | Total assets $ | £* |
|---|---|---|---|---|
| 1. | Dai-Ichi Kangyo Bank | Japan | 289,720,000,000 | 171,432,000,000 |
| 2. | Sumimoto Bank | Japan | 271,390,000,000 | 160,586,000,000 |
| 3. | Fuji Bank | Japan | 264,330,000,000 | 156,408,000,000 |
| 4. | Mitsubishi Bank | Japan | 246,510,000,000 | 145,864,000,000 |
| 5. | Mitsubishi Trust & Banking Corporation | Japan | 238,820,000,000 | 141,314,000,000 |
| 6. | Sanwa Bank | Japan | 234,690,000,000 | 138,870,000,000 |
| 7. | Sumimoto Trust & Banking Co | Japan | 225,500,000,000 | 133,432,000,000 |
| 8. | Caisse Nationale du Crédit Agricole | France | 214,380,000,000 | 126,852,000,000 |
| 9. | Industrial Bank of Japan | Japan | 205,210,000,000 | 121,426,000,000 |
| 10. | Citicorp | USA | 203,610,000,000 | 120,479,000,000 |
| 18. | *Barclays* | *UK* | *164,300,000,000* | *97,219,000,000* |

*calculated at rate prevailing in April 1989

## INDUSTRY, COMMERCE & COMMUNICATIONS

The Royal National Lifeboat Institution, Britain's No 1 charity, saves over 1,000 lives every year.

# BRITAIN'S TOP 10 DONORS TO CHARITY

| | Company | Donation*<br>£ |
|---|---|---|
| 1. | British Petroleum | 2,900,000 |
| 2. | Hanson Trust | 2,600,000 |
| 3. | Marks and Spencer | 2,580,000 |
| 4. | Trustee Savings Bank | 1,929,000 |
| 5. | Barclays Bank | 1,863,000 |
| 6. | ICI | 1,800,000 |
| 7. | National Westminster Bank | 1,651,000 |
| 8. | BAT Industries | 1,488,000 |
| 9. | Shell UK | 1,050,000 |
| 10. | Van Leer (UK) | 1,011,000 |

*figures for 1987/88

The National Trust

Imperial Cancer
Research Fund

# BRITAIN'S TOP 10 CHARITIES

| | Charity | Total voluntary income<br>£ |
|---|---|---|
| 1. | Royal National Lifeboat Institution | 35,933,000 |
| 2. | National Trust | 34,233,000 |
| 3. | Oxfam | 33,923,000 |
| 4. | Imperial Cancer Research Fund | 28,809,000 |
| 5. | Cancer Research Campaign | 24,739,000 |
| 6. | Salvation Army | 24,023,000 |
| 7. | Barnardo's | 23,666,000 |
| 8. | Save the Children Fund | 21,349,000 |
| 9. | Guide Dogs for the Blind Association | 15,944,000 |
| 10. | National Society for the Prevention of Cruelty to Children | 15,915,000 |

*There are over 162,000 registered charities in England and Wales alone. The order of the Top 10 is for voluntary income only. Most charities also receive income from other sources, such as rents and interest on investments. In 1987 the total income of the largest, the National Trust, from all sources was £87,880,000, and the Salvation Army was second with £55,800,000. The order of the largest ones, and the amounts donated to them, have changed dramatically over recent years: in 1984/85, for example, Band Aid was the largest with a total income of £56,500,000. Now it is not even in the Top 50.*

## INDUSTRY, COMMERCE & COMMUNICATIONS

# THE TOP 10 ITEMS OF BRITISH CONSUMERS' EXPENDITURE

| Item | Expenditure* £ |
|------|------------|
| 1. Transport | 43,377,000,000 |
| 2. Housing | 38,862,000,000 |
| 3. Food | 33,643,000,000 |
| 4. Recreation, entertainment and education | 23,682,000,000 |
| 5. Catering (restaurants and hotels) | 18,066,000,000 |
| 6. Clothing and footwear | 17,788,000,000 |
| 7. Alcohol | 17,309,000,000 |
| 8. Household goods and services | 16,763,000,000 |
| 9. Life assurance, etc. | 11,467,000,000 |
| 10. Fuel and power | 11,082,000,000 |

*T*he costs of transport include £14,303,000,000 spent on buying vehicles and £15,700,000,000 on running them. The costs of category 2 include £5,703,000,000 spent on television and video and £3,529,000,000 on books and newspapers. The 11th largest single item on the list would be the £7,653,000,000-worth of tobacco we managed to burn our way through in 1987.

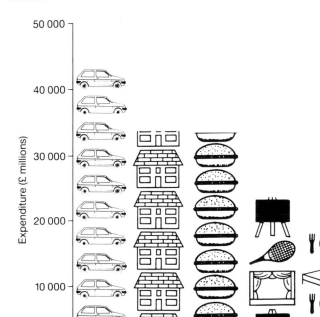

# THE TOP 10 EXPORTING COUNTRIES TO THE UK

| Country | Value £ |
|---------|---------|
| 1. West Germany | 15,783,900,000 |
| 2. United States | 9,136,000,000 |
| 3. France | 8,382,000,000 |
| 4. Netherlands | 7,148,000,000 |
| 5. Japan | 5,463,100,000 |
| 6. Italy | 5,216,800,000 |
| 7. Belgium and Luxembourg | 4,362,500,000 |
| 8. Irish Republic | 3,488,400,000 |
| 9. Switzerland | 3,298,000,000 |
| 10. Norway | 3,290,300,000 |

• • • • • • • • • • • • • • •

# THE TOP 10 EXPORT MARKETS FOR BRITISH GOODS

| Country | Value £ |
|---------|---------|
| 1. United States | 11,014,200,000 |
| 2. West Germany | 9,404,300,000 |
| 3. France | 7,781,500,000 |
| 4. Netherlands | 5,856,200,000 |
| 5. Italy | 4,145,700,000 |
| 6. Belgium and Luxembourg | 3,857,700,000 |
| 7. Irish Republic | 3,831,700,000 |
| 8. Sweden | 2,322,200,000 |
| 9. Spain | 2,164,200,000 |
| 10. Saudi Arabia | 1,978,400,000 |

# THE UK GOVERNMENT'S TOP 10 SOURCES OF TAX REVENUE

| Source | Amount £ |
|---|---|
| 1. Income tax | 46,900,000,000 |
| 2. Value added tax (VAT) | 30,000,000,000 |
| 3. Corporation tax | 22,400,000,000 |
| 4. Petrol and oil tax | 8,800,000,000 |
| 5. Tobacco tax | 5,100,000,000 |
| 6. Alcohol tax | 4,700,000,000 |
| 7. Vehicle excise duties and driving licence fees | 2,900,000,000 |
| 8. Stamp duties | 2,400,000,000 |
| 9. Capital gains tax | 2,100,000,000 |
| 10. Customs duties | 1,800,000,000 |

*I*n addition to these taxes, the Government receives £34,000,000,000 from National Insurance and £7,000,000,000 from interest and dividends. The Government's total income for 1989/90 from all sources, as announced in the 1989 Budget, is estimated to be £206,400,000,000 – £3,628 for every man, woman and child in the country.

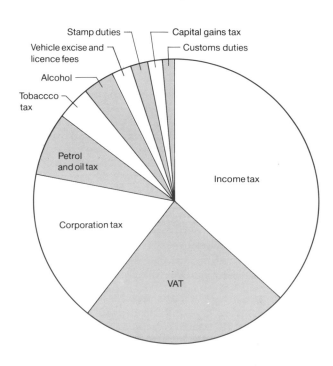

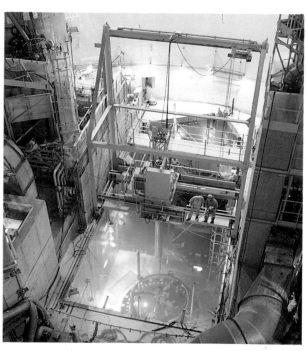

Inside the Prairie Island nuclear power plant, a contributor to the USA's colossal electricity output.

# THE TOP 10 ELECTRICITY-PRODUCING COUNTRIES

| Country | Production kw per hr |
|---|---|
| 1. United States | 2,469,072,000,000 |
| 2. USSR | 1,545,000,000,000 |
| 3. Japan | 667,000,000,000 |
| 4. Canada | 446,412,000,000 |
| 5. West Germany | 408,713,000,000 |
| 6. China | 407,300,000,000 |
| 7. France | 323,575,000,000 |
| 8. United Kingdom | 297,050,000,000 |
| 9. Italy | 195,213,000,000 |
| 10. Brazil | 175,710,000,000 |
| *World total* | *9,675,000,000,000* |

INDUSTRY, COMMERCE & COMMUNICATIONS

# THE TOP 10 OIL-PRODUCING COUNTRIES

| | Country | Production per annum tonnes |
|---|---|---|
| 1. | USSR | 595,048,000 |
| 2. | United States | 438,950,000 |
| 3. | Saudi Arabia | 172,953,000 |
| 4. | Mexico | 142,684,000 |
| 5. | United Kingdom | 127,527,000 |
| 6. | China | 125,000,000 |
| 7. | Iran | 112,952,000 |
| 8. | Venezuela | 88,179,000 |
| 9. | Nigeria | 73,077,000 |
| 10. | Canada | 72,141,000 |
| | *World total* | *2,669,000,000* |

An oil-rig on the Caspian, one of the USSR's giant oilfields.

# THE TOP 10 MINERALS EXTRACTED IN GREAT BRITAIN

| | Mineral | Production per annum tonnes |
|---|---|---|
| 1. | Sand and gravel (from land) | 94,499,000 |
| 2. | Limestone | 93,912,000 |
| 3. | Igneous rock | 39,616,000 |
| 4. | Clay and shale | 17,763,000 |
| 5. | Dolomite | 17,280,000 |
| 6. | Sand and gravel (marine-dredged) | 16,220,000 |
| 7. | Chalk | 13,444,000 |
| 8. | China clay | 4,054,000 |
| 9. | Industrial sand | 4,029,000 |
| 10. | Gypsum | 3,363,000 |

Sand and gravel, Britain's major minerals.

# THE TOP 10 URANIUM-PRODUCING COUNTRIES

| | Country | Production per annum tonnes |
|---|---|---|
| 1. | Canada | 11,720 |
| 2. | United States | 5,200 |
| 3. | South Africa | 4,600 |
| 4. | Australia | 4,154 |
| 5. | Namibia | 3,300 |
| 6. | France | 3,247 |
| 7. | Niger | 3,110 |
| 8. | Gabon | 900 |
| 9. | Spain | 215 |
| 10. | India | 200 |

*T*he amount of uranium produced in the USSR is a closely-guarded secret, but is assumed to be several thousand tonnes per annum. It is estimated that Australia has the greatest reserves of uranium – some 463,000 tonnes.

# THE 10 COMMONEST COMPLAINTS BY CONSUMERS IN GREAT BRITAIN

### GOODS

| | | |
|---|---|---|
| 1. | Miscellaneous (not listed below) | 93,452 |
| 2. | Household appliances | 88,469 |
| 3. | Motor vehicles and accessories | 73,919 |
| 4. | Furniture and floor coverings | 60,853 |
| 5. | Clothing and textiles | 48,734 |
| 6. | Food and drink | 33,207 |
| 7. | Footwear | 18,937 |
| 8. | Toys, games, sports good, etc. | 10,626 |
| 9. | Solid and liquid fuels | 4,577 |
| 10. | Toilet requisites, soaps and detergents | 2,133 |

### SERVICES

| | | |
|---|---|---|
| 1. | Professional services | 31,458 |
| 2. | Public utilities and transport | 31,458 |
| 3. | Consumer credit | 22,633 |
| 4. | General services, etc. | 22,201 |
| 5. | Home repairs and improvements | 21,603 |
| 6. | Holidays | 13,754 |
| 7. | Repairs and servicing (other than motor vehicles) | 12,770 |
| 8. | Repairs and servicing of motor vehicles | 11,981 |
| 9. | Entertainment and accommodation | 9,957 |
| 10. | Cleaning | 8,179 |

Figures are for 1987 from the report of the Director General of Fair Trading. 'Miscellaneous' covers a very wide range of complaints, including those relating to double glazing and house insulation.

Britain is still a nation of shopkeepers – and newsagents come out on top.

# THE 10 COMMONEST SHOPS IN BRITAIN

| | Type of shop | Number |
|---|---|---|
| 1. | Confectionery, tobacco and newsagents' shops | 47,744 |
| 2. | Small grocery shops | 32,942 |
| 3. | Women's and children's clothes shops | 27,135 |
| 4. | Butchers and poulterers | 20,721 |
| 5. | Greengrocers and fruiterers | 16,805 |
| 6. | Electrical, gas and music goods shops | 16,304 |
| 7. | Chemists | 12,538 |
| 8. | Furniture shops | 11,639 |
| 9. | Shoe shops | 11,447 |
| 10. | General clothing shops | 11,282 |

*The figures show that Britain is still a 'nation of shopkeepers', with small, single outlet retailers outnumbering large chain stores and other multiple stores. It is the Government's method of classifying businesses that gives rise to such odd groupings as 'Electrical, gas and music goods'!*

## INDUSTRY, COMMERCE & COMMUNICATIONS

# MARKS AND SPENCER'S 10 BESTSELLING LINES

1. Whole chickens
2. Ladies' knickers
3. Ladies' skirts
4. Ladies' slips
5. Ladies' jumpers
6. Men's suits
7. Ladies' white blouses
8. Men's white shirts
9. Men's socks
10. Ladies' nightdresses

*M*ichael Marks, a Polish refugee, set up his 'Penny Bazaar', a stall in the Leeds open-air market, in 1884. Marks and Spencer, the company that grew out of it, was created in 1926. Today it is the 16th largest company in Great Britain, employing nearly 70,000 people and achieving sales in 1988 of over £4,500,000,000.

• • • • • • • • • • • • • • • •

# THE 10 BESTSELLING COMPUTERS IN EUROPE

1. Atari ST
2. Amstrad PC 1512
3. Commodore Amega
4. Olivetti M24
5. IBM PS2 Model 30
6. Amstrad PC 1640
7. IBM PC 80
8. IBM PS2 Model 50
9. Apple Macintosh SE
10. IBM PC XT

# THE 10 COUNTRIES WITH THE HIGHEST INFLATION

|    | Country | Currency unit | Inflation rate % |
|----|---------|---------------|------------------|
| 1. | Nicaragua | Cordoba | 911.8 |
| 2. | Uganda | Shilling | 238.1 |
| 3. | Brazil | Cruzado | 229.1 |
| 4. | Sierra Leone | Leone | 178.7 |
| 5. | Mexico | Peso | 131.8 |
| 6. | Argentina | Austral | 131.3 |
| 7. | Yugoslavia | Dinar | 120.8 |
| 8. | Zaire | Zaire | 90.4 |
| 9. | Peru | Inti | 85.8 |
| 10. | Uruguay | New Peso | 63.6 |

*T*hese figures are for 1987, the latest year for which complete figures exist. High as they are, these inflation rates seem almost insignificant when compared with the multi-million per cent hyper-inflation experienced by Germany in 1923, and Hungary in 1946. They have also been far exceeded in recent times by Bolivia's rate of inflation, which was over 24,000% in 1985. Britain's highest annual rate was in 1974/5 when it reached almost 27%. It has been in single figures for the past few years.

## INDUSTRY, COMMERCE & COMMUNICATIONS

# THE 10 COUNTRIES THAT MAKE THE MOST INTERNATIONAL PHONE CALLS

| | Country | International calls per head | Total international calls |
|---|---|---|---|
| 1. | United States | 2.0 | 478,770,000 |
| 2. | West Germany | 7.7 | 468,198,000 |
| 3. | United Kingdom | 4.3 | 245,600,000 |
| 4. | Canada | 6.5 | 167,370,000 |
| 5. | Switzerland | 24.7 | 160,500,000 |
| 6. | Italy | 2.5 | 141,138,000 |
| 7. | Netherlands | 9.6 | 140,000,000 |
| 8. | Belgium | 10.8 | 106,900,000 |
| 9. | Spain | 2.6 | 99,554,000 |
| 10. | Sweden | 8.8 | 73,470,000 |

*A*fter Switzerland, *Denmark, which does not even appear in the Top 10, makes the second highest number of international calls per person (13.4).*

# THE 10 COUNTRIES WITH THE MOST TELEPHONES

| | Country | Telephones per 1,000 population |
|---|---|---|
| 1. | Monaco | 733 |
| 2. | Sweden | 642 |
| 3. | Switzerland | 520 |
| 4. | Denmark | 513 |
| 5. | Canada | 512 |
| 6. | United States | 506 |
| 7. | Finland | 462 |
| 8= | Norway | 439 |
| 8= | Liechtenstein | 439 |
| 10. | West Germany | 438 |
| | *United Kingdom* | *382* |

*T*here are many countries in *the world with fewer than ten telephones per 1,000 population, including China (6.2 phones per 1,000), Pakistan (5.2), India (4.6), Indonesia (3.9) and most of Africa – Niger, for example has only 1.4 telephones per 1,000.*

Spoilt for choice in the USA, the country with the most public telephones per person.

# THE 10 COUNTRIES WITH THE MOST PUBLIC TELEPHONES

| | Country | Public phones per 1,000 | Total public phones |
|---|---|---|---|
| 1. | United States | 1.42 | 1,565,707 |
| 2. | Japan | 6.86 | 834,000 |
| 3. | Italy | 7.70 | 440,779 |
| 4. | France | 3.69 | 204,538 |
| 5. | West Germany | 2.65 | 161,795 |
| 6. | Korea | 3.33 | 138,491 |
| 7. | Brazil | 0.81 | 112,580 |
| 8. | Taiwan | 4.77 | 92,973 |
| 9. | United Kingdom | 1.38 | 78,100 |
| 10. | Switzerland | 9.06 | 58,919 |

# Wealth

## THE 10 HIGHEST-EARNING ACTORS IN THE WORLD

| | Actor | 1987/88 income $ | £* |
|---|---|---|---|
| 1. | Bill Cosby | 97,000,000 | 57,000,000 |
| 2. | Sylvester Stallone | 63,000,000 | 37,000,000 |
| 3. | Eddie Murphy | 62,000,000 | 36,000,000 |
| 4. | Arnold Schwarzenegger | 43,000,000 | 25,000,000 |
| 5. | Paul Hogan | 29,000,000 | 17,000,000 |
| 6. | Tom Selleck | 25,000,000 | 15,000,000 |
| 7. | Jane Fonda | 23,000,000 | 13,500,000 |
| 8. | Steve Martin | 22,000,000 | 13,000,000 |
| 9. | Jack Nicholson | 21,000,000 | 12,000,000 |
| 10. | Michael J. Fox | 19,000,000 | 11,000,000 |

*calculated at rate prevailing in April 1989

*Based on Forbes Magazine's survey of top entertainers' income in the years 1987 and 1988. Bill Cosby was also number 1 in the 1987 list of all entertainers (including pop stars, professional sportsmen and others), with earnings of $57,000,000, but in 1988 he was overtaken by Michael Jackson. Bruce Willis did not quite make it into the Top 10, with earnings in the two-year period of only $17,000,000/£10,000,000.*

*Used by permission of Forbes Magazine.*

Bill Cosby, the world's highest-paid actor.

# WEALTH

# THE 10 HIGHEST-EARNING POP STARS IN THE WORLD

Those dark glasses don't fool anybody. Jacko shows the strain of being the world's highest-earning pop star.

| | Artist(s) | 1987/88 income | |
|---|---|---|---|
| | | $ | £* |
| 1. | Michael Jackson | 97,000,000 | 57,000,000 |
| 2. | Bruce Springsteen | 61,000,000 | 36,000,000 |
| 3. | Madonna | 46,000,000 | 27,000,000 |
| 4. | U2 | 42,000,000 | 25,000,000 |
| 5. | George Michael | 38,000,000 | 22,500,000 |
| 6. | Bon Jovi | 34,000,000 | 20,000,000 |
| 7. | Whitney Houston | 30,000,000 | 18,000,000 |
| 8. | Pink Floyd | 29,000,000 | 17,000,000 |
| 9. | Julio Iglesias | 26,000,000 | 16,500,000 |
| 10. | Kenny Rogers | 26,000,000 | 15,500,000 |

*calculated at rate prevailing in April 1989

*B*ased on Forbes Magazine's survey of top entertainers' income in the years 1987 and 1988. Other high-earning singers in this two-year period include Tina Turner and Van Halen ($25,000,000/£15,000,000 each), Sting and Prince ($24,000,000/£14,000,000 each), John Cougar Mellencamp and Grateful Dead ($23,000,000/£13,500,000 each), Wayne Newton ($21,000,000/£12,000,000), Billy Joel ($18,000,000/£10,500,000) and Frank Sinatra ($16,000,000/£9,500,000). Even a number of dead singers earned a lot, among them (in 1988 alone) Elvis Presley ($15,000,000/£9,000,000) and John Lennon ($5,000,000/£3,000,000).

*Used by permission of Forbes Magazine.*

## WEALTH

More than $1,000,000 a week – Steven Spielberg, the world's wealthiest film producer and director.

# THE 10 HIGHEST-EARNING ENTERTAINERS IN THE WORLD*

| | Name | Profession | 1987/88 income | |
|---|---|---|---|---|
| | | | $ | £† |
| 1. | Steven Spielberg | Film producer/director | 64,000,000 | 38,000,000 |
| 2. | Charles M. Schulz | 'Peanuts' cartoonist | 62,000,000 | 36,500,000 |
| 3. | Mike Tyson | Boxer | 55,000,000 | 32,500,000 |
| 4. | Johnny Carson | TV host/producer | 40,000,000 | 23,500,000 |
| 5. | Oprah Winfrey | TV host/producer | 37,000,000 | 22,000,000 |
| 6. | Jim Davis | 'Garfield' cartoonist | 36,000,000 | 21,500,000 |
| 7. | Sugar Ray Leonard | Boxer | 27,000,000 | 16,000,000 |
| 8. | Stephen King | Novelist/ screenwriter | 25,000,000 | 15,000,000 |
| 9. | Andrew Lloyd Webber | Composer | 24,000,000 | 14,000,000 |
| 10. | Michael Spinks | Boxer | 17,000,000 | 10,000,000 |

*other than actors and pop stars   †calculated at rate prevailing in April 1989

*B*ased on Forbes Magazine*'s survey of top entertainers' income in the years 1987 and 1988. Used by permission of* Forbes Magazine.

# THE 10 RICHEST PEOPLE IN THE USA

In 1988, according to *Forbes Magazine*, at least 50 Americans were reckoned to be dollar billionaires – that is, with assets in excess of $1,000,000,000/ £591,000,000. The ten at the top of this enviable pile are:

1. Samuel Moore Walton – $6,700,000,000/ £3,964,000,000

*N*umber 1 in the list of America's richest people for several years, Sam Walton is president of Wal-Mart Stores, based in Bentonville, Arkansas. In 1940 he worked for the J.C. Penney store as a shirt salesman, earning $85/£50 per month. He opened his first 'Ben Franklin' store in Newport, Arkansas, in 1945, but lost the lease five years later. With his brother, James, he restarted in Bentonville, developing a chain of discount retail outlets serving predominantly rural areas. He now owns the third-largest chain of retail stores in the USA, his 1,200 Wal-Mart stores achieving annual sales of $15,900,000,000/£9,408,000,000.

2. John Werner Kluge – $3,200,000,000/£1,893,000,000

*F*ounder of the Metromedia Company of Charlottesville, Virginia. The family of German-born Kluge settled in Detroit in 1922, where he worked on the Ford assembly line. He won a scholarship to Columbia University and gained a degree in economics. He started a radio station and in 1959, with partners, acquired the Metropolitan Broadcasting Company, developing it into Metromedia, a corporation that owns TV and radio stations (and the Harlem Globetrotters basketball team). Kluge sold Metromedia in 1984 and has diversified his interests into such areas as films, printing and restaurants.

3. Henry Ross Perot – $3,000,000,000/£1,775,000,000

*F*ormer president of Electronic Data Systems. Son of a Texan horse-trader, Perot once sold saddles and served in the US Navy before becoming IBM's star salesman. In 1962, with $1,000/£600, he founded Electronic Data Systems of Dallas. It crashed in 1970, losing a record $600,000,000/£355,000,000 in a single day's trading. Perot got the firm back on its feet and in 1984 sold it to General Motors for $991,000,000/£586,000,000. A subsequent management dispute led to his being bought out in 1986 for $742,000,000/£439,000,000. He now runs an investment company which has backed other high-tech entrepreneurs, such as Steve Jobs (the founder of Apple Computers) in the launch of NExT, Inc. – to the tune of $20,000,000/£12,000,000.

4. Samuel Irving Newhouse Jr and Donald Edward Newhouse – $5,200,000,000/£3,000,000,000 (shared)

*T*he New York City-based Newhouse brothers are owners of America's largest privately-owned chain of newspapers, with interests including cable television and book publishing. Samuel ('Si') Newhouse runs book publishers Random House and magazine publishers Condé Nast. Donald controls their jointly-owned newspaper group. Both have children working in their businesses.

5. Henry Lea Hillman – $2,500,000,000+/£1,479,000,000+

*B*ased in Pittsburgh, Hillman is an industrialist and venture capitalist who has moved his family business (founded in coal, steel and gas) through light industry into high technology.

6. Lester Crown – $2,300,000,000+/£1,360,000,000+

*T*he son of Chicago financier Henry Crown, who was born to poor Latvian immigrants, Lester Crown has enlarged the family fortunes through his directorship of TWA, ownership of the Empire State Building (sold in 1961 for $31,000,000/£18,000,000 profit) and the Hilton Hotel chain.

7. Barbara Cox Anthony and Anne Cox Chambers – $4,500,000,000+/£2,662,000,000+ (shared)

*D*aughters of a former schoolteacher who bought the Dayton Daily News in 1898. The family business grew into a media empire encompassing newspapers, magazines, TV and radio stations and many other interests.

8. J. Arthur Pritzker and Robert Alan Pritkzer – $4,400,000+/£2,603,000,000+ (shared)

*O*f Russian ancestry, the Pritzker brothers are Chicago-based financiers, the owners of Hyatt Hotels (run by J.A 'Jay' Pritzker's son Thomas), McCall's magazine, real estate and other interests.

9. Warren Edward Buffett – $2,200,000,000/£1,300,000,000

*B*uffett was born and still lives in Omaha, Nebraska. He started as a pinball service engineer, after which he published a horse-race tip sheet. His diverse business interests include the major textile company, Berkshire Hathaway.

## WEALTH

10.  David Packard – $2,000,000,000+/£1,183,000,000+

*P*resident of Hewlett-Packard of Palo Alto, California. In 1939 Packard launched his electronics company with his Stanford college friend, William Hewlett. They were among the pioneers in the development of calculators and computers, and the first US company to introduce flexitime. Packard was Deputy Defense Secretary under President Richard Nixon (1969–71). In 1986 he gave $70,000,000/£41,000,000 to his old college.

Sam Walton, America's richest man, claims 'All I own is a pickup truck and a little Wal-Mart stock".

# THE 10 RICHEST BRITISH PEOPLE

1.  The Duke of Westminster – £3,200,000,000/$4,992,000,000

*G*erald Grosvenor owns 300 acres in Mayfair and Belgravia (part of which was once a cabbage-patch, acquired in 1677 as the dowry of the 12-year-old bride of Sir Thomas Grosvenor), Eaton Hall near Chester and its 13,000-acre estate, and 100,000 acres of Scottish Forest, as well as property around the world.

2.  The Sainsbury Family – £2,000,000,000/$3,120,000,000

*F*ounded in 1869, Sainsbury's were among the first to develop American-style supermarkets in the UK. Today Lord (Alan) Sainsbury, Sir Robert Sainsbury, Sir John Sainsbury and David Sainsbury own the majority of the shares in the chain which has an annual turnover in excess of £5,000,000,000.

3= Sir John Moores – £1,700,000,000/$2,652,000,000

*O*riginally a post office messenger, Sir John Moores founded Littlewoods in 1923. Now Britain's largest private company, it operates Littlewoods Football Pools and the Littlewoods retail and mail-order stores group.

3= Garfield Weston – £1,700,000,000/$2,652,000,000

*A*s Chairman of Associated British Foods, Garfield Weston runs the British arm of the family firm which made a fortune in the bakery business in Canada.

5.  Lord Samuel and Edmund Vestey – £1,200,000,000/$1,872,000,000

*B*uilt up during the nineteenth century from a cattle-ranching and meat-shipping business, cousins Lord Samuel and Edmund Vestey's company is today the world's largest retail butcher.

6.  Sir James Goldsmith – £750,000,000/$1,170,000,000

*P*rincipally a financier, Sir James was the one-time owner of a diverse group of businesses ranging from food companies to the French newspaper, L'Express – as well as 2.5 million acres of American forests.

7.  Robert Maxwell – £675,000,000/$1,053,000,000

*B*orn Jan Ludwig Hoch, the son of a poor Czechoslovakian labourer, Robert Maxwell served in the British army during the Second World War and went on to found a global printing and communications empire that today includes Mirror Group Newspapers, Macdonald Publishers and Pergamon Press in the UK, and Macmillan in the USA.

8= Gerald Ronson – £500,000,000/$780,000,000

*R*onson's Heron Group owns garages and is involved in property development. After Littlewoods, it is Britain's largest privately-owned company.

8= Sir Adrian and John Swire – £500,000,000/ $780,000,000

*T*he Swire brothers inherited a business based on shipping. Today the John Swire Group includes Cathay Pacific Airline and extensive interests in property, hotels and insurance.

10.  The Earl of Cadogan – £450,000,000/$702,000,000

*T*he basis of the Cadogan family fortunes is the Cadogan Estates, a large amount of property it owns in Chelsea, an area that became increasingly fashionable in the nineteenth century.

# THE TOP 10 GOLD PRODUCERS IN THE WORLD

| | Country | Annual production tonnes |
|---|---|---|
| 1. | South Africa | 607.0 |
| 2. | USSR | 270.6* |
| 3. | United States | 154.9 |
| 4. | Canada | 120.3 |
| 5. | Australia | 108.0 |
| 6. | Brazil | 83.8 |
| 7. | China | 59.1* |
| 8. | Philippines | 39.5 |
| 9. | Papua New Guinea | 33.9 |
| 10. | Colombia | 26.3 |

*1985 figures; others 1987

*In 1987 the non-Communist world mined a total of 2,008 tonnes of gold, of which South Africa produced over 30%.*

• • • • • • • • • • • • • • •

# THE TOP 10 DIAMOND-PRODUCING COUNTRIES IN THE WORLD

| | Country | Production carats per annum |
|---|---|---|
| 1. | Australia | 30,000,000 |
| 2. | Zaire | 24,000,000 |
| 3. | Botswana | 14,000,000 |
| 4. | USSR | 12,000,000 |
| 5. | South Africa | 9,000,000 |
| 6= | Namibia | 1,000,000 |
| 6= | Angola | 1,000,000 |
| 8. | Guinea | 450,000 |
| 9. | Central African Republic | 400,000 |
| 10. | Brazil | 300,000 |

# THE 10 LARGEST UNCUT DIAMONDS IN THE WORLD

The weight of diamonds is measured in carats (the word derives from the carob bean which grows on the *Ceratonia siliqua* tree and which is remarkable for its consistent weight of 0.2 of a gram). There are approximately 142 carats to the ounce.

The value of large diamonds is truly astonishing: at Sotheby's New York on 19 November 1988, the London firm of Graff Diamonds paid a record $9,310,000 for an 85.91-carat diamond, ending the eight-year reign of the 41.28-carat Polar Star which had been sold in Geneva on 21 November 1980 for £2,100,000. On 20 April 1988 at Christie's New York, a 52.59-carat stone made $7,980,000, a record $151,740 per carat. Just eight days later, a tiny rare red diamond weighing just 0.95 of a carat made $938,250/£500,000, equivalent to $987,632/£526,316 per carat.

Fewer than 100 uncut diamonds weighing more than 100 carats have ever been found. The ten largest of these are:

### 1. THE CULLINAN (3,106.00 carats)
The largest diamond ever found, the *Cullinan* was named after Thomas Cullinan, president of De Beers, the diamond mining corporation. Measuring approximately 10 × 6.5 × 5 cm/4 × 2½ × 2 in and weighing almost 6,237 g/1 lb 6 oz, it was unearthed in 1905 at the Premier Mine in South Africa. Bought by the Transvaal Government for £150,000 ($730,000*), it was presented to King Edward VII on the occasion of his 66th birthday on 9 November 1907. The King decided to have it cut, and called upon Dutch expert Joseph Asscher who spent weeks making meticulous calculations before commencing his task. At 2.45 p.m. on 10 February 1908, surrounded by assistants in his Amsterdam workshop, Asscher started work, knowing that the slightest mistake could cause the world's largest diamond to shatter into fragments. His first blade immediately snapped, but on his second attempt the diamond was cleft in two – precisely along the plane Asscher intended. Further cutting resulted in 105 separate gems, the most important of which are now among the British Crown Jewels. The largest of them are:
The *Great Star of Africa* – a pear shape of 530.20 carats, mounted in the Queen's Sceptre. This is the largest cut diamond in the world.
The *Second Star of Africa* – a square-shaped gem of 317.40 carats, the third largest cut diamond in the world, set in the Imperial State Crown beneath the Black Prince's Ruby.
The *Third Star of Africa* – a 94.40-carat pear shape – and the *Fourth Star of Africa* – a heart shape of 63.60 carats, both originally set in Queen Mary's Crown, but now set in a brooch which, along with other lesser gems cut from the *Cullinan*, are worn by Queen Elizabeth II.

## WEALTH

### 2. THE BRAGANZA (1,680.00 carats)

All trace of this enormous stone has been lost. Found in Brazil in the 18th century, there is much dispute about whether it was really a diamond at all, some authorities believing it to have been a giant white sapphire, a topaz or an aquamarine. Its position in the Top 10 is thus somewhat dubious. (If the *Braganza* is disqualified from the list, the tenth largest uncut diamond becomes a 620.14-carat stone that to date has not yet been finally named).

### 3. EXCELSIOR (995.20 carats)

The native worker who found this diamond (in 1893 – in a shovelful of gravel at the Jagersfontein Mine in South Africa) hid it and took it directly to the mine manager, who rewarded him with a horse, a saddle and £500. Cut by the celebrated Amsterdam firm of Asscher in 1903, it produced 21 superb stones, which were sold mainly through Tiffany's of New York and entered private hands. The largest, *Excelsior I*, weighing 69.68 carats, has since reappeared and was sold in London in 1984.

### 4. STAR OF SIERRA LEONE (968.80 carats)

Found in Sierra Leone on St Valentine's Day, 1972, the uncut diamond weighed 225 g/8 oz and measured 6.5 × 4 cm/2¹/₂ × 1¹/₂ in. Acquired by the famous New York diamond dealer, Harry Winston (who is celebrated in the song, *Diamonds Are a Girl's Best Friend*), it was cut into 11 individual stones, the largest weighing 143.20 carats. This in turn was cut into seven, and all but the largest set in the magnificent *Star of Sierra Leone Brooch*.

### 5. ZALE CORPORATION/'GOLDEN GIANT' (890.00 carats)

Its origin is so shrouded in mystery that it is not even known which country this stone came from. Bought uncut in 1984, it took three years to cut it to a 407-carat, 65-facet yellow stone – after the *Great Star of Africa*, the second largest cut stone of all time. On 19 October 1988 it came up for auction at Christie's, New York, with press speculation that it might smash all previous records by fetching $30,000,000. However, although the bidding went up to $12,000,000, which would have broken the world record, it failed to reach its unknown but clearly much higher reserve price, and will presumably come on to the market again at some future date – unless it finds a private buyer willing to spend more than $12,000,000.

### 6. GREAT MOGUL (787.50 carats)

When found in 1650 in the Gani Mine, India, this diamond was presented to Shah Jehan, the builder of the Taj Mahal. It is said that when his son Aurangzeb gave it to the cutter, Hortensio Borgio, he reduced its size so much (to 280 carats) that Aurangzeb flew into a rage and fined him 10,000 rupees. After Nadir Shah conquered Delhi in 1739, it entered the Persian treasury and apparently vanished from history, but it has been claimed that it merely changed its name and is the *Orlov* diamond, one of the Russian Imperial diamonds held in the Soviet Union by the USSR Diamond Fund.

### 7. WOYIE RIVER (770.00 carats)

Found in 1945 beside the river in Sierra Leone whose name it now bears, it was cut into 30 stones. The largest of these, known as *Victory* and weighing 31.35 carats, was auctioned at Christie's, New York in 1984 for $880,000.

### 8. PRESIDENTE VARGAS (726.60 carats)

Discovered in the Antonio River, Brazil, in 1938 and named after the then president, Getulio Vargas, Harry Winston paid a reputed $700,000 for it in 1939 and had it cut into no fewer than 29 gems, the whereabouts of most of which are now unknown.

### 9. JONKER (726.60 carats)

In 1934 Jacobus Jonker, a previously unsuccessful diamond prospector, found this massive diamond after it had been exposed by a heavy storm. Acquired by Harry Winston, it was exhibited in the American Museum of Natural History and attracted enormous crowds. It was cut into 13 gems, the largest of which, bearing the name *Jonker* and said to be the most perfect cut diamond in the world, was sold to King Farouk of Egypt. After he was deposed in 1952, it disappeared, resurfaced in the Queen of Nepal's collection and was finally sold in Hong Kong in 1977 for a reputed £1,300,000 ($2,340,000*).

### 10. REITZ (650.80 carats)

Like the *Excelsior*, the *Reitz* was found in the Jagersfontein Mine in South Africa in 1895 and was named after the President of the Orange Free State, Francis William Reitz. Two years later, it was cut and the principal gem renamed the *Jubilee* to celebrate Queen Victoria's Diamond Jubilee. At 245.35 carats, one of the largest cut diamonds in the world, the *Jubilee* is also said to be the most precisely cut, capable of being balanced on one of its facets measuring only 2 mm/¹/₁₂ in across. It was first acquired by an Indian industrialist and later by Paul-Louis Weiller, a French millionaire.

*conversions calculated at rate prevailing at time of sale

LEFT The Imperial State Crown, in which the Second Star of Africa, cut from the Cullinan, is mounted (front, bottom).

BELOW The Cullinan in its uncut state.

**WEALTH**

# THE 10 LEADING MAKERS OF GOLD JEWELLERY IN THE WORLD

| Country | Gold used in jewellery tonnes per annum |
|---------|------------------|
| 1. Italy | 210.0 |
| 2. India | 159.2 |
| 3. United States | 94.4 |
| 4. Japan | 84.0 |
| 5. Turkey | 72.4 |
| 6. Taiwan | 48.3 |
| 7. Saudi Arabia and Yemen | 47.0 |
| 8. West Germany | 39.2 |
| 9. Egypt | 29.2 |
| 10. Indonesia | 29.1 |

*The Top 10 gold jewellery-manufacturing nations consumed more gold (including recycled scrap gold) in 1988 than the entire annual gold production of South Africa, and more than half the gold mined in the entire non-Communist world. The rest of the world's gold is made into ingots and is used in electronics (123.7 tonnes worldwide in 1987), dentistry (48 tonnes) and for other industrial and decorative purposes. Issues of official coins also comprise a large sector of the gold market (206.6 tonnes worldwide in 1987), but because gold is in such relatively limited supply, a single special issue of a gold coin can swallow up a large proportion of world output. This happened in 1986 when the Japanese government issued a coin to commemorate the 60th anniversary of the accession of Emperor Hirohito, thereby consuming 182 tonnes of gold.*

# H. SAMUEL'S 10 BESTSELLING ITEMS OF JEWELLERY

| | |
|---|---|
| 1. | 9 ct gold gate bracelet |
| 2. | 18 ct gold three-stone diamond ring |
| 3. | 18 ct gold diamond solitaire ring |
| 4. | 9 ct gold ladies' watch |
| 5. | 9 ct gold engraved bangle |
| 6. | 18 ct gold two-stone diamond ring |
| 7. | 18 ct gold diamond and sapphire cluster ring |
| 8. | 9 ct gold coin signet ring |
| 9. | 9 ct gold chain |
| 10. | 9 ct gold hoop earrings |

H. Samuel, Britain's largest jeweller, has over 400 branches

RIGHT India is one of the world's leading gold jewellery makers.

# THE 10 HIGHEST AUCTION PRICES FOR PRECIOUS STONES

| Gem/Sale | Price $ | £* | Gem/Sale | Price $ | £* |
|---|---|---|---|---|---|
| 1. Pear-shaped, 85.91-carat diamond Sotheby's, New York, 19 April 1988 | 9,310,000 | 5,509,000 | 9. The Porter-Rhodes Diamond, rectangular-cut 54.99 carats Sotheby's, New York, 20 October 1987 | 3,850,000 | 2,278,000 |
| 2. Rectangular-cut, 52.59-carat diamond Christie's, New York, 20 April 1988 | 7,480,000 | 4,426,000 | | | |
| 3. Pear-shaped, 64.83-carat diamond Christie's, New York, 21 October 1987 | 6,380,000 | 3,775,000 | | | |
| 4. Pear-shaped, 59.00-carat diamond Christie's, New York, 19 April 1988 | 5,560,000 | 3,290,000 | | | |
| 5. The Polar Star Diamond, cushion-cut 41.28 carats Christie's, Geneva, 19 November 1980 (SF8,800,000) | 5,086,705 | | | | |

*Named after the Porter-Rhodes claim in the Kimberley Mine, South Africa, where it was found in 1880. In its uncut state it weighed 153.50 carats. Cut to 73 carats, it was given by the Duke of Westminster to his third wife, Loelia Ponsonby, in 1926. It was later sold and recut to its present weight.*

| Gem/Sale | Price $ | £* |
|---|---|---|
| 10. Cushion-cut, 15.97-carat Burmese ruby Sotheby's, New York, 18 October 1988 | 3,630,000 | 2,148,000 |

*calculated at rate prevailing in April 1989

*Said to be the brightest diamond known, it probably came from India and was once owned by Joseph Bonaparte, Emperor Napoleon's brother. After changing hands several times, it entered the possession of Lady Deterding, widow of oil magnate Sir Henry Deterding. Its present owner has not been disclosed.*

| | | |
|---|---|---|
| 6. Rectangular-cut, fancy pink 20.00-carat diamond Sotheby's, New York, 19 April 1988 | 4,730,000 | 2,799,000 |
| 7. Pear-shaped, fancy blue, 42.92-carat diamond pendant Christie's, Geneva, 14 November 1984 (SF11,000,000) | 4,508,196 | 2,667,000 |
| 8. The Ashoka Diamond, oblong cushion-cut 41.37 carats Sotheby's, St Moritz, 20 February 1988 (SF5,390,000) | 3,880,000 | 2,296,000 |

*Found in the Golconda Mine, India, and named after Ashoka, a Buddhist emperor, (268–233 BC); bought by Harry Winston in 1947, recut and mounted in a ring.*

A flawless diamond, at $9,310,000/£5,509,000 the holder of the world record price for any gem.

**WEALTH**

The Berkeley Hotel, Piccadilly, pictured in the nineteenth century.

## THE 10 MOST EXPENSIVE HOTELS IN LONDON

| Hotel | Rate*<br>£ |
|---|---|
| 1. Berkeley | 230 |
| 2= Le Meridien | 220 |
| 2= Ritz | 220 |
| 4. Hyatt Carlton Tower | 218 |
| 5. Inn on the Park | 212 |
| 6= Claridge's | 210 |
| 6= Savoy | 210 |
| 8. Intercontinental | 207 |
| 9. Dorchester | 201 |
| 10. Connaught | 200 |

*as at April 1989

*These prices are per night for the best standard double room; they include VAT at the current rate (15%) and service, but not breakfast.*

*Suites, which most of these hotels can also provide, are even more expensive. If you really want to splash out, the Intercontinental can offer their Royal Suite at £1,235 per day – the most expensive in Britain.*

## HARRODS' 10 MOST EXPENSIVE BOTTLES OF PERFUME

| Perfume | Price*<br>£ |
|---|---|
| 1. Amouage (10 ml) | 1,250 |
| (20 ml) | 1,600 |
| 2. Bijan | 360 |
| 3. Chapard with Diamonds | 195 |
| 4. Mille | 193 |
| 5. L'Air d'Or (27 ml) | 175 |
| 6. Joy | 168 |
| 7. Obsession | 150 |
| 8. Nikki | 145 |
| 9. Panthère | 110 |
| 10. L'Air du Temps | 105 |

*as at January 1989

*All bottles contain 30 ml unless otherwise stated. Number 1 is sold in a sterling silver bottle decorated with gold plate and a tiger's eye stone, and number 10 is in a Lalique crystal bottle.*

# Food & Drink

## THE 10 LEADING CALORIE-CONSUMING NATIONS

| | Country | Average daily consumption |
|---|---|---|
| 1. | Belgium | 3,850 |
| 2. | East Germany | 3,800 |
| 3. | United Arab Emirates | 3,713 |
| 4. | Ireland | 3,692 |
| 5. | Greece | 3,688 |
| 6. | USA | 3,642 |
| 7. | Bulgaria | 3,634 |
| 8. | Libya | 3,611 |
| 9. | Yugoslavia | 3,542 |
| 10. | Hungary | 3,541 |
| | *United Kingdom* | *3,218* |

*The* Calorie requirement of the average man is 2,700 and of a woman 2,500; inactive people need less, while those engaged in heavy labour might require to increase, perhaps even to double, these figures. Calories that are not consumed as energy turn to fat, which is why calorie-counting is one of the key aspects of most diets. The high Calorie intake of certain countries, such as those in Eastern Europe, is a reflection of the high proportion of starchy foods, such as potatoes and bread, in the national diet; in many Western countries the high figures simply reflect over-eating. It should also be noted that these figures are averages, which means that at least part of the population of each country is pigging out at mega levels. While weight-watchers of the West guzzle their way through 30% more than they need, the Calorie consumption in Bangladesh and some of the poorest African nations falls below 2,000, while in Ghana it drops as low as 1,733.

Bon appetit! Little belt-tightening in evidence for the Belgians – or most of us Western overeaters.

**FOOD & DRINK**

Labelling Heinz baked bean cans by hand, c.1905.

# THE WORLD'S TOP 10 CONSUMERS OF HEINZ BAKED BEANS

| Country | Retail sales £ |
|---|---|
| 1. United Kingdom | 105,000,000 |
| 2. Sweden | 610,000 |
| 3. Greece | 290,000 |
| 4. West Africa | 272,000 |
| 5. Spain | 250,000 |
| 6. NAAFI, West Germany | 213,000 |
| 7. Dubai | 141,000 |
| 8. Bahrain | 102,000 |
| 9. Kuwait | 78,000 |
| 10. Saudi Arabia | 77,000 |

*These figures are not a mistake: the United Kingdom really did munch its way through £105,000,000-worth of Heinz Baked Beans in 1988 – more than 172 times as much as the next most important international market, Sweden.*

*Of all their '57 Varieties', baked beans are Heinz's most famous product. They were originally test-marketed in the North of England in 1901, and imported from the USA up to 1928 when they were first canned here.*

*The slogan 'Beanz Meanz Heinz' was invented in 1967 over a drink in the Victoria pub in Mornington Terrace by Young & Rubicam advertising agency executive Maurice Drake.*

# THE TOP 10 HEINZ PRODUCTS WORLDWIDE

| | |
|---|---|
| 1. | Tomato ketchup |
| 2. | Tuna |
| 3. | Frozen potatoes |
| 4. | Baby foods |
| 5. | Cat food |
| 6. | Frozen meals |
| 7. | Corn syrup, shakes and by-products |
| 8. | Beans (all varieties) |
| 9. | Weightwatchers' Low-Calorie meals |
| 10. | Soup |

*Heinz's product range in the United States and elsewhere is quite different from that with which the British consumer is familiar, which accounts for this league table.*

*Henry John Heinz was born in the United States in 1844 and dreamed up his '57 Varieties' slogan in 1896. Even though his successful company was already marketing more than 57 products, he thought it sounded memorable. When he first visited London to sell his wares, he astonished the distinguished grocery store, Fortnum & Mason, by having the audacity to enter through the front door. By the time he died, he had become a multi-millionaire and his descendants are still numbered among the wealthiest Americans.*

# THE TOP 10 SMITH'S CRISP FLAVOURS

1. Plain (ready salted)
2. Cheese & onion
3. Salt 'n' vinegar
4. Bacon
5. Beef
6. Bovril
7. Chicken
8. Tomato sauce
9. Gammon
10. Spring onion

# THE 10 FOODS SLIMMERS BLAME MOST FOR THEIR SURPLUS WEIGHT

1. Chocolate
2. Bread
3. Biscuits
4. Sweets
5. Cakes
6. Cheese
7. Crisps
8. Alcohol
9. Sugar
10. Chips

Based on the 1988/89 Slimming Survey conducted by *Slimming Magazine*

# DAYVILLE'S 10 BESTSELLING ICE CREAM FLAVOURS

1. Vanilla
2. English Toffee
3. Burgundy Cherry
4. Chocolate (chocolate ice cream with chocolate chips)
5. Dutch Chocolate (plain chocolate)
6. Strawberry
7. Mocca Almond Fudge
8. Butterscotch Toffee
9. Rum and Raisin
10. Mint Chocolate Chip

*D*ayvilles opened its first 'American Ice Cream Parlour' in London in 1975, offering 32 flavours, many of them previously unknown in the UK. They now supply a nationwide chain of ice cream parlours, as well as supermarkets and freezer centres.

# WALL'S 10 BESTSELLING ICE CREAMS

1. Cornetto
2. Feast
3. Calippo
4. Strawberry Split
5. Snofruit and Cream
6. Twister
7. Chunky Choc Bar
8. Orange Frutie
9. Bonanza
10. Snofruit and Juice

# PAXTON & WHITFIELD'S 10 BESTSELLING CHEESES

1. Extra mature Cheddar
2. Stilton
3. Mature Cheddar
4. Brie de Meaux
5. Farmhouse camembert
6. Cambozola
7. Leicester/Smoked Leicester
8. Blue Cheshire
9. Emmenthal
10. Crottin de Chavignol

*Paxton & Whitfield of Jermyn Street, London, have been cheesemongers since 1797. Their top five bestsellers among the 250 different types of cheese they stock remain the same throughout the year, but sales of numbers 6–10 fluctuate seasonally.*

· · · · · · · · · · · · · · · · ·

# TESCO'S 10 BESTSELLING CHEESES

1. Mild white Cheddar
2. Full-flavoured Cheddar
3. Farmhouse Cheddar
4. Medium-matured Cheddar
5. Edam
6. Red Leicester
7. Stilton
8. Brie
9. Double Gloucester
10. Gouda

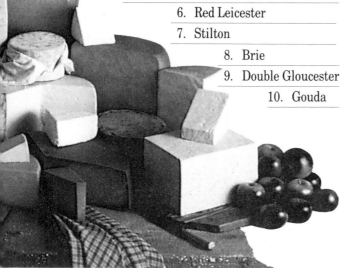

# THE 10 LARGEST CHEESES EVER MADE

**1. 18,171 kg/40,060 lb**
Making gigantic cheeses is not a modern eccentricity: in his *Natural History*, the Roman historian Pliny describes a 454-kg/1,000-lb cheese that was made in the Tuscan town of Luni. The current world record-holder is this monster Cheddar manufactured on 13–14 March 1988 by Simon's Specialty Cheese of Little Chute, Wisconsin, USA. It was then taken on tour in a refrigerated 'cheesemobile'.

**2. 15,690 kg/34,591 lb**
Made on 20–22 January 1964 for the World's Fair, New York, by the Wisconsin Cheese Foundation, it was 4.35 m/14.5 ft long, 1.95 m/6.5 ft wide and 1.80 m/6 ft high and took 183 tonnes of milk – equivalent to a day's output by a herd of 16,000 cows. It was toured and displayed until 1968, when it was cut up and sold. As late as 1978, the last two chunks were sold at a charity auction for $200 each.

**3. 6,096 kg/13,440 lb**
Using the milk from 6,000 cows, production was started on 12 July 1937 and the cheese was exhibited at the New York State Fair in Syracuse.

**4. 5,359 kg/11,815 lb**
This Cheddar was made in January 1957 in Flint, Michigan, from the milk pooled by a group of 367 farmers from their 6,600 cows.

**5. 3,629 kg/8,000 lb**
This large Canadian Cheddar was made for the 1883 Toronto Fair.

**6. 669 kg/1,474 lb**
A cheese 3.90 m/13 ft in circumference made by James Elgar of Peterborough, Northamptonshire, in 1849.

**7. 653 kg/1,400 lb**
A Cheddar given to President Andrew Jackson. After maturing for two years in the White House, it was given to the people of Washington, DC, on Washington's birthday.

**8= 544 kg/1,200 lb**
A huge Cheshire given in 1801 to President Thomas Jefferson by a preacher, John Leland, it was appropriately made by the town of Cheshire, Massachusetts.

**8= 544 kg/1,200 lb**
Made on 3 March 1989 in the village of West Pennard, Somerset, by John Green, to recreate the 'Great Pennard Cheese' (see number 10) and as an exhibit at the May 1989 Festival of British Food and Farming. It took 5,455 lit/1,200 gallons of milk and measures 75 cm/3 ft in diameter and 2.7 m/9 ft in circumference.

**10. 499 kg/1,100 lb**
This 2.7-m/9-ft circumference Cheddar, named the 'Great Pennard Cheese' after the Somerset village in which it was made, was presented to Queen Victoria as a wedding gift in 1840. It was taken to London and exhibited at the Egyptian Hall in Piccadilly, but on its return was found to have suffered so much in the heat of the exhibition that she refused to accept it.

# THE TOP 10 CHEESE-PRODUCING NATIONS

| | Country | Annual production tonnes |
|---|---|---|
| 1. | United States | 2,836,000 |
| 2. | USSR | 1,905,000 |
| 3. | France | 1,313,000 |
| 4. | West Germany | 966,044 |
| 5. | Italy | 684,264 |
| 6. | Netherlands | 555,000 |
| 7. | Poland | 450,443 |
| 8. | Egypt | 303,750 |
| 9. | United Kingdom | 289,200 |
| 10. | Canada | 278,470 |
| | *World total* | *13,709,802* |

# THE 10 SMELLIEST FRENCH CHEESES

| | Cheese | Region |
|---|---|---|
| 1. | Epoisses | Burgundy |
| 2. | Munster | Alsace and Vosges |
| 3. | Maroilles | Flanders |
| 4. | Livarot | Normandy |
| 5. | Boulette d'Avesnes | Flanders |
| 6. | Camembert | Normandy |
| 7. | Langres | Champagne |
| 8. | Chaumes | Dordogne |
| 9. | Dauphin | Flanders |
| 10. | Carré de l'Est | Champagne and Lorraine |

TOP Choosing the ripest (or smelliest!) cheese is a serious business in France.

RIGHT Gruyère in the making – a contribution to France's annual cheese production of over 1,300,000 tonnes.

**'S**melliest' tends to be a subjective assessment, but this list has been prepared by experts in the field who have the experience and noses for their subject.

## FOOD & DRINK

# FORTNUM & MASON'S 10 BESTSELLERS

1. Smoked Scottish salmon
2. Russian caviar
3. Game pie (made on the premises)
4. Champagne and claret
5. Vintage port
6. English handmade chocolates
7. Tea
8. Jam
9. Biscuits
10. Christmas puddings

*F*ortnum & Mason Ltd of Piccadilly dates from the 18th century when William Fortnum, a former footman in Queen Anne's household, joined forces with Hugh Mason to found a grocery store that soon became one of the most famous in the world. It was the first to stock the products of H. J. Heinz and has a long-standing reputation for producing food hampers, including, in 1985, the world's largest, a 180 × 120 × 120-cm/6 × 4 × 4-ft wicker basket of food and drink costing £20,000 – although it came complete with the services of a butler for one day!

# BRITAIN'S 10 BESTSELLING SWEETS

| | Product | Manufacturer | Sales per annum £ |
|---|---|---|---|
| 1. | Kit Kat | Rowntree | 153,000,000 |
| 2. | Mars Bar | Mars | 139,000,000 |
| 3. | Twix | Mars | 90,000,000 |
| 4. | Dairy Milk | Cadbury | 80,000,000 |
| 5. | Quality Street | Mackintosh | 52,000,000 |
| 6= | Maltesers | Mars | 50,000,000 |
| 6= | Roses | Cadbury | 50,000,000 |
| 8= | Wispa | Cadbury | 46,000,000 |
| 8= | Flake | Cadbury | 46,000,000 |
| 10. | Milk Tray | Cadbury | 43,000,000 |

*T*he bestselling Kit Kat bar is also the 5th bestselling chocolate bar in both the USA and Japan.
    Of Britain's Top 20 bestselling sweets, only one – Polo Mints, at number 17 (£31,000,000 per annum) – is not based on chocolate. Britain leads the world in its consumption of chocolate.

Some of Britain's best-loved sweets go back a long way. For Kit Kat and Mars Bars at least, the wrappers have hardly changed.

# THE 10 LEADING CONSUMERS OF KELLOGG'S CORN FLAKES

1. Ireland
2. United Kingdom
3. Denmark
4. Australia
5. Sweden
6. Norway
7. Canada
8. United States
9. Venezuela
10. Mexico

Based on per capita consumption. Reproduced by kind permission of Kellogg Company.

## THE 10 BESTSELLING CHOCOLATE BRANDS IN HARRODS

1. Harrods' own brand (loose boxed)
2. Gartner
3. Harrods' truffles
4. Leonidas
5. Harrods' mints
6. Godiva
7. Panache
8. Harrods' French range by Pierre Koenig
9. Assorted loose Belgian chocolates
10. Harrods' own brand (loose)

## CADBURY'S 10 BESTSELLING CHOCOLATE PRODUCTS

1. Dairy Milk
2. Roses
3. Wispa
4. Flake
5. Crunchie
6. Milk Tray
7. Whole Nut
8. Fruit and Nut
9. Double Decker
10. Creme Eggs

*T*he firms of Fry's and Cadbury's were founded in the early 18th and 19th centuries respectively by Quakers (who viewed drinking chocolate as a healthy alternative to alcohol) and merged in 1919. Many of their best-known products date back longer than one might suppose: Dairy Milk, famed for its 'glass-and-a-half of full cream milk in every half pound' (the slogan of a campaign started in 1928), has been around since 1905, and Milk Tray since 1915. Flake, Fruit and Nut and Crunchie bars all date from the 1920s, and Roses and Whole Nut from the 1930s. The sales of even the 10th product on the list are an amazing 200,000,000 a year.

## SMITH'S 10 BESTSELLING SNACKS

1. Hula Hoops
2. Quavers
3. Square Crisps
4. Wotsits
5. Skips
6. Monster Munch
7. Snaps
8. Crispy Tubes
9. French Fries
10. Nik Naks

*S*mith's is Britain's largest snack manufacturer, followed by Golden Wonder, Walkers, KP, Rowntree – and everyone else.

# PIZZA EXPRESS'S 10 BESTSELLING PIZZA FLAVOURS

1. American Hot
   (Pepperoni sausage, hot green peppers, mozzarella, tomato)

2. Four Seasons
   (Mushrooms, pepperoni sausage, capers, anchovy, olives, mozzarella, tomato)

3. La Reine
   (Ham, olives, mushrooms, mozzarella, tomato)

4. American
   (Pepperoni sausage, mozzarella, tomato)

5. Mushroom
   (Mushrooms, mozzarella, tomato)

6. Fiorentina
   (Spinach, egg, parmesan, olives, mozzarella, tomato)

7. Giardiniera
   (Sliced tomato, mushrooms, olives, pepperonata, leeks, parmesan, petits pois, mozzarella, tomato)

8. Veneziana
   (Onions, capers, olives, pine kernels, sultanas, mozzarella, tomato)

9. Quattro Formaggi
   (Four cheeses, tomato)

10. Capricciosa
    (Ham, pepperonata, anchovy, egg, capers, olives, mozzarella, tomato)

*P*izza Express was the first Italian-style pizza restaurant chain to be established in Britain. Founded in London in 1965, it now has 53 branches.

An American Hot pizza, Pizza Express's bestseller.

# BIRDS EYE'S 10 BESTSELLING FROZEN FOODS IN THE UK

| Food | Tonnes per annum |
|---|---|
| 1. Garden peas | 27,519 |
| 2. Fish fingers | 13,000 |
| 3. Beefburgers | 12,000 |
| 4. Potato waffles | 6,600 |
| 5. Cod in sauce | 6,250 |
| 6. Pies | 6,000 |
| 7. Cod steaks in crispy batter | 5,000 |
| 8. Cod steaks in breadcrumbs | 4,500 |
| 9. Sliced beans | 3,600 |
| 10. Grillsteaks | 3,500 |

*O*ur annual consumption of Birds Eye Garden Peas is equivalent to the weight of over 72 fully-laden jumbo jets or 2,200 London double-decker buses. Fish-finger consumption equals the weight of 1,040 buses.

RIGHT Birds Eye's No 2 bestseller.

. . . . . . . . . . . . . . .

# THE UK'S 10 MOST POPULAR HERBS AND SPICES

1. Pepper
2. Garlic
3. Mixed herbs
4. Parsley
5. Chili powders
6. Oregano
7. Paprika
8. Ginger
9. Cumin
10. Tarragon

*I*n the decade from 1978 to 1988, our taste in herbs and spices altered considerably: in 1978 only 15% of our pepper was black; now it is 40%, while traditional English herbs such as sage and thyme, though still popular, have dropped out of the Top 10.

## FOOD & DRINK

Busy bees: world honey production totals over 1,000,000 tonnes.

# THE TOP 10 FOOD AND DRINK ITEMS CONSUMED IN GREAT BRITAIN

| | Product | Average consumption per head per annum kg | lb | oz |
|---|---|---|---|---|
| 1. | Milk and cream | 135.1 | 297 | 13 |
| 2. | Potatoes and potato products | 112.4 | 247 | 13 |
| 3. | Beer | 108.1 | 238 | 5 |
| 4. | Fruit | 90.8 | 200 | 3 |
| 5. | Vegetables | 85.7 | 188 | 15 |
| 6. | Grain products (bread, breakfast cereals, etc.) | 70.3 | 155 | 0 |
| 7. | Meat | 55.4 | 122 | 2 |
| 8. | Sugar, honey and glucose | 43.6 | 96 | 2 |
| 9. | Oils and fats | 22.9 | 50 | 8 |
| 10. | Eggs | 13.2 | 29 | 2 |

# THE TOP 10 HONEY-PRODUCERS IN THE WORLD

| | Country | Annual production tonnes | Equivalent in 454-g/1-lb jars |
|---|---|---|---|
| 1. | USSR | 190,000 | 418,878,800 |
| 2. | China | 168,050 | 370,486, 639 |
| 3. | United States | 102,000 | 224,871,240 |
| 4. | India | 52,000 | 114,640,240 |
| 5. | Mexico | 49,000 | 108,026,380 |
| 6. | Canada | 39,000 | 85,980,180 |
| 7. | Turkey | 36,000 | 79,366,320 |
| 8. | Argentina | 35,000 | 77,161,700 |
| 9. | Australia | 28,000 | 61,729,360 |
| 10. | Ethiopia | 22,200 | 48,942,564 |
| | *United Kingdom* | *1,500* | *3,306,930* |

*W*orld honey production is estimated at 1,073,384 tonnes – equivalent to 2,364,281,938 jars.

# THE WORLD'S TOP 10 CHAMPAGNE IMPORTERS

| | Country | Bottles imported |
|---|---|---|
| 1. | United Kingdom | 20,648,226 |
| 2. | United States | 14,507,582 |
| 3. | West Germany | 12,307,361 |
| 4. | Switzerland | 8,564,639 |
| 5. | Italy | 8,434,712 |
| 6. | Belgium | 5,447,784 |
| 7. | Netherlands | 1,594,168 |
| 8. | Australia | 1,374,224 |
| 9. | Canada | 1,067,990 |
| 10. | Spain | 893,383 |

*In 1988 a total of 237,300,000 bottles of Champagne were produced. The French kept most of it for themselves and continued to be the world-leading Champagne consumers, with a staggering 147,300,000 bottles drunk – equivalent to an annual consumption of 2.6 bottles for every man, woman and child in the country. But some 90,000,000 bottles of Champagne were exported, and for many years the United Kingdom has led the world as its principal importer. In 1988 UK imports of it increased 7.28% on 1987, to 0.36 of a bottle per head of the population.*

# THE 10 MOST POPULAR COCKTAILS AT THE SAVOY HOTEL'S AMERICAN BAR

1. Dry Martini
   (Gin and vermouth)
2. Whisky Sour
   (Whisky and fresh lemon juice)
3. Manhattan
   (Canadian Club whisky or bourbon, sweet vermouth and dash of angostura bitters)
4. White Lady
   (Gin, lemon juice, Cointreau)
5. Tom Collins
   (Gin, lemon juice, gomme syrup, soda water)
6. Moscow Mule
   (Vodka, lime juice and ginger beer)
7. Bloody Mary
   (Vodka, tomato juice and spices)
8. Champagne Cocktail
   (Champagne, brandy and sugar soaked in angostura bitters)
9. Marguerita
   (Tequila, lemon juice, Cointreau, gomme syrup, served in a glass rimmed with salt)
10. Frozen Daiquiri
    (White rum, lime juice, maraschino)

*Cocktails originated in the United States around the early 19th century, eventually reaching London in the 1850s; they became particularly fashionable in the 1920s. The Savoy Hotel, London, was opened in 1889. The 'American Bar' (so-called because it served ice in drinks – once regarded as a shocking innovation) became world famous for its cocktails. Its barman, Harry Craddock, even compiled* The Savoy Cocktail Book *(1930).*

LEFT French champagne consumers lead the world. An advertisement for Monopole, 1922.

# THE TOP 10 BEER-DRINKING COUNTRIES IN THE WORLD

| Country | Annual consumption per head lit | pt |
|---|---|---|
| 1. West Germany | 146.5 | 257.8 |
| 2. East Germany | 142.1 | 250.1 |
| 3. Czechoslovakia | 133.4 | 234.8 |
| 4. Denmark | 130.0 | 228.8 |
| 5. New Zealand | 120.1 | 211.4 |
| 6. Belgium | 120.0 | 211.2 |
| 7. Austria | 116.0 | 204.1 |
| 8. Australia | 110.8 | 195.9 |
| 9. United Kingdom | 107.9 | 189.8 |
| 10. Republic of Ireland | 104.0 | 183.0 |

# THE TOP 10 ALCOHOL CONSUMERS IN THE WORLD

| Country | Annual consumption per head of 100% alcohol lit | pt |
|---|---|---|
| 1. France | 13.7 | 24.1 |
| 2. East Germany | 13.3 | 23.4 |
| 3. Portugal | 12.4 | 21.4 |
| 4. West Germany | 12.2 | 21.8 |
| 5. Spain | 11.7 | 20.6 |
| 6= Hungary | 11.1 | 19.5 |
| 6= Austria | 11.1 | 19.5 |
| 8. Czechoslovakia | 10.9 | 19.1 |
| 9. Switzerland | 10.7 | 18.8 |
| 10. Belgium | 10.1 | 17.8 |
| 21. *United States* | *7.6* | *13.4* |
| 22. *United Kingdom* | *7.1* | *12.5* |

*E*ven though France's total consumption has recently gone down from 17.4 lit/30.6 pt per head, it has held the lead in this list for many years. In the same period, Britain's consumption rose from 5.2 lit/9.1 pt to a peak of 7.2 lit/12.6 pt in 1985, but is now declining.

German beer drinkers doing their best to maintain their world record.

The French: boozers *extraordinare* according to official figures.

# THE 10 LARGEST BREWERIES IN THE WORLD

| | Brewery | Country | Beer sales lit | pt |
|---|---|---|---|---|
| 1. | Anheuser-Busch Inc | USA | 9,010,000,000 | 15,855,000,000 |
| 2. | Miller Brewing Co | USA | 4,720,000,000 | 8,306,000,000 |
| 3. | Heineken NV | Netherlands | 4,300,000,000 | 7,567,000,000 |
| 4. | Kirin Brewery Co Ltd | Japan | 3,040,000,000 | 5,350,000,000 |
| 5. | Bond Corp | Australia | 2,990,000,000 | 5,262,000,000 |
| 6. | The Stroh Brewery Co | USA | 2,580,000,000 | 4,540,000,000 |
| 7. | Elders Brewing Group | Australia | 2,100,000,000 | 3,695,000,000 |
| 8. | Groupe BSN | France | 1,980,000,000 | 3,484,000,000 |
| 9. | Adolphe Coors Co | USA | 1,920,000,000 | 3,379,000,000 |
| 10. | Companhia Cervejaria Brahma | Brazil | 1,800,000,000 | 3,168,000,000 |
| 18. | *Bass PLC* | *UK* | *70,000,000* | *123,000,000* |

*A*nheuser-Busch, the world's largest brewery, produces every year the equivalent of more than 2.7 lit/5 pt for every person in the world.

• • • • • • • • • • • • • • • • • • • • • • • • • • • • •

# THE WORLD'S TOP 10 BEER BRANDS

| | Brand | Company/Country | Sales lit | pt |
|---|---|---|---|---|
| 1. | Budweiser | Anheuser-Busch, USA | 60,000,000,000 | 105,600,000,000 |
| 2. | Kirin Beer | Kirin Brewing Co Ltd, Japan | 25,000,000,000 | 44,000,000,000 |
| 3. | Miller Lite | Miller Brewing Co, USA | 23,000,000,000 | 45,000,000,000 |
| 4. | Heineken | Heineken NV, Netherlands | 15,600,000,000 | 27,500,000,000 |
| 5. | Antartica | Companhia Antartica Paulista, Brazil | 13,000,000,000 | 22,900,000,000 |
| 6. | Brahma Chopp | Companhia Cervejaria Brahama, Brazil | 12,500,000,000 | 22,000,000,000 |
| 7. | Miller High Life | Miller Brewing Co, USA | 11,600,000,000 | 20,400,000,000 |
| 8. | Polar | Polar CA, Venezuela | 10,800,000,000 | 19,000,000,000 |
| 9. | Coors Lite | Adolph Coors Co, USA | 9,800,000,000 | 17,200,000,000 |
| 10. | Castle Lager | South African Breweries Ltd | 9,500,000,000 | 16,700,000,000 |
| 20. | *Guinness* | *Guinness PLC, Ireland* | *7,200,000,000* | *12,650,000,000* |

based on 1987 figures

## FOOD & DRINK

# THE 10 LONGEST-NAMED BRITISH PUBS

1. The Old Thirteenth Cheshire Astley Volunteer Rifleman Corps Inn (55 letters), Astley Street, Stalybridge, Manchester. In order to maintain its pre-eminence, it was renamed from the earlier 39-letter version: The Thirteenth Mounted Cheshire Rifleman Inn.

2. Henry J. Bean's but His Friends All Call Him Hank Bar and Grill (49), originally in Raphael Street, Knightsbridge, but now in Abingdon Road, London W8, and Kings Road, London SW3.

3. The Fellows, Moreton and Clayton Brewhouse Company (43), Canal Street, Nottingham.

4. The Ferret and Firkin in the Balloon up the Creek (40), Lots Road, London SW10.

5. The London Chatham and Dover Railway Tavern (37), Cabul Road, London SW11.

6= The Argyll and Sutherland Highlander Inn (35), Eastham, Cheshire.

6= The Football and Cricketers Public House (35), Linlithgow, Lothian.

8= The Shoulder of Mutton and Cucumbers Inn (34), Yapton, Sussex.

8= The Green Man and Black's Head Royal Hotel (34), Ashbourne, Derbyshire.

10= The Queen Victoria and Railway Tavern (32), Paddington, London W2.

10= The Nightingale Theatre Public House (32), Brighton, Sussex.

# THE 10 COMMONEST PUB NAMES IN GREAT BRITAIN

1. The Red Lion*
2. The Crown
3. The Royal Oak
4. The White Hart
5. The King's Head
6. The Bull
7. The Coach and Horses
8. The George
9. The Plough
10. The Swan

*There are over 600 Red Lions in Britain.

*The shortest-named public house in Britain is the X at Westcott, two miles south of Collumpton, Devon.*

**FOOD & DRINK**

Vineyards in Tuscany. Italy outstrips even France in wine production.

## PETER DOMINIC'S 10 BESTSELLING WINES

1. Liebfraumilch Rosentor
2. Bulgarian Cabernet Sauvignon BVC
3. Lambrusco Bianco Amatti
4. Piesporter Michelsberg QBA
5. Côtes du Rhone Rouge Marcel Baron
6. Bereich Bernkastel QBA
7. Moët et Chandon NV Champagne
8. Bulgarian Merlot BVC
9. Muscadet AC Henri Clairville
10. Bulgarian Chardonnay BVC

Peter Dominic are the leading wine retailers in the United Kingdom.

## THE TOP 10 WINE-PRODUCING COUNTRIES IN THE WORLD

| | Country | Annual production tonnes |
|---|---|---|
| 1. | Italy | 7,320,000 |
| 2. | France | 7,079,000 |
| 3. | Spain | 3,800,000 |
| 4. | USSR | 2,000,000 |
| 5. | Argentina | 1,900,000 |
| 6. | United States | 1,695,000 |
| 7. | Portugal | 1,020,000 |
| 8. | Romania | 1,000,000 |
| 9. | West Germany | 865,000 |
| 10. | South Africa | 800,000 |

*These countries account for over 86% of the world total annual production of 31,790,000 tonnes.*

## FOOD & DRINK

# THE 10 MOST EXPENSIVE SINGLE BOTTLES OF WINE EVER SOLD AT AUCTION*

| | Wine | Price £ |
|---|---|---|
| 1. | Château Lafite 1787<br>Sold by Christie's, London, 5 December 1985 to Christopher Forbes; the highest price paid for a bottle of red wine, prized because it was initialled by US President Thomas Jefferson. | 105,000 |
| 2. | Château d'Yquem 1784<br>Sold by Christie's, London, 4 December 1986 – the highest price for a bottle of white wine. | 36,000 |
| 3. | Château Lafite Rothschild 1832 (double magnum)<br>Sold by international Wine Auctions, London, 9 April 1988. | 24,000 |
| 4. | Château Lafite 1811 (tappit-hen – equivalent to three bottles)<br>Sold by Christie's, London, 23 June 1988. | 20,000 |
| 5. | Château Margaux 1784 (half-bottle)<br>Sold by Christie's, at Vin Expo, France, 26 June 1987; the highest price for a half-bottle. | 18,000 |
| 6. | Château Latour 1888 (magnum)<br>Sold by Sotheby's, London, December 1987 – Sotheby's highest ever price for a single bottle. | 16,000 |
| 7. | Château d'Yquem 1811<br>Sold by Christie's, London, 1 December 1988. | 15,000 |
| 8. | Château Lafite-Rothschild 1806<br>Sold at a Heublein auction, San Francisco, 24 May 1979 ($28,000). | 14,000† |
| 9. | Château Lafite 1822<br>Sold at a Heublein auction, San Francisco, 28 May 1980 ($31,000). | 13,400† |
| 10. | Château Lafite Rothschild 1811<br>Sold by International Wine Auctions, London, 26 June 1985. | 12,000 |

*Rare bottles of wine have also been sold privately for sums in excess of £25,000.
†calculated at rate then prevailing

*O*n 25 April 1989, another bottle of wine initialled by Thomas Jefferson, a 1784 Château Margaux with an asking price of $500,000/£304,878, was smashed by a waiter's tray while displayed at a tasting in the Four Seasons restaurant, New York.

# THE WORLD'S TOP 10 BESTSELLING SPIRITS

| | Brand | Type | Sales of 75-cl bottles* |
|---|---|---|---|
| 1. | Bacardi | Rum | 248,400,000 |
| 2. | Smirnoff | Vodka | 171,600,000 |
| 3. | Ricard | Anise/pastis | 88,800,000 |
| 4. | Gordon's | Gin | 82,800,000 |
| 5. | Johnnie Walker Red | Scotch whisky | 74,400,000 |
| 6. | Suntory Old | Japanese whisky | 62,400,000 |
| 7. | J & B Rare | Scotch whisky | 57,600,000 |
| 8. | De Kuyper | Liqueur | 56,400,000 |
| 9= | Seagram's 7 Crown | American-blended whisky | 55,200,000 |
| 9= | Jim Beam | Bourbon | 55,200,000 |

*based on 1987 figures

*G*lobal sales of Bacardi are equivalent to more than a bottle for every US citizen, or over four bottles for every person in the UK.

The Jefferson Château Lafite 1787, the most expensive bottle of wine ever sold at auction.

FOOD & DRINK

# THE TOP 10 COFFEE-DRINKING NATIONS

| | Country | kg | lb | oz | cups* |
|---|---|---|---|---|---|
| | | **Annual consumption per head** | | | |
| 1. | Finland | 12.61 | 27 | 13 | 1,892 |
| 2. | Sweden | 11.71 | 25 | 13 | 1,757 |
| 3. | Norway | 10.81 | 23 | 13 | 1,622 |
| 4. | Denmark | 10.65 | 23 | 8 | 1,598 |
| 5. | Netherlands | 10.48 | 23 | 2 | 1,578 |
| 6. | Austria | 8.18 | 17 | 0 | 1,227 |
| 7. | West Germany | 8.17 | 17 | 0 | 1,226 |
| 8. | Switzerland | 7.11 | 15 | 11 | 1,067 |
| 9. | Belgium and Luxembourg | 6.92 | 15 | 4 | 1,038 |
| 10. | France | 5.83 | 12 | 14 | 875 |
| 11. | *United States* | *4.52* | *9* | *15* | *678* |
| 18. | *United Kingdom* | *2.48* | *5* | *7* | *372* |

*based on 150 cups per kg/2.2lb

*C*offee is drunk mainly in affluent countries. Finland has led the rankings since the early 1980s. The average Finn is revealed to drink more than five cups of coffee a day compared with just over one for the United Kingdom. As the comparative table of Top 10 Tea-Drinking Nations shows, the Brits are still a nation of tea-drinkers.

# THE 10 LEADING TEA-DRINKING NATIONS

| | Country | kg | lb | oz | cups* |
|---|---|---|---|---|---|
| | | **Annual consumption per head** | | | |
| 1. | United Kingdom | 3.08 | 6 | 13 | 1,355 |
| 2. | Irish Republic | 2.96 | 6 | 8 | 1,302 |
| 3. | New Zealand | 2.02 | 4 | 7 | 889 |
| 4. | Turkey | 1.48 | 3 | 4 | 651 |
| 5. | Australia | 1.46 | 3 | 4 | 642 |
| 6. | Sri Lanka | 1.45 | 3 | 3 | 638 |
| 7. | Egypt | 1.31 | 2 | 14 | 576 |
| 8. | Chile | 0.97 | 2 | 2 | 427 |
| 9. | Kenya | 0.81 | 1 | 13 | 356 |
| 10. | USSR | 0.74 | 1 | 10 | 326 |

*based on 440 cups per kg/2.2lb

*T*he USA drinks 0.35 kg/0.77 lb per head – an average of only 154 cups per person per annum.

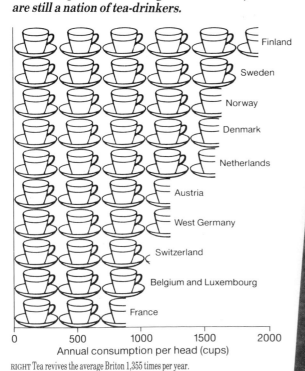

RIGHT Tea revives the average Briton 1,355 times per year.

# Crime & Punishment

## THE 10 LARGEST PRISONS IN ENGLAND & WALES

| Prison | Inmates |
|---|---|
| 1. Strangeways, Manchester | 1,652 |
| 2. Wandsworth, London | 1,506 |
| 3. Walton, Liverpool | 1,323 |
| 4. Armley, Leeds | 1,212 |
| 5. Wormwood Scrubs, London | 1,083 |
| 6. Durham | 1,063 |
| 7. Brixton, London | 1,048 |
| 8. Winston Green, Birmingham | 1,013 |
| 9. Pentonville, London | 897 |
| 10. Stafford | 798 |

*Figures as at 31 December 1988, when the total for all local and long-term prisons (which tend to be smaller) was 47,961. Armley is said to be the most overcrowded prison in the whole of England and Wales.*

ABOVE Strangeways Prison, the largest in England.

Selling guns can be a casual business in the USA.

# THE 10 COMMONEST METHODS OF MURDER IN ENGLAND & WALES

| Weapon | Victims |
| --- | --- |
| 1. Sharp instrument | 210 |
| 2. Hitting and kicking | 101 |
| 3. Strangulation and asphyxiation | 93 |
| 4. Blunt instrument | 82 |
| 5. Shooting | 80 |
| 6. Burning | 19 |
| 7. Poison and drugs | 12 |
| 8. Motor vehicle | 11 |
| 9. Drowning | 6 |
| 10. Explosives | 1 |

*According to Home Office figures, in 1987 there were 635 homicides in England and Wales. In addition to those in the list, 16 methods are described as 'other' and four of unknown cause.*

# THE 10 COMMONEST MURDER WEAPONS IN THE USA

| Weapon | Victims |
| --- | --- |
| 1. Handguns | 7,807 |
| 2. Cutting and stabbing instruments | 3,619 |
| 3. 'Personal weapons' (hands, feet, fists, etc.) | 1,162 |
| 4. Shotguns | 1,095 |
| 5. Blunt objects (hammers, clubs, etc.) | 1,039 |
| 6. Firearms (other than handguns and rifles) | 866 |
| 7. Rifles | 772 |
| 8. Items for strangulation (ropes, etc.) | 357 |
| 9. Fire | 199 |
| 10. Items for asphyxiation (plastic bags, etc.) | 115 |

*In 1987, the year to which these figures relate, 'other weapons or weapons not stated' were also used in 691 murders. Relatively less common methods included drowning (51 cases), explosives (12) and poison (34). The total number of murders for the year amounted to 17,859 (equivalent to one person in every 13,653 of the population). In the same year, there were 635 homicides in the United Kingdom (one in 78,740). In other words, an American is almost six times as likely to be murdered as a British person.*

## CRIME & PUNISHMENT

# THE 10 MOST DANGEROUS PLACES IN THE UK

| | Area | Homicides | Homicide rate per million |
|---|---|---|---|
| 1. | Greater London | 177 | 26.10 |
| 2. | Strathclyde | 54 | 23.03 |
| 3. | Tayside | 9 | 22.94 |
| 4. | Northern Ireland | 24 | 15.22 |
| 5. | Norfolk | 11 | 15.11 |
| 6. | Kent | 20 | 13.32 |
| 7. | West Midlands | 35 | 13.29 |
| 8. | Merseyside | 19 | 12.95 |
| 9. | Greater Manchester | 33 | 12.79 |
| 10. | Northamptonshire | 7 | 12.62 |

*These figures are for 1986, when there were a total of 685 homicides in the United Kingdom. In that year, Warwickshire was the safest place, with no homicides recorded. The figure for Northern Ireland excludes terrorist killings.*

# THE 10 DIPLOMATIC MISSIONS WITH THE MOST UNPAID PARKING FINES

| | | Total unpaid fines* | |
|---|---|---|---|
| | Mission | 1987 | 1988 |
| 1. | Egypt | 799 | 668 |
| 2. | USSR | 622 | 656 |
| 3. | Saudia Arabia | 382 | 357 |
| 4. | Poland | 329 | 340 |
| 5. | Cameroon | 159 | 311 |
| 6. | Spain | 435 | 310 |
| 7. | Ivory Coast | 138 | 300 |
| 8. | Sudan | 236 | 286 |
| 9. | Brunei | 127 | 281 |
| 10. | Iraq | 424 | 274 |

*For many years diplomats used their immunity from prosecution to avoid paying parking fines. In 1984 they managed to clock up a record 108,845 unpaid tickets. Since 1985, however, this practice has been challenged and pressure brought to bear on the offending embassies and international organizations to make their staffs behave responsibly. The most recent report on how this policy has succeeded showed that the 1988 total (10,079) was 30% less than 1987 (14,437), and only 9% of the 1984 figure. Egypt and the USSR have headed the list for several years. China and France used to be serious offenders, but have improved their records, reducing their 1987/88 totals from 551 and 513 respectively to 167 and 112. Since 1987 only five embassies have had perfect records: Malta, New Zealand, Grenada, Tonga and the Holy See do not have a single unpaid ticket between them.*

The Metropolitan Police deal with another incident in the capital.

# THE 10 MOST PROLIFIC MURDERERS IN THE UK

### 1. Mary Ann Cotton
Cotton (b. 1832) disposed of 14–20 victims by poisoning them and was hanged at Durham on 24 March 1873.

### 2. Dr William Palmer
Known as the 'Rugeley Poisoner', Palmer (b. 1824) may have killed 13–16 men in order to rob them to pay off his gambling debts. He was hanged at Stafford on 14 June 1856. The true number of his victims remains uncertain.

### 3= Bruce Lee
In 1981 Lee was convicted of arson that resulted in the deaths of 26 old people's home residents. He was later cleared by the Court of Appeal of 11 of the deaths. He is currently in a mental hospital.

### 3= William Burke and William Hare
Two Irishmen living in Edinburgh, Burke and Hare murdered at least 15 people in order to sell their bodies (for £8 to £14 each) to anatomists in the period before human dissection was legal. Burke was hanged on 28 January 1829 while Hare, having turned king's evidence against him, was released a week later and allegedly died a blind beggar in London in the 1860s.

### 3= Dennis Andrew Nilsen
Nilsen (b. 1948) admitted to murdering 15 men between 1978 and 1983. On 4 November 1983 he was sentenced to life imprisonment on six charges of murder and two attempted murders.

### 3= Michael Ryan
On 19 August 1987 in Hungerford, Berkshire, Ryan (b. 1960) shot 15 dead and wounded 15 others before shooting himself.

### 7. Peter Sutcliffe
Known as the 'Yorkshire Ripper', Sutcliffe (b. 1946) was caught on 2 January 1981 and on 22 May 1981 found guilty of murdering 13 women and seven attempted murders between 1975 and 1980. He was sentenced to life imprisonment on each charge and is currently in Parkhurst Prison, Isle of Wight.

### 8. Judith Minna Ward
Ward (b. 1949) was found guilty of the 1974 bombing of an Army coach in Yorkshire, killing 12 soldiers.

### 9. Peter Thomas Anthony Manuel
Found guilty of murdering 12 men, Manuel was hanged at Barlinnie Prison on 11 July 1958.

### 10. John George Haigh
The so-called 'Acid Bath Murderer' killed at least nine and was hanged on 10 August 1949.

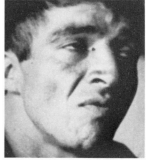

'Countess Dracula' (top) and Pedro Alonso López.

LEFT The trial of Dr William Palmer, the 'Rugeley Poisoner', who may have murdered as many as 16 men.

# THE 10 MOST PROLIFIC MURDERERS IN THE WORLD

## 1. Behram
The leader of the Thug cult in India in the period 1790–1840, he was reputed to have committed over 931 ritual strangulations.

## 2. Countess Erszebet Bathory
In the period up to 1610 in Hungary, Bathory (1560–1614), known as 'Countess Dracula', murdered 300–650 girls in the belief that drinking their blood would prevent her from ageing. She was eventually arrested in 1611. Tried and found guilty, she died on 21 August 1614 walled up in her castle.

## 3. Pedro Alonso López
Known as the 'Colombian Monster' and the 'Monster of the Andes', up to his 1980 capture he murdered over 300 young girls in Colombia, Ecuador and Peru. He was caught by Ayacucho Indians in Peru, whose children he had been abducting, and escorted to Ecuador by a female missionary. He was arrested and led police to 53 graves; further bodies were revealed when a river flooded, but others were devoured by wild animals or buried under roads and on construction sites and were never discovered. López was convicted and sentenced to life imprisonment.

## 4. William Estel Brown
On 17 July 1961 Brown admitted that on 18 March 1937 he had deliberately loosened the gas pipes in his school basement in New London, Texas, thereby causing an explosion that killed 282 children and 24 teachers.

## 5. Gilles de Rais
A fabulously wealthy French aristocrat, de Rais (b.1404) was accused of having kidnapped and killed between 60 and 200 children. He was strangled and his body burnt at Nantes on 25 October 1440.

## 6. Herman Webster Mudgett
Also known as 'H.H. Holmes', Mudgett (b.1860) was believed to have lured over 150 women to his 63rd Street 'Castle' in Chicago which was fully equipped for torturing and murdering them and disposing of the bodies. Charged with 27 murders, he was hanged on 7 May 1896.

## 7. Bruno Lüdke
Lüdke (b.1909) was a German who confessed to murdering 85 women between 1928 and 29 January 1943. During the war, on 8 April 1944, he was executed by lethal injection in a Vienna hospital.

## 8. Wou Bom-Kon
An off-duty policeman, on 26–27 April 1982 in South Korea he went on a drunken rampage with guns and grenades, killing 57 before blowing himself up with a grenade.

## 9. Ted Bundy
After spending nine years on death row, Bundy was executed at Florida State Prison on 24 January 1989 for the murder of 12-year-old Kimberley Leach. He confessed to 23 murders during his last hours. Police linked him conclusively to the murders of 36 girls and he once admitted that he might have killed as many as 100 times.

## 10. John Wayne Gacy
On 13 March 1980 Gacy (b.1943) was sentenced to death by electrocution for the Chicago murders of 33 men. The sentence was never carried out and he is currently in prison.

*Other possible contenders for this unenviable Top 10 are Fritz Haarman of Hanover, West Germany, who at the end of the First World War may have murdered as many as 40 refugees in order to steal their clothes and sell their bodies as meat. He was charged with 27 murders and executed in 1924.*

*Dr Marcell Petiot is known to have killed at least 27 but admitted to 63 murders at his Paris house during the Second World War. He claimed that they were Nazi collaborators, but it is probable that they were wealthy Jews whom he robbed and killed after pretending to help them escape from occupied France. He was guillotined on 26 May 1946.*

Behram was the leading exponent of the Thugs' technique of assassination. One distracts an unwary traveller while an accomplice creeps up from behind and strangles him.

# Military

## THE 10 LARGEST ARMED FORCES IN THE WORLD

| Country | Estimated total active forces |
|---|---|
| 1. USSR | 5,096,000 |
| 2. China | 3,200,000 |
| 3. United States | 2,163,000 |
| 4. India | 1,362,000 |
| 5. Vietnam | 1,252,000 |
| 6. Iraq | 1,000,000 |
| 7. North Korea | 842,000 |
| 8. Turkey | 635,000 |
| 9. South Korea | 629,000 |
| 10. Iran | 604,000 |
| *United Kingdom* | *320,000* |

The Chinese army, depicted here during
Chairman Mao's period in power, is the
second largest in the world.

## THE TOP 10 'THIRD WORLD' MAJOR WEAPON IMPORTING COUNTRIES

| Country | % of total Third World imports |
|---|---|
| 1. Egypt | 10.6 |
| 2. Syria | 10.5 |
| 3. Iraq | 10.3 |
| 4. India | 7.5 |
| 5. Libya | 6.9 |
| 6. Saudi Arabia | 6.7 |
| 7. Israel | 4.8 |
| 8. Cuba | 3.7 |
| 9. Argentina | 3.1 |
| 10. Jordan | 2.1 |

MILITARY

# THE 10 LARGEST ARMS EXPORTERS IN THE WORLD

| | Country | % of world trade | $ | Value £* |
|---|---|---|---|---|
| 1. | United States | 27.5 | 2,069,000,000 | 1,224,000,000 |
| 2. | USSR | 24.8 | 1,863,000,000 | 1,102,500,000 |
| 3. | France | 13.5 | 1,018,000,000 | 602,500,000 |
| 4. | United Kingdom | 8.4 | 634,000,000 | 375,000,000 |
| 5. | West Germany | 7.3 | 549,000,000 | 325,000,000 |
| 6. | China | 5.7 | 430,000,000 | 255,000,000 |
| 7. | Italy | 4.1 | 311,000,000 | 184,000,000 |
| 8. | Switzerland | 0.6 | 45,000,000 | 27,000,000 |
| 9. | Netherlands | 0.3 | 20,000,000 | 12,000,000 |
| 10. | Czechoslovakia | 0.2 | 15,000,000 | 9,000,000 |
| | *Total yearly world arms business:* | | *7,519,000,000* | *4,450,000,000* |

*calculated at rate prevailing in April 1989

## MILITARY

Marching to the front. The Russian army was the largest military body during the First World War.

# THE 10 COUNTRIES WITH THE LARGEST TOTAL MOBILIZED FORCES, 1914–18

| Country | Personnel* |
|---|---|
| 1. Russia | 12,000,000 |
| 2. Germany | 11,000,000 |
| 3. British Empire† | 8,904,467 |
| 4. France | 8,410,000 |
| 5. Austria–Hungary | 7,800,000 |
| 6. Italy | 5,615,000 |
| 7. United States | 4,355,000 |
| 8. Turkey | 2,850,000 |
| 9. Bulgaria | 1,200,000 |
| 10. Japan | 800,000 |

*total at peak strength
†including Australia, Canada, India, New Zealand, South Africa, etc.

# THE 10 COUNTRIES WITH THE LARGEST TOTAL MOBILIZED FORCES, 1939–45

| Country | Personnel* |
|---|---|
| 1. USSR | 12,500,000 |
| 2. United States | 12,364,000 |
| 3. Germany | 10,000,000 |
| 4. Japan | 6,095,000 |
| 5= France | 5,000,000 |
| 5= China | 5,000,000 |
| 7. United Kingdom | 4,683,000 |
| 8. Italy | 4,500,000 |
| 9. India | 2,150,000 |
| 10. Poland | 1,000,000 |

*total at peak strength

# THE 10 FASTEST FIGHTER AIRCRAFT OF WORLD WAR II

| | Aircraft | Country | kph | mph |
|---|---|---|---|---|
| 1. | Messerschmitt Me 163 | Germany | 959 | 596 |
| 2. | Messerschmitt Me 262 | Germany | 901 | 560 |
| 3. | Heinkel He 162A | Germany | 890 | 553 |
| 4. | P-51-H | USA | 784 | 487 |
| 5. | Lavochkin La11 | USSR | 740 | 460 |
| 6. | Spitfire XIV | UK | 721 | 448 |
| 7. | Yakolev Yak-3 | USSR | 719 | 447 |
| 8. | P-51-D Mustang | USA | 708 | 440 |
| 9. | Tempest VI | UK | 705 | 438 |
| 10. | Focke Wulf FW109D | Germany | 700 | 435 |

# THE 10 LARGEST BATTLESHIPS OF WORLD WAR II

| Name | Country | Tonnage |
|---|---|---|
| 1= *Yamato* (sunk 7 April 1945) | Japan | 72,809 |
| 1= *Musashi* (sunk 25 October 1944) | Japan | 72,809 |
| 3= *Iowa* (still in service with US Navy) | USA | 55,710 |
| 3= *New Jersey* (still in service with US Navy) | USA | 55,710 |
| 3= *Missouri* (still in service with US Navy) | USA | 55,710 |
| 3= *Wisconsin* (still in service with US Navy) | USA | 55,710 |
| 7= *Bismarck* (sunk 27 May 1941) | Germany | 50,153 |
| 7= *Tirpitz* (sunk 12 November 1944) | Germany | 50,153 |
| 9= *Richelieu* (survived war, later scrapped) | France | 47,500 |
| 9= *Jean Bart* (survived war, later scrapped) | France | 47,500 |

The Messerschmitt Me 163 *Komet* rocket-powered fighter achieved remarkable speeds, but a maximum duration of barely ten minutes before its fuel was exhausted limited its effectiveness.

The Japanese battleship *Yamato* (left) and her sister ship *Musashi* were the largest ever built.

## MILITARY

# THE 10 SMALLEST ARMED FORCES IN THE WORLD

| | Country | Estimated total active forces |
|---|---|---|
| 1= | The Bahamas | 600 |
| 1= | The Gambia | 600 |
| 3. | Belize | 700 |
| 4. | Luxembourg | 800 |
| 5. | Malta | 1,216 |
| 6= | Cape Verde | 1,300 |
| 6= | Seychelles | 1,300 |
| 8. | Equatorial Guinea | 1,400 |
| 9. | Jamaica | 2,500 |
| 10. | Trinidad & Tobago | 2,750 |

# THE 10 COUNTRIES WITH THE SMALLEST DEFENCE BUDGETS

| | Country | Budget $ | £* |
|---|---|---|---|
| 1. | The Bahamas | 9,600,000 | 5,680,000 |
| 2. | Seychelles | 9,710,000 | 5,746,000 |
| 3. | Belize | 11,320,000 | 6,698,000 |
| 4. | Fiji | 13,790,000 | 8,160,000 |
| 5. | Central African Republic | 18,640,000 | 11,029,000 |
| 6. | Malawi | 19,070,000 | 11,284,000 |
| 7. | Malta | 23,180,000 | 13,716,000 |
| 8. | Botswana | 27,260,000 | 16,130,000 |
| 9. | Togo | 27,440,000 | 16,237,000 |
| 10. | Djibouti | 34,460,000 | 20,390,000 |

*calculated at rate prevailing in April 1989
Includes only those countries that declare defence budgets.

MILITARY

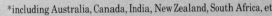

# THE 10 COUNTRIES SUFFERING THE GREATEST MILITARY LOSSES IN WORLD WAR I

| Country | Killed |
| --- | --- |
| 1. Germany | 1,773,700 |
| 2. Russia | 1,700,000 |
| 3. France | 1,357,800 |
| 4. Austria-Hungary | 1,200,000 |
| 5. British Empire* | 908,371 |
| 6. Italy | 650,000 |
| 7. Romania | 335,706 |
| 8. Turkey | 325,000 |
| 9. United States | 116,516 |
| 10. Bulgaria | 87,500 |

*including Australia, Canada, India, New Zealand, South Africa, etc.

# THE 10 COUNTRIES SUFFERING THE GREATEST MILITARY LOSSES IN WORLD WAR II

| Country | Losses |
| --- | --- |
| 1. USSR | 13,600,000 |
| 2. Germany | 3,300,000 |
| 3. China | 1,324,516 |
| 4. Japan | 1,140,429 |
| 5. British Empire* of which United Kingdom | 357,116 264,000 |
| 6. Romania | 350,000 |
| 7. Poland | 320,000 |
| 8. Yugoslavia | 305,000 |
| 9. United States | 292,131 |
| 10. Italy | 279,800 |

*including Australia, Canada, India, New Zealand, South Africa, etc.

# THE 10 CAMPAIGNS IN WHICH THE MOST VICTORIA CROSSES HAVE BEEN WON

| Campaign | VCs |
| --- | --- |
| 1. World War I (1914–18) | 634 |
| 2= Indian Mutiny (1857–58) | 182 |
| 2= World War II (1939–45) | 182 |
| 4. Crimean War (1854–56) | 111 |
| 5. Second Boer War (1899–1902) | 78 |
| 6. Zulu War (1879) | 23 |
| 7. Second Afghan War (1878–80) | 16 |
| 8. Maori War (1863–66) | 13 |
| 9= Basuto War (1879–82) | 6 |
| 9= First Boer War (1880–81) | 6 |

• • • • • • • • • • • • • • • •

# THE 10 REGIMENTS OF THE BRITISH ARMY THAT HAVE WON THE MOST VICTORIA CROSSES

| Regiment | VCs |
| --- | --- |
| 1. Royal Artillery | 62 |
| 2. Royal Engineers | 44 |
| 3. Royal Army Medical Corps | 29* |
| 4. Rifle Brigade | 27 |
| 5= South Wales Borderers | 22 |
| 5= King's Royal Rifle Corps | 22 |
| 7. Royal Fusiliers | 19 |
| 8= Lancashire Fusiliers | 18 |
| 8= Seaforth Highlanders | 18 |
| 10. Gordon Highlanders | 17 |

*including two bars

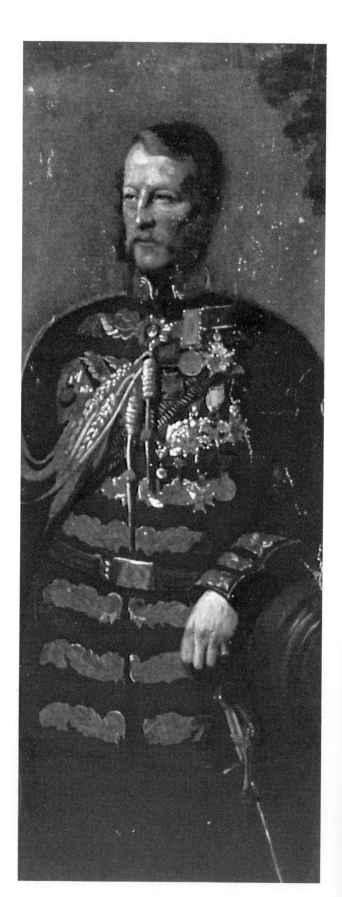

RIGHT General Sir Collingwood Dickson, VC, GCB, the first Gunner to be awarded the VC, which he won in the Crimea in 1854.

# THE TOP 10 U-BOAT ACES OF WORLD WAR II

| | Name | U-boats commanded | Ships sunk |
|---|---|---|---|
| 1. | Otto Kretschmer | U23, U99 | 45 |
| 2. | Wolfgang Luth | U9, U138, U43, U181 | 44 |
| 3. | Joachim Schepko | U3, U19, U100 | 39 |
| 4. | Erich Topp | U57, U552 | 35 |
| 5. | Victor Schutze | U25, U103 | 34 |
| 6. | Heinrich Leibe | U38 | 30 |
| 7= | Karl F. Merten | U68 | 29 |
| 7= | Gunther Prien | U47 | 29 |
| 7= | Johann Mohr | U124 | 29 |
| 10. | Georg Lassen | U160 | 28 |

# THE 10 NATIONS WITH THE MOST PRISONERS OF WAR, 1914–18

| | Country | Taken prisoner |
|---|---|---|
| 1. | Russia | 2,500,000 |
| 2. | Austria-Hungary | 2,200,000 |
| 3. | Germany | 1,152,800 |
| 4. | Italy | 600,000 |
| 5. | France | 537,000 |
| 6. | Turkey | 250,000 |
| 7. | British Empire* of which: | 191,652 |
| | United Kingdom | 170,309 |
| 8. | Serbia | 152,958 |
| 9. | Romania | 80,000 |
| 10. | Belgium | 34,659 |

*including Australia, Canada, India, New Zealand, South Africa, etc.

# THE TOP 10 LUFTWAFFE ACES OF WORLD WAR II

| | Pilot | Kills claimed |
|---|---|---|
| 1. | Eric Hartmann | 352 |
| 2. | Gerhard Barkhorn | 301 |
| 3. | Gunther Rall | 275 |
| 4. | Otto Kittel | 267 |
| 5. | Walther Nowotny | 255 |
| 6. | Wilhelm Batz | 237 |
| 7. | Erich Rudorffer | 222 |
| 8. | Heinrich Baer | 220 |
| 9. | Herman Graf | 212 |
| 10. | Heinrich Ehrler | 209 |

RIGHT Luftwaffe ace Eric Hartmann is fêted by his comrades.

## MILITARY

# THE TOP 10 AIR ACES OF WORLD WAR I

| | Pilot | Country | Kills claimed |
|---|---|---|---|
| 1. | Manfred von Richthofen | Germany | 80 |
| 2. | René Paul Fonck | France | 75 |
| 3. | Edward Mannock* | Great Britain | 73 |
| 4. | William Avery Bishop | Great Britain | 72 |
| 5. | Ernst Udet | Germany | 62 |
| 6. | Raymond Collishaw | Canada | 60 |
| 7. | James Thomas Byford McCudden* | Great Britain | 57 |
| 8= | Anthony Wetherby Beauchamp-Proctor | Great Britain | 54 |
| 8= | Donald Roderick MacLaren | Great Britain | 54 |
| 8= | Georges-Marie Guynemer* | France | 54 |

*killed in action

RIGHT The 'Red Baron', Manfred von Richthofen, the First World War's leading air ace.

FAR RIGHT Edward Mannock's 73 kills made him the foremost British air ace.

*R*ittmeister Manfred Freiherr, Baron von Richthofen's claim of 80 kills has been disputed, since only 60 of them have been completely confirmed. Recent evidence has also suggested that Major Raymond Collishaw may have achieved as many as 81 kills, but that inter-service rivalries led to many of them not being confirmed. It certainly seems that he had more witnessed kills than any other flier (only 13 of Bishop's 72, for example, were actually witnessed).

If the German and French aces are excluded altogether so that the list consists of RFC, RNAS and RAF pilots only, the runners-up are: William George Barker (53), Robert Alexander Little (47), Philip Fletcher Fuller and George Edward Henry McElroy (46 each).

# Religion

## THE WORLD'S 10 LEADING ORGANIZED RELIGIONS

| Religion | Followers |
|---|---|
| 1. Christianity | 1,644,396,000 |
| 2. Islam | 860,388,300 |
| 3. Hinduism | 655,695,200 |
| 4. Buddhism | 309,626,100 |
| 5. Judaism | 18,075,400 |
| 6. Sikhism | 16,604,150 |
| 7. Confucianism | 5,914,400 |
| 8. Baha'ism | 4,627,900 |
| 9. Jainism | 3,462,820 |
| 10. Shintoism | 3,403,010 |

*T*his list excludes the *followers of various folk religions and shamanism which, if lumped together, would make up substantial groups.*

LEFT More than half the world's Christians belong to the Roman Catholic church.

BELOW Comparative religion: the top four.

## RELIGION

<table>
<tr><td>

# THE 10 LEADING RELIGIONS IN THE UK

| | Religion | Membership |
|---|---|---|
| 1. | Roman Catholicism | 2,059,000 |
| 2. | Anglicanism | 1,928,000 |
| 3. | Presbyterianism | 1,346,000 |
| 4. | Islam | 900,000 |
| 5. | Methodism | 517,000 |
| 6. | Baptist | 241,000 |
| 7. | Sikhism | 200,000 |
| 8. | Hinduism | 150,000 |
| 9. | Mormonism | 142,000 |
| 10. | Judaism | 109,000 |

*This list is based on figures for adult membership, as recorded in, for example, the electoral rolls of the Church of England. Adherents are thus held to be practising rather than nominal members of each religion.*

</td><td>

# THE TOP 10 CHRISTIAN DENOMINATIONS IN THE WORLD

| | Denominations | Adherents |
|---|---|---|
| 1. | Roman Catholic | 872,104,646 |
| 2. | Slavonic Orthodox | 92,523,987 |
| 3. | United (including Lutheran/Reformed) | 65,402,685 |
| 4. | Pentecostal | 58,999,862 |
| 5. | Anglican | 52,499,051 |
| 6. | Baptist | 50,321,923 |
| 7. | Lutheran (excluding United) | 44,899,837 |
| 8. | Reformed (Presbyterian) | 43,445,520 |
| 9. | Methodist | 31,718,508 |
| 10. | Disciples (Restorationists) | 8,783,192 |

*The Top 10 is based on 1985 estimates supplied by MARC Europe, a Christian research and information organization. The Vatican's 1987 estimate increased the figure for Roman Catholics to 911,000,000 while retaining the 52,000,000 figure for Anglicans – which indicates something of the problem of arriving even at 'guesstimates' when it comes to global memberships.*

</td></tr>
</table>

# RELIGION

# THE 10 LARGEST CHRISTIAN POPULATIONS IN THE WORLD

| | Country | % | Christian population total |
|---|---|---|---|
| 1. | United States | 88.0 | 197,344,000 |
| 2. | Brazil | 94.0 | 118,856,000 |
| 3. | USSR | 36.1 | 96,726,500 |
| 4. | Mexico | 97.0 | 67,866,900 |
| 5. | West Germany | 92.8 | 57,557,300 |
| 6. | United Kingdom | 86.9 | 49,964,000 |
| 7. | Philippines | 94.3 | 49,201,700 |
| 8. | Italy | 83.6 | 47,104,500 |
| 9. | France | 80.1 | 44,110,800 |
| 10. | Spain | 97.0 | 35,932,700 |

*A*lthough Christian communities are found in almost every country in the world, it is more difficult to put a precise figure on nominal membership than on active participation. David Barrett's World Christian Encyclopaedia *(1982) contained the most recent attempt to estimate global Christian populations, and the Top 10 is based on his findings.*

# THE 10 COMMANDMENTS

1. Thou shalt have no other gods before me.
2. Thou shalt not make unto thee any graven image.
3. Thou shalt not take the name of the Lord thy God in vain.
4. Remember the sabbath day, to keep it holy.
5. Honour thy father and thy mother.
6. Thou shalt not kill.
7. Thou shalt not commit adultery.
8. Thou shalt not steal.
9. Thou shalt not bear false witness against thy neighbour.
10. Thou shalt not covet thy neighbour's house, thou shalt not covet thy neighbour's wife, nor his manservant, nor his maidservant, nor his ox, nor his ass, not any thing that is thy neighbour's.

*Exodus* 20.iii

An audience with the Pope: Roman Catholics in St Peter's Square.

Bar mitzvah, one of the great Jewish celebrations.

Muslims at prayer. Islam is attracting increasingly large numbers of followers.

# THE 10 LARGEST JEWISH POPULATIONS IN THE WORLD

| Country | Total Jewish population |
|---|---|
| 1. United States | 5,834,650 |
| 2. Israel | 3,575,000 |
| 3. USSR | 2,200,000 |
| 4. France | 700,000 |
| 5. United Kingdom | 385,000 |
| 6. Canada | 304,000 |
| 7. Argentina | 300,000 |
| 8. Brazil | 175,000 |
| 9. South Africa | 118,000 |
| 10. Australia | 88,000 |

*The Diaspora or scattering of Jewish people has been in progress for nearly 2,000 years, and as a result Jewish communities are found in virtually every country in the world. In 1939 it was estimated that the total world Jewish population was 17,000,000. Some 6,000,000 fell victim to Nazi persecution, reducing it to about 11,000,000. Today it is put at 14,317,764, approximately equivalent to that of a medium-sized country such as the Netherlands.*

# THE 10 LARGEST MUSLIM POPULATIONS IN THE WORLD

| Country | Muslim population % | total |
|---|---|---|
| 1. India | 11.6 | 80,540,000 |
| 2. Pakistan | 96.8 | 80,320,350 |
| 3. Bangladesh | 85.9 | 72,848,640 |
| 4. Indonesia | 43.4 | 67,213,000 |
| 5. Turkey | 99.2 | 45,018,800 |
| 6. Iran | 97.9 | 37,694,300 |
| 7. Egypt | 81.8 | 34,648,360 |
| 8. Nigeria | 45.0 | 32,668,000 |
| 9. USSR | 11.3 | 30,297,000 |
| 10. Afghanistan | 99.3 | 21,885,280 |

*The phenomenal growth of Islam in recent years suggests that these figures, compiled in 1982, are already out of date, although the order of the Top 10 is probably unchanged. At the time they were prepared, the global population was said to be under 600,000,000; by 1987 a total figure of 860,388,300 was claimed by one authoritative source.*

## THE 10 SHORTEST-SERVING POPES

| | | Year in office | Duration (days) |
|---|---|---|---|
| 1. | Urban VII | 1590 | 12 |
| 2. | Valentine | 827 | c.14 |
| 3. | Boniface VI | 896 | c.14 |
| 4. | Celestine IV | 1241 | 16 |
| 5. | Sisinnius | 708 | 20 |
| 6. | Sylvester III | 1045 | 21 |
| 7. | Theodore II | 897 | c.21 |
| 8. | Marcellus II | 1555 | 22 |
| 9. | Damasus II | 1048 | 23 |
| 10= | Pius III | 1503 | 26 |
| 10= | Leo XI | 1605 | 26 |

*E*leven popes have reigned for less than a month. Some authorities give Stephen's two- or three-day reign in March 757 as the shortest, but although he was elected, he died before he was enthroned and is therefore not included in the official list of popes; in fact, his successor was given his title, Stephen II, and reigned for five years (although some call the uncrowned Stephen 'Stephen II' and his successors are confusingly known as 'Stephen II (III)', and so on. The life of a pope is not always tranquil: Boniface VI, the third shortest-serving, was deposed, and Damasus II probably poisoned. Pope Johns have been particularly unfortunate: John XXI lasted nine months but was killed in 1277 when a ceiling collapsed on him, while John XII was beaten to death by the husband of a woman with whom he was having an affair. In modern times, John Paul I was pontiff for just 33 days in 1978, and was succeeded by the present Pope John Paul II.

## THE 10 LONGEST-SERVING POPES

| | Pope | Period in office | Years |
|---|---|---|---|
| 1. | Pius IX | 16 Jun 1846 – 7 Feb 1878 | 31 |
| 2. | Peter | c.42 – 67 | c.25 |
| 3. | Leo XIII | 20 Feb 1878 – 20 Jul 1903 | 25 |
| 4. | Pius VI | 15 Feb 1775 – 29 Aug 1799 | 24 |
| 5. | Adrian I | 1 Feb 772 – 25 Dec 795 | 23 |
| 6. | Pius VII | 14 Mar 1800 – 20 Aug 1823 | 23 |
| 7. | Alexander III | 7 Sep 1159 – 30 Aug 1181 | 21 |
| 8. | Sylvester | 31 Jan 314 – 31 Dec 335 | 21 |
| 9. | Leo I | 29 Sep 440 – 10 Nov 461 | 21 |
| 10. | Urban VIII | 6 Aug 1623 – 29 Jul 1644 | 20 |

*P*opes are usually chosen from the ranks of cardinals, who are customarily men of mature years (although Pope Benedict IX, elected in 1033, is believed to have been about 15!). As a result, it is unusual for a pope to remain in office for more than 20 years. Although St Peter is regarded as the first pope, some authorities doubt the historical accuracy of his reign. If he is omitted as unhistorical, numbers 3–10 all move up one place and 10th becomes Clement XI (23 Sep 1700–19 Mar 1721, a reign of 20 years).

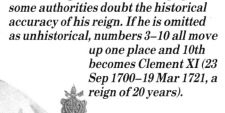

Pope Pius IX was in office for 31 turbulent years until his death at the age of 85.

# Sports, Games & Pastimes

........................

American (above) and Soviet (right) Olympic gold medal winners...

...over 1,000 gold medals have been won between the two countries.

## THE TOP 10 SUMMER OLYMPIC GOLD MEDAL-WINNERS, 1896–1988

| | | |
|---|---|---:|
| 1. | United States | 753 |
| 2. | USSR | 395 |
| 3. | United Kingdom | 172 |
| 4. | East Germany | 160 |
| 5. | France | 155 |
| 6. | West Germany | 152 |
| 7. | Italy | 148 |
| 8. | Sweden | 134 |
| 9. | Hungary | 124 |
| 10. | Finland | 98 |

*The USSR first entered the Olympic Games in 1952, and boycotted the 1984 Games. The United States boycotted the 1980 Games.*

## THE TOP 10 WINTER OLYMPICS GOLD MEDAL-WINNERS, 1924–88

| | | |
|---|---|---:|
| 1. | USSR | 79 |
| 2. | Norway | 54 |
| 3. | East Germany | 43 |
| 4. | United States | 42 |
| 5. | Sweden | 33 |
| 6. | Finland | 32 |
| 7. | Austria | 28 |
| 8. | Switzerland | 23 |
| 9. | West Germany | 21 |
| 10= | Canada | 14 |
| 10= | Italy | 14 |

# THE TOP 10 INDIVIDUAL OLYMPIC GOLD MEDAL-WINNERS

| Medal winner | Total gold medals |
|---|---|
| 1.  Ray C. Ewry (USA) – Athletics<br>1900, 1904, 1906, 1908 | 10 |
| 2= Larissa Latynina (USSR) – Gymnastics<br>1956, 1960, 1964<br>(also 5 silver and 4 bronze medals) | 9 |
| 2= Paavo Nurmi (Finland) – Athletics<br>1920, 1924, 1928<br>(also 3 silver medals) | 9 |
| 2= Mark Spitz (USA) – Swimming<br>1968, 1972<br>(also 1 silver and 1 bronze medal) | 9 |
| 5.  Sawao Kato (Japan) – Gymnastics<br>1968, 1972, 1976<br>(also 3 silver and 1 bronze medals) | 8 |
| 6= Nikolai Andrianov (USSR) – Gymnastics<br>1972, 1976, 1980<br>(also 5 silver and 3 bronze medals) | 7 |
| 6= Boris Shakhlin (USSR) – Gymnastics<br>1956, 1960, 1964<br>(also 4 silver and 2 bronze medals) | 7 |
| 6= Vera Caslavska (Czechoslovakia) –<br>Gymnastics<br>1960, 1964, 1968<br>(also 4 silver medals) | 7 |
| 6= Victor Tshukarin (USSR) – Gymnastics<br>1952, 1956<br>(also 4 silver and 2 bronze medals) | 7 |
| 6= Aldar Gerevich (Hungary) – Fencing<br>1932, 1936, 1948, 1952, 1956, 1960<br>(also 1 silver and 2 bronze medals) | 7 |

*The* only British Olympic *Games competitor to have won four gold medals is Henry Taylor (1885–1951), for swimming. He competed in 1906, 1908, 1912 and 1920, and also won one silver and three bronze medals.*

Ray Ewry, the leading male Olympic gold medal winner.

# THE 10 BRITISH FOOTBALL LEAGUE CLUBS WITH THE LARGEST GROUND CAPACITY*

| Club | Capacity |
| --- | --- |
| 1. Arsenal | 57,000 |
| 2. Manchester United | 56,385 |
| 3. Sheffield Wednesday | 54,101 |
| 4. Manchester City | 52,500 |
| 5. Everton | 50,059 |
| 6. Aston Villa | 46,000 |
| 7. Liverpool | 45,500 |
| 8. Sheffield United | 44,010 |
| 9. Chelsea | 43,900 |
| 10. Leeds United | 40,176 |

*all capacities are now being reviewed in the light of the Taylor report on the Hillsborough tragedy.

Old Trafford, Manchester United's home ground, with a capacity of over 56,000.

# THE 10 BIGGEST WINNERS ON LITTLEWOODS' FOOTBALL POOLS

| Winner | Amount £ |
| --- | --- |
| 1. Jimmy Anderson (Anderton, Northamptonshire) | 1,339,358 |
| 2. Vic Larkins and syndicate (Dagenham, Essex) | 1,198,852 |
| 3. Vi Bowden (Dorking, Surrey) | 1,082,928 |
| 4. Anonymous man (Poole, Dorset) | 1,059,679 |
| 5. Geoff Hoyle and syndicate (Stockport, Greater Manchester) | 1,049,813 |
| 6. Anonymous man (Glasgow, Scotland) | 1,046,109 |
| 7. Anonymous woman (Bexley, London) | 1,032,088 |
| 8. Anonymous woman (Oldham, Lancashire) | 1,021,024 |
| 9. Eddie Turner and syndicate (Manchester) | 1,018,404 |
| 10. Margaret Francis and syndicate (Devizes, Wiltshire) | 1,017,890 |

*L*ittlewoods' Football Pools was started in February 1923 by John (now Sir John) Moores (b.25 January 1896), one of Britain's richest men. The first dividend ever paid was £2 12s (£2.60). Today the company, Britain's largest privately-owned firm, encompasses mail-order and retail stores, but the pools business is still one of its mainstays. Littlewoods' turnover contributes over 70% of the total £500,000,000-plus of the three companies that comprise the Pools Promoters' Association (Littlewoods, Vernons, Zetters).

Jimmy Anderson receives his £1,339,358.30 cheque from Elaine Page.

## SPORTS, GAMES & PASTIMES

# BRITAIN'S 10 MOST POPULAR PARTICIPATION SPORTS, GAMES AND PHYSICAL ACTIVITIES

| | Pursuit | Average annual participation* |
|---|---|---|
| 1. | Walking two miles or more | 20.0 |
| 2. | Snooker/billiards/pool | 7.9 |
| 3. | Darts | 4.3 |
| 4. | Swimming (indoor) | 4.1 |
| 5. | Athletics/jogging | 3.0 |
| 6. | Keep fit/yoga | 2.7 |
| 7. | Cycling | 2.3 |
| 8. | Swimming (outdoor) | 2.2 |
| 9. | Gymnastics/indoor athletics | 2.1 |
| 10. | Football | 1.9 |

*The figures, derived from an official survey, relate to the average number of days during the year on which each adult participated in the pursuit.

Walking leads the list of Britain's top activities.

# THE 10 CATEGORIES OF SPORTSPEOPLE WITH THE LARGEST HEARTS

| | |
|---|---|
| 1. | Tour de France cyclists |
| 2. | Marathon runners |
| 3. | Rowers |
| 4. | Boxers |
| 5. | Sprint cyclists |
| 6. | Middle-distance runners |
| 7. | Weightlifters |
| 8. | Swimmers |
| 9. | Sprinters |
| 10. | Decathletes |

*B*ased on average medical measurements. The heart size of a person who engages regularly in a demanding sport enlarges according to the strenuousness of the sport.

Big-hearted athletes: Tour de France cyclists engage in the most physically demanding of all sports.

# THE 10 FASTEST WOMEN'S TIMES FOR THE LONDON MARATHON

Steve Jones alongside Ingrid Kristiansen, winners of the 1985 London Marathon, both with record-breaking times.

| | Runner | Country | Year | hr | min | sec |
|---|---|---|---|---|---|---|
| 1. | Ingrid Kristiansen | Norway | 1985 | 2 | 21 | 6 |
| 2. | Ingrid Kristiansen | Norway | 1987 | 2 | 22 | 48 |
| 3. | Ingrid Kristiansen | Norway | 1984 | 2 | 24 | 26 |
| 4. | Grete Waitz | Norway | 1986 | 2 | 24 | 54 |
| 5. | Grete Waitz | Norway | 1983 | 2 | 25 | 29 |
| 6. | Ingrid Kristiansen | Norway | 1988 | 2 | 25 | 41 |
| 7. | Véronique Marot | UK | 1989 | 2 | 25 | 56 |
| 8. | Priscilla Welch | UK | 1987 | 2 | 26 | 51 |
| 9. | Wanda Paufil | Poland | 1989 | 2 | 27 | 05 |
| 10. | Sarah Rowell | UK | 1985 | 2 | 28 | 06 |

# THE 10 FASTEST MEN'S TIMES FOR THE LONDON MARATHON

| | Runner | Country | Year | hr | min | sec |
|---|---|---|---|---|---|---|
| 1. | Steve Jones | UK | 1985 | 2 | 8 | 16 |
| 2. | Charlie Spedding | UK | 1985 | 2 | 8 | 33 |
| 3. | Douglas Wakiihuri | Kenya | 1989 | 2 | 9 | 3 |
| 4. | Steve Moneghetti | Australia | 1989 | 2 | 9 | 6 |
| 5. | Ahmed Salah | Djibouti | 1989 | 2 | 9 | 9 |
| 6. | Alister Hutton | UK | 1985 | 2 | 9 | 16 |
| 7. | Christoph Herle | West Germany | 1985 | 2 | 9 | 23 |
| 8. | Hugh Jones | UK | 1982 | 2 | 9 | 24 |
| 9= | Mike Gratton | UK | 1983 | 2 | 9 | 43 |
| 9= | Henrik Jorgensen | Denmark | 1985 | 2 | 9 | 43 |
| 9= | Manuel Mattias | Portugal | 1989 | 2 | 9 | 43 |

# THE 10 FASTEST TIMES FOR THE OXFORD AND CAMBRIDGE BOAT RACE

| Crew | Year | Lengths | min | sec |
|------|------|---------|-----|-----|
| 1. Oxford | 1984 | $3^3/_4$ | 16 | 45 |
| 2. Oxford | 1976 | $3^3/_4$ | 16 | 58 |
| 3. Oxford | 1985 | $4^3/_4$ | 17 | 11 |
| 4= Oxford | 1974 | $5^1/_2$ | 17 | 35 |
| 4= Oxford | 1988 | $5^1/_2$ | 17 | 35 |
| 6. Cambridge | 1948 | 5 | 17 | 50 |
| 7= Cambridge | 1971 | 10 | 17 | 58 |
| 7= Cambridge | 1986 | 7 | 17 | 58 |
| 9. Cambridge | 1934 | $4^1/_4$ | 18 | 3 |
| 10. Cambridge | 1969 | 4 | 18 | 4 |

*T*he Oxford and Cambridge Boat Race was first rowed at Henley in 1829, but the course from Putney to Mortlake (6.78 km/4 miles 374 yd) has been used since 1845 (Mortlake to Putney in 1863). The course time has steadily improved from the 25 minutes or more of the early years to the record-breaking times of the post-war period. Cambridge has won 69 times, Oxford 65 (to 1989), and there has been one dead heat (1877). The largest margin was the 20 lengths by which Cambridge won in 1900. Cambridge sank in 1859 and 1978 and Oxford in 1925; both crews sank in 1912 and Oxford won when the race was re-rowed a week later; Oxford sank near the start in 1951 and the race took place two days later, with Cambridge the winner.

Oxford in the lead in their record-breaking 1984 University boat race.

# THE 10 COMMONEST SPORTING INJURIES*

| Common name | Medical term |
| --- | --- |
| 1. Sprained ankle | Sprain of the lateral ligament |
| 2. Sprained knee | Sprain of the medial collateral ligament |
| 3. Hamstring tear | Muscle tear of the hamstrings |
| 4. Bruise | Soft tissue contusion |
| 5. Low back strain | Lumbar joint dysfunction |
| 6. Jumper's knee | Patella tendinitis |
| 7. Achilles tendinitis | Tendinitis of the Achilles tendon |
| 8. Shin splints | Medial periostitis of the tibia |
| 9. Tennis elbow | Lateral epicondylitis |
| 10. Shoulder strain | Rotator cuff tendinitis |

*Excluding fractures.

Lloyd Honeyghan celebrates his 45-second victory over Gene Hatcher.

# THE 10 FASTEST WORLD TITLE FIGHTS

| Winner/Loser | Duration sec |
| --- | --- |
| 1= Lloyd Honeyghan (GB) v Gene Hatcher (USA)<br>Welterweight, 30 August 1987 | 45 |
| 1= Al McCoy (USA) v George Chip (USA)<br>Middleweight, 7 April 1914 | 45 |
| 3. James J. Jeffries (USA) v Jack Finnegan (USA)<br>Heavyweight, 6 April 1900 | 55 |
| 4. Emile Pladner (France) v Frankie Genaro (USA)<br>Flyweight, 2 March 1929 | 58 |
| 5. Jackie Paterson (GB) v Peter Kane (GB)<br>Flyweight, 19 June 1943 | 61 |
| 6. Michael Dokes (USA) v Mike Weaver (USA)<br>Heavyweight, 10 December 1982 | 63 |
| 7. Tony Canzoneri (USA) v Al Singer (USA)<br>Lightweight, 14 November 1930 | 66 |
| 8. Marvin Hagler (USA) v Caveman Lee (USA)<br>Middleweight, 7 March 1982 | 67 |
| 9. Terry McGovern (USA) v Pedlar Palmer (GB)<br>Bantamweight, 12 September 1899 | 75 |
| 10. Santos Laciar (Argentina) v Shin-Hi Sop (S. Korea)<br>Flyweight, 16 July 1983 | 79 |

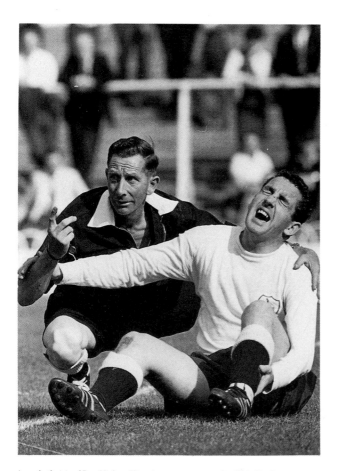

Agony for the injured Dave Mackay of Spurs in a reserve team match at White Hart Lane.

*T*here are also on record several professional (but non-title) fights that have ended in under ten seconds.

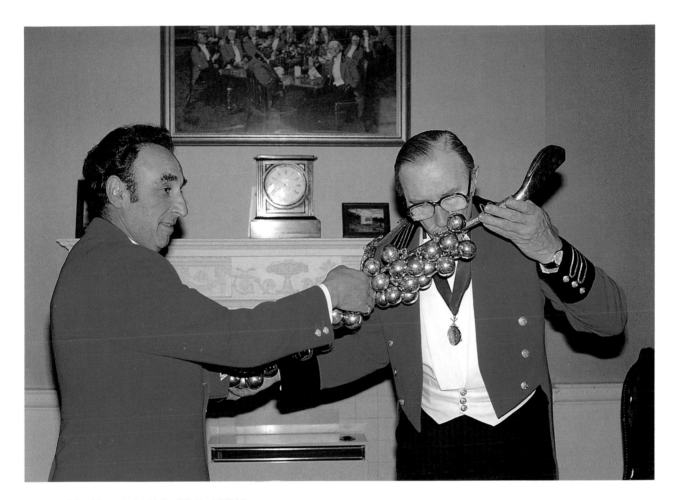

The Secretary (left) and Captain (right) of the Royal Blackheath Golf club.

# THE 10 OLDEST GOLF CLUBS IN THE UK

| Club | Founded |
|------|---------|
| 1. Royal Blackheath Golf Club | 1608 |
| 2. Royal Burgess Golfing Society of Edinburgh | 1735 |
| 3. Honourable Company of Edinburgh Golfers | 1744 |
| 4. Royal and Ancient Golf Club of St Andrews | 1754 |
| 5. Bruntsfield Links Golf Club | 1761 |
| 6. Royal Musselburgh Golf Club | 1774 |
| 7. Royal Aberdeen Golf Club | 1780 |
| 8. Crail Golfing Society | 1786 |
| 9. Glasgow Killermont Golf Club | 1787 |
| 10. Burntisland Golf Club | 1797 |

# THE 10 MOST POPULAR SPORTS USED BY SLIMMERS TO GET INTO BETTER SHAPE

1. Aerobics/keep fit
2. Swimming
3. Walking
4. Cycling
5. Weight training
6. Running/jogging
7. Exercise bike/multi-gym
8. Badminton
9. Dancing
10. Squash

Based on *Slimming Magazine's* 'Slimming Survey', 1988/89

## SPORTS, GAMES & PASTIMES

Lester Piggott, the jockey with the most classic wins.

## THE 10 MOST SUCCESSFUL JOCKEYS OF ALL TIME

|  | Jockey | Country | Total wins to end 1988 |
|---|---|---|---|
| 1. | Bill Shoemaker* | USA | 8,621 |
| 2 | L. Pincay, Jr* | USA | 6,517 |
| 3. | Johnny Longden | USA | 6,032 |
| 4. | A. Cordero, Jr* | USA | 5,867 |
| 5. | J. Velasquez* | USA | 5,736 |
| 6. | L. Snyder* | USA | 5,491 |
| 7. | S. Hawley* | USA | 5,095 |
| 8. | Dave Gall* | USA | 5,024 |
| 9. | Gordon Richards | GB | 4,870 |
| 10. | Eddie Arcaro | USA | 4,779 |

*still riding

Bill Shoemaker, the most successful jockey of all time.

## THE 10 JOCKEYS WITH THE MOST CLASSIC WINS

|  | | Year of first Classic win | a | b | c | d | e | Total |
|---|---|---|---|---|---|---|---|---|
| 1. | Lester Piggott | 1954 | 4 | 2 | 9 | 6 | 8 | 29 |
| 2. | Frank Buckle | 1792 | 5 | 6 | 5 | 9 | 2 | 27 |
| 3. | Jem Robinson | 1817 | 9 | 5 | 6 | 2 | 2 | 24 |
| 4. | Fred Archer | 1874 | 4 | 2 | 5 | 4 | 6 | 21 |
| 5= | Bill Scott | 1821 | 3 | 0 | 4 | 3 | 9 | 19 |
| 5= | Jack Watts | 1883 | 2 | 4 | 4 | 4 | 5 | 19 |
| 7= | John Barham Day | 1826 | 4 | 5 | 0 | 5 | 2 | 16 |
| 7= | George Fordham | 1859 | 3 | 7 | 1 | 5 | 0 | 16 |
| 9. | Joe Childs | 1912 | 2 | 2 | 2 | 6 | 2 | 15 |
| 10= | Frank Butler | 1843 | 2 | 2 | 2 | 6 | 2 | 14 |
| 10= | Steve Donoghue | 1915 | 3 | 1 | 6 | 2 | 2 | 14 |
| 10= | Charlie Elliot | 1923 | 5 | 4 | 3 | 2 | 0 | 14 |
| 10= | Gordon Richards | 1930 | 3 | 3 | 1 | 2 | 5 | 14 |

Key: a) 2,000 Guineas; b) 1,000 Guineas; c) Derby; d) Oaks;
e) St Leger

# THE 10 MOST VALUABLE FLAT RACES IN GREAT BRITAIN

| | Race | Prize* £ |
|---|---|---|
| 1. | Ever Ready Derby | 500,000 |
| 2. | Gold Seal Oaks | 250,000 |
| 3. | King George VI and Queen Elizabeth Diamond Stakes | 240,000 |
| 4. | Swettenham Stud Sussex Stakes | 200,000 |
| 5. | Queen Elizabeth II Stakes | 190,000 |
| 6. | Matchmaker International | 150,000 |
| 7. | Dubai Championship Stakes | 130,000 |
| 8. | Holsten Pils St Leger | 125,000 |
| 9. | Coral-Eclipse Stakes | 115,000 |
| 10. | Tote Diamond Jubilee Ebor | 110,000 |

*Rhyme 'n' Reason takes the last jump in the Grand National, Britain's most valuable steeplechase.*

# THE 10 MOST VALUABLE HURDLE RACES IN GREAT BRITAIN

| | Race | Prize* £ |
|---|---|---|
| 1. | Waterford Crystal Champion Hurdle Challenge Trophy | 70,000 |
| 2. | Tote Gold Trophy Handicap | 50,000 |
| 3. | Waterford Crystal Stayers | 45,000 |
| 4. | Top Rank Christmas Hurdle Race | 40,000 |
| 5. | William Hill Imperial Cup | 30,500 |
| 6= | Daily Express Triumph Hurdle | 30,000 |
| 6= | Mecca Bookmakers Handicap Hurdle | 30,000 |
| 8= | Waterford Crystal Supreme Novices Hurdle | 25,000 |
| 8= | Sun Alliance Hurdle Race | 25,000 |
| 8= | Glenlivet Anniversary | 25,000 |
| 8= | Sandeman Aintree | 25,000 |
| 8= | Swinton Insurance Trophy | 25,000 |
| 8= | Mercury Communications | 25,000 |

# THE 10 MOST VALUABLE STEEPLECHASES IN GREAT BRITAIN

| | Steeplechase | Prize* £ |
|---|---|---|
| 1. | Seagram Grand National | 105,000 |
| 2. | Tote Cheltenham Gold Cup | 90,000 |
| 3. | Whitbread Gold Cup | 70,000 |
| 4= | Queen Mother Champion Steeple Chase | 60,000 |
| 4= | King George VI Rank Steeple Chase | 60,000 |
| 6. | Arkle Challenge Trophy | 45,000 |
| 7= | Sun Alliance Novices Steeple Chase | 40,000 |
| 7= | William Hill Scottish National | 40,000 |
| 8= | Lee Cooper Gainsborough Handicap | 30,000 |
| 8= | H & T Walker Gold Cup Handicap | 30,000 |

# THE 10 MOST SUCCESSFUL EUROPEAN RACEHORSES OF ALL TIME

| | Horse | Country | Foaled | Starts | Wins | Total earnings $ |
|---|---|---|---|---|---|---|
| 1. | Triptych | Fr | 1982 | 41 | 14 | 2,706,175 |
| 2. | Tony Bin | GB | 1983 | 26 | 14 | 2,176,548 |
| 3. | Miesque | Fr | 1984 | 16 | 12 | 2,096,517 |
| 4. | Dancing Brave | GB | 1983 | 10 | 8 | 1,766,723 |
| 5. | Dahlia | Fr | 1970 | 48 | 15 | 1,535,443 |
| 6. | Mtoto | GB | 1983 | 17 | 8 | 1,394,980 |
| 7. | Allez France | Fr | 1970 | 21 | 13 | 1,380,565 |
| 8. | Reference Point | GB | 1984 | 10 | 7 | 1,252,819 |
| 9. | Indian Skimmer | Fr | 1984 | 13 | 8 | 1,244,651 |
| 10. | Kahyasi | GB | 1985 | 7 | 5 | 1,124,622 |

*N*umbers 4, 5, 7 and 8 have retired, but the others are still running as of February 1989.

Triptych wins by a length, adding further to his record earnings.

# THE 10 MOST SUCCESSFUL RACEHORSES OF ALL TIME

| | Horse | Foaled | Starts | Wins | Total earnings $ | Total earnings £* |
|---|---|---|---|---|---|---|
| 1. | Alysheba | 1980 | 26 | 11 | 6,679,242 | 3,952,214 |
| 2. | John Henry | 1975 | 83 | 39 | 6,591,860 | 3,900,508 |
| 3. | Spend a Buck | 1982 | 15 | 10 | 4,220,689 | 2,497,449 |
| 4. | Creme Fraiche† | 1982 | 60 | 17 | 4,009,727 | 2,372,619 |
| 5. | Ferdinand | 1983 | 29 | 8 | 3,777,978 | 2,235,490 |
| 6. | Slew o'Gold | 1980 | 21 | 12 | 3,533,534 | 2,090,848 |
| 7. | Precisionist | 1981 | 46 | 20 | 3,485,398 | 2,062,365 |
| 8. | Snow Chief | 1983 | 24 | 13 | 3,383,210 | 2,001,899 |
| 9. | Bet Twice | 1984 | 26 | 10 | 3,308,599 | 1,957,751 |
| 10. | Gulch | 1984 | 32 | 13 | 3,095,521 | 1,831,669 |

*calculated at rate prevailing in April 1989          † still running as of February 1989

*A*ll are USA horses and their earnings reflect the level of prize money paid there compared with the rest of the world.

# THE WORLD'S 10 RICHEST HORSE RACES

| | Race | Country | First prize* $ | First prize* £† |
|---|---|---|---|---|
| 1. | Breeders' Cup Classic | USA | 1,350,000 | 798,816 |
| 2. | Belmont Stakes | USA | 1,303,720 | 771,432 |
| 3. | Breeders' Cup Turf | USA | 900,000 | 532,544 |
| 4. | Japan Cup | Jap | 885,714 | 524,091 |
| 5. | Melbourne Cup | Aus | 848,250 | 501,923 |
| 6. | Prix de l'Arc de Triomphe | Fr | 787,500 | 465,976 |
| 7. | Cartier Million | Ire | 716,461 | 423,941 |
| 8. | Travers Stakes | USA | 653,100 | 386,450 |
| 9. | Jockey Club Gold Cup | USA | 637,800 | 377,396 |
| 10. | Tancred Stakes | Aus | 620,000 | 366,864 |

*as at February 1989          † calculated at rate prevailing in April 1989

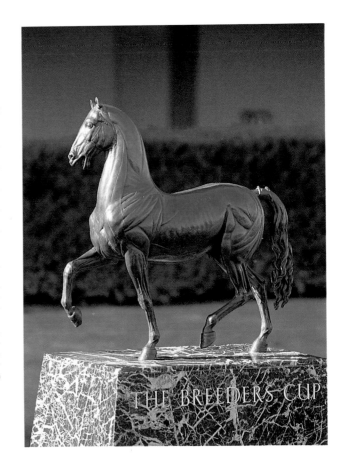

The Breeders' Cup, the richest prize in the racing world.

# THE 10 HIGHEST-SCORING SCRABBLE WORDS

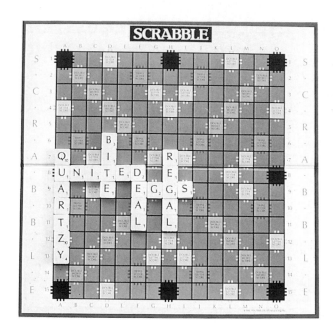

| | Score |
|---|---|
| 1. QUARTZY | |
| (i) Play across a triple-word-score (red) square with the Z on a double-letter-score (light blue square) | 164 |
| (ii) Play across two double-word-score (pink squares) with Q and Y on pink squares | 162 |
| 2= BEZIQUE | |
| (i) Play across a red square with either the Z or the Q on a light blue square | 161 |
| (ii) Play across two pink squares with the B and second E on two pink squares | 158 |
| 2= CAZIQUE | |
| (i) Play across a red square with either the Z or the Q on a light blue square | 161 |
| (ii) Play across two pink squares with the C and E on two pink squares | 158 |
| 4= ZINKIFY | |
| Play across a red square with the Z on a light blue square | 158 |
| 5= QUETZAL | |
| Play across a red square with either the Q or the Z on a light blue square | 155 |
| 5= JAZZILY | |
| (Using a blank as one of the Zs) Play across a red square with the non-blank Z on a light blue square | 155 |
| 5= QUIZZED | |
| (Using a blank as one of the Zs) Play across a red square with the non-blank Z or the Q on a light blue square | 155 |
| 8= ZEPHYRS | |
| Play across a red square with the Z on a light blue square | 152 |
| 8= ZINCIFY | |
| Play across a red square with the Z on a light blue square | 152 |
| 8= ZYTHUMS | |
| Play across a red square with the Z on a light blue square | 152 |

*A*ll the Top 10 words contain seven letters and therefore earn the premium of 50 for using all the letters in the rack. Being able to play them depends on there already being suitable words on the board to which they can be added. In an actual game, the face values of the perpendicular words to which they are joined would also be counted, but these are discounted here as the total score variations would be infinite. Under circumstances where eight-letter words are played to cover two red squares, multiplying the face values of the tiles by three and three again, even higher-scoring words are encountered, for example: QUETZALS (Q and S on red squares, Z on a light blue) – score 364; CONQUERS (C and S on red squares, Q on a light blue) – score 311. Theoretically, given the right existing layout of letters on the board, words could traverse three red squares in one move, multiplying the face value by three, three and three again, achieving totals in excess of 1,000 points, for example, BENZOXYCAMPHORS – 1,643 points.

Like 'Monopoly', 'Scrabble' was invented in the USA during the Depression by an unemployed architect, Alfred Butts. He developed it during the 1930s, changing its name from 'Lexiko' to 'It' and 'Criss-Cross'. It was developed in the late 1940s by James Brunot, who decided on the name 'Scrabble' after rejecting several others that were in use for other products. By 1953 over 1,000,000 sets had been sold. Versions in languages other than English include different ratios of letters appropriate to the language; in Dutch, for example, there are 18 Es, ten Ns and two Js. The German version has 119 rather than 100 letters, and players have eight letters rather than seven on their racks.

# THE 10 MOST VALUABLE PROPERTIES IN 'MONOPOLY'*

| Atlantic City | Value $/£ | London |
|---|---|---|
| 1. Boardwalk | 400 | Mayfair |
| 2. Park Place | 350 | Park Lane |
| 3. Pennsylvania Avenue | 320 | Bond Street |
| 4= North Carolina Avenue | 300 | Oxford Street |
| 4= Pacific Avenue | 300 | Regent Street |
| 6. Marvin Gardens | 280 | Piccadilly |
| 7= Atlantic Avenue | 260 | Coventry Street |
| 7= Ventnor Avenue | 260 | Leicester Square |
| 9. Illinois Avenue | 240 | Trafalgar Square |
| 10= Indiana Avenue | 220 | Fleet Street |
| 10= Kentucky Avenue | 220 | Strand |

*'MONOPOLY' is a registered trademark of Parker Brothers division of Tonka Coporation, USA, under licence to Waddington Games Ltd.

*'M*ONOPOLY', *for 50 years the world's most popular board game, was invented by an American, Charles B. Darrow, in 1933. During the Depression years he dreamed of visiting the New Jersey resort of Atlantic City, but could not afford the fare. Instead, he created a game in which players could imagine themselves there, trading in property and getting rich. Initially rejected by the games firm, Parker Brothers – and never looked back: Darrow became a millionaire and to date more than 100,000,000 sets of 'MONOPOLY' have been sold worldwide. It has been played underwater and even been made in solid gold and chocolate. It is now available in 23 languages, Russian being the latest addition (based on the streets of Moscow). Some countries use the original Atlantic City names, or the London street names, but other national editions feature the streets of such cities as Dublin, Athens, Hong Kong, Tel Aviv, Oslo and Tokyo.*

A section of the 250-mile Pennine Way at Airton, North Yorkshire.

# THE 10 LONGEST WALKS IN GREAT BRITAIN

| Walk | Length km | miles |
|---|---|---|
| 1. Southwest Coastal Path | 829 | 515 |
| 2. Pennine Way | 402 | 250 |
| 3. Southern Upland Way | 341 | 212 |
| 4. Pembrokeshire Coastal Path | 290 | 180 |
| 5. Offa's Dyke Path | 270 | 168 |
| 6. North Downs Way | 227 | 141 |
| 7. West Highland Way | 153 | 95 |
| 8= Cleveland Way | 150 | 93 |
| 8= Peddars Way and Norfolk Coast Path | 150 | 93 |
| 10. Ridgeway Path | 137 | 85 |

*T*he Top 10 are all official walks, as designated by the Countryside Commission (England) and the Countryside Commission for Scotland. There are several other long walks that have not been designated.

Monopoly, the ultimate capitalist game, has been produced in Russian to be sold in the Soviet Union. In the Russian version Boardwalk/Mayfair becomes Arbat, Marvin Gardens/Piccadilly is Smolenskaya Square and Kentucky Avenue/Strand changes to Gorky Street.

# THE 10 MOST POPULAR FANCY DRESS COSTUMES

### Women

1. Saloon girl
2. 1920s 'flapper'
3. Victorian crinoline
4. Georgian
5. Elizabethan
6. Edwardian
7. Egyptian
8. Eastern
9. Spanish
10. Showgirl

### Men

1. Cowboy
2. Clown
3. Rhett Butler (from *Gone With the Wind*)
5. Medieval
6. Roman soldier
7. Toy soldier
8. Eastern/Indian
9. Spaceman
10. Henley Regatta (striped blazer and boater)

Based on hirings from Bermans & Nathans Ltd, the international theatrical, television and film costumiers.

# THE 10 BESTSELLING TOYS OF 1988

| Toy | Manufacturer |
| --- | --- |
| 1. Legoland Town | Lego |
| 2. Sylvanian Families | Tomy |
| 3. Transformers | Hasbro |
| 4. Barbie | Mattel |
| 5. Thundercats | Rainbow |
| 6. Duplo | Lego |
| 7. Tomytime Pre-School Toys | Tomy |
| 8. Legoland Space | Lego |
| 9. Fisher Price Pre-School Toys | Fisher Price |
| 10. MASK | Kenner Parker |

Based on data supplied by 9,000 specialist toyshops, F.W. Woolworth, W.H. Smith, Argos and other retailers which together account for nearly 80% of all toy sales.

Legoland Town, Britain's bestselling toy of 1988. Lego was invented in Denmark by Ole Kirk Christiansen. Its name comes from the Danish *leg-godt*, meaning 'play well'.

Scalextric: Hamley's biggest seller at Christmas.

# HAMLEY'S TOP 10 TOYS

| | Toy |
| --- | --- |
| 1. (2) | Scalextric sets |
| 2. (10) | Pictionary (board game) |
| 3. (–) | Pass the Pigs (game) |
| 4. (3) | Paddington Bears |
| 5. (5) | Barbie dolls |
| 6. (8) | Hamley's chemistry sets |
| 7. (–) | Dingbats (board game) |
| 8. (4) | Taiyo Aero Hopper RC |
| 9. (6) | Walkie-talkie |
| 10. (7) | Fluppets |

Based on Hamley's Christmas 1988 figures; previous year's position in brackets.

## SPORTS, GAMES & PASTIMES

# WOOLWORTH'S TOP 10 TOYS

1. Ghostbusters Ecto 1 Vehicle
2. My Little Pony Crimp 'n' Curl Salon
3. L'il Miss Make-Up
4. Trivial Pursuit
5. Neighbours (board game)
6. Mickey Mouse Wind-Up Train
7. Scalextric Monaco Racing Set (exclusive to Woolworths)
8. Pound Puppies
9. Lego
10. Tiny Tears

Based on Christmas 1988 figures.

. . . . . . . . . . . . . . . .

# JUST GAMES' 10 BESTSELLING INDOOR GAMES

1. Pass the Pigs
2. Scrabble'
3. Trivial Pursuit
4. Chess
5. Backgammon
6. Risk
7. Monopoly
8. 221B Baker Street
9. Black Monday
10. Six-Day Race

*Based on sales in Just Games, a London specialist games shop that stocks a large range of indoor games, including chess sets ranging in price from £1.95 to £1,100 and backgammon sets from £3.95 to £1,400. Numbers 9 and 10 are both German games, revolving round stocks and shares and a bicycle race respectively.*

# THE 10 MOST EXPENSIVE TOYS SOLD AT SOTHEBY'S

| Toy | Year sold | Price £ |
|---|---|---|
| 1. William and Mary wooden doll, English, *c.*1690 | 1987 | 67,000 |
| 2. Tinplate Gauge I 'Rocket' by Märklin, German, *c.*1909 | 1984 | 28,050 |
| 3. Gauge I armoured trainset by Märklin, German, *c.*1902 | 1988 | 26,400 |
| 4. Charles II oak baby house on stand, English, *c.*1675 | 1988 | 25,300 |
| 5. Bisque character doll by Kammer and Reinhardt, German, *c.*1909 | 1986 | 24,200 |
| 6. Tinplate brake by Gebrüder Bing, German, *c.*1902 | 1987 | 23,100 |
| 7. Automaton of a pumpkin-eater by Gustave Vichy, French, *c.*1870 | 1988 | 22,000 |
| 8. Tinplate limousine by Märklin, German, *c.*1907 | 1987 | 18,700 |
| 9. Tinplate spirit-fired fire-engine by Märklin, German, *c.*1902 | 1988 | 15,620 |
| 10. Tinplate riverboat by Märklin, German, *c.*1910 | 1987 | 15,400 |

*As the list shows, toys by the German tinplate maker, Märklin, are highly prized among collectors. The two most expensive tinplate toys ever sold by Christie's were also by Märklin, with those produced by another German firm, Bing, closely following. The William and Mary doll holds the world record price for a doll.*

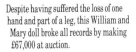

Despite having suffered the loss of one hand and part of a leg, this William and Mary doll broke all records by making £67,000 at auction.

# Air & Space

## THE FIRST 10 PEOPLE TO FLY IN HEAVIER-THAN-AIR AIRCRAFT

1. Orville Wright (1871–1948; American)
   On 17 December 1903 at Kitty Hawk, North Carolina, Wright made the first ever manned flight in his Wright Flyer I. It lasted 12 seconds and covered a distance of 37 m/120 ft.

2. Wilbur Wright (1867–1912; American)
   On the same day, Orville Wright's brother made his first flight in the Wright Flyer I (59 sec; 260 m/852 ft).

3. Alberto Santos-Dumont (1873–1932; Brazilian)
   On 12 November 1906 at Bagatelle, France, in his Santos-Dumont 14-bis (21.2 sec; 220 m/722 ft).

4. Léon Delagrange (1873–1910; French)
   On 5 November 1907 at Issy, France, in his Voisin-Delagrange I (40 sec; 500 m/1,640 ft).

5. Robert Esnault-Pelterie (1881–1957; French)
   On 16 November 1907 at Buc, France, in his REP 1 (55 sec; 600 m/1,969 ft).

6. Henri Farman (1874–1958; British – later French)
   On 11 January 1908 at Issy, France, in his Voisin-Farman I (1 min 45 sec; distance not recorded). This was the first European flight of more than one minute; on 13 January Farman flew the first circle in Europe in the same aircraft.

7. Charles W. Furnas (American)
   On 14 May 1908 at Dayton, Ohio, Wilbur Wright took Furnas, his mechanic, for a spin in the Wright Flyer III (29 sec; 600 m/1,968 ft). He was thus the first aeroplane passenger.

8. Louis Blériot (1872–1936; French)
   On 29 June 1908 at Issy, France, in his Blériot VIII (50 sec; 700 m/2,297 ft). By 6 July 1908, Blériot had made a flight of 8 min 25 sec (distance not recorded); he flew across the English Channel on 25 July 1909.

9. Glenn Hammond Curtiss (1878–1930; American)
   On 4 July 1908 at Hammondsport, New York, in an AEA June Bug (1 min 42.5 sec; 1,551 m/5,090 ft), the first official public flight in the USA.

10. Thérèse Peltier (French)
    On 8 July 1908 at Turin, Italy, in a Voisin piloted by Delagrange. This short hop of 500 ft made her the first woman air passenger.

*While most of the flyers listed flew on numerous subsequent occasions and broke their first-time records, most other 'flights' of the 1906–8 period, other than those of the Wright brothers, were no more than short hops of a few seconds' duration; meanwhile, the Wrights were so far in advance of their competitors that they were flying under full control for more than an hour and over distances of 80 km/50 miles.*

*The first flight in Britain was by an American, Samuel Franklin Cody, at Farnborough on 16 October 1908; it lasted barely 27 seconds and covered just 424 m/1,390 ft.*

ABOVE Orville Wright takes to the air for the first time ever. This flight lasted all of 12 seconds.

AIR & SPACE

# THE 10 BUSIEST AIRPORTS IN THE WORLD

| | Airport | Country/State | Passengers per annum |
|---|---|---|---|
| 1. | Chicago O'Hare | Illinois | 53,338,056 |
| 2. | Atlanta | Georgia | 45,191,480 |
| 3. | Los Angeles | California | 41,417,867 |
| 4. | Dallas/Fort Worth | Texas | 39,945,326 |
| 5. | London Heathrow | England | 34,700,000 |
| 6. | Denver | Colorado | 34,685,944 |
| 7. | Newark | New Jersey | 29,433,046 |
| 8. | San Francisco | California | 28,607,363 |
| 9. | New York JFK | New York | 27,223,733 |
| 10. | Tokyo | Japan | 27,217,761 |

# THE 10 BUSIEST AIRPORTS IN THE UK

| | Airport | Passengers per annum |
|---|---|---|
| 1. | London Heathrow | 34,700,000 |
| 2. | London Gatwick | 19,400,000 |
| 3. | Manchester | 8,600,000 |
| 4. | Glasgow | 3,400,000 |
| 5= | Birmingham | 2,600,000 |
| 5= | Luton | 2,600,000 |
| 7. | Belfast Aldergrove | 2,100,000 |
| 8. | Edinburgh | 1,800,000 |
| 9. | Aberdeen | 1,500,000 |
| 10= | Newcastle-upon-Tyne | 1,300,000 |
| 10= | East Midlands | 1,300,000 |

Flying is rather less glamorous nowadays. A busy scene at Gatwick airport.

# THE FIRST 10 MANNED BALLOON FLIGHTS

1. The first ten pioneering balloon flights all took place within a year. The Montgolfier brothers, Joseph and Étienne, tested their first unmanned hot-air balloon in the French town of Annonay on 5 June 1783. They were then invited to demonstrate it to Louis XVI at Versailles. On 19 September 1783 it took off with the first ever airborne passengers – a sheep, a rooster and a duck. On 21 November 1783 François Laurent (Marquis d'Arlandes) and Jean-François Pilâtre de Rozier took off from the Bois de Boulogne, Paris, in a Montgolfier hot-air balloon. This first ever manned flight covered a distance of about 9 km/5.5 miles in 23 minutes, landing safely near Gentilly. On 15 June 1785 de Rozier and his passenger were killed near Boulogne when their hydrogen balloon burst into flames during an attempted Channel crossing, making them the first ever air fatalities.

2. On 1 December 1783, watched by a crowd of 400,000, Jacques A. C. Charles and Nicholas-Louis Robert made the first ever flight in a hydrogen balloon. They took off from the Tuileries, Paris, and travelled about 27 miles north to Nesle in a time of about two hours. Charles then took off again alone, thus becoming the first solo flyer.

3. 25 February 1784 – Chevalier Paolo Andreani and the brothers Augustino and Carlo Giuseppi Gerti made the first ever flight outside France, near Milan.

4. 2 March 1784 – Jean Pierre François Blanchard, after experimental hops during the preceding months, made his first flight from the Champ de Mars, Paris.

5. 25 April 1784 (and 12 June) – Guyton de Morveau, a French chemist, and l'Abbé Bertrand flew at Dijon.

6. On 15 May 1784 M. Adorne and an unnamed passenger crash-landed near Strasbourg.

7. On 4 June 1784 M. Fleurand made a flight at Lyons accompanied by Mme Thiblé, an opera singer, who was thus the first woman to fly. (The Marchioness de Montalembert had ascended on 20 May 1784, but in a tethered balloon.)

8. On 19 July 1784 (following the 15 July failure of a flight by Nicholas-Louis Robert and the Duke of Chartres that lasted barely five minutes), Robert and his brother, Anne-Jean, flew 255 km/159 miles from Paris to Béthune.

9. On 27 August 1784 James Tytler (known as 'Balloon Tytler'), a doctor and newspaper editor, took off from Comely Gardens, Edinburgh, achieving a 127-m/350-ft hop in a home-made balloon – the first (and until Smeath in 1837, the only) hot-air balloon flight in Great Britain.

10. On 15 September 1784, watched by a crowd of 200,000, Vincenzo Lunardi ascended from the Artillery Company Ground, Moorfields, London, flying to Standon near Ware in Hertfordshire, the first ever balloon flight in England. (An attempt the previous month by a Dr Moret ended with the balloon catching fire and the crowd rioting.) Lunardi went on to make further flights in Edinburgh and Glasgow.

*After the first ten flights, the pace of ballooning accelerated rapidly: on 7 January 1785 Jean-Pierre Blanchard achieved the first Channel crossing with Dr John Jeffries (the first American to fly). They also carried the first airmail letter. As they lost height, they had to reduce weight, so they threw everything overboard, including their clothes.*

*On 19 January 1785 the first flight in Ireland took place, from Ranelagh Gardens, Dublin. In the same year Rear-Admiral (later Admiral) Sir Edward Vernon flew from Tottenham Court Road, London, to Horsham, Sussex, and in the summer to Colchester, Essex. On 5 May 1785 James Sadler became the first English pilot.*

*On 29 June 1785 Lunardi took George Biggin and Letitia Sage, the first Englishwoman to fly, from St George's Fields, London, to Harrow, Middlesex. (Miss Sage was, apparently, rather overweight and there was some concern that the balloon might not get airborne.)*

*On 9 January 1793 in Philadelphia, Blanchard made the first flight in America, watched by George Washington. There is an earlier claim, that of Edward Warren, aged 13, who is said to have flown a hot-air balloon made by Peter Carnes on 23 June 1784 at Baltimore, but this seems improbable.*

The first ever manned balloon flight, which took place on 21 November 1783.

# THE 10 LARGEST HOT-AIR BALLOONS IN THE WORLD

| | | Capacity | |
|---|---|---|---|
| Owner | | cubic m | cubic ft |
| 1. Virgin | | 63,713 | 2,250,000 |
| 2= Zanussi | | 24,069 | 850,000 |
| 2= Nashua | | 24,069 | 850,000 |
| 4. Semiramis | | 15,008 | 530,000 |
| 5. Heineken | | 14,159 | 500,000 |
| 6. Virgin | | 11,327 | 400,000 |
| 7= ICI | | 10,619 | 375,000 |
| 7= Julian Nott | | 10,619 | 375,000 |
| 9= Safaris | | 8,495 | 300,000 |
| 9= Safaris | | 8,495 | 300,000 |

*T*he average size of a hot-air balloon is 2,180 cubic m/77,000 cubic ft, so these are all big balloons! Larger helium balloons, usually flown unmanned, have been constructed, as well as unregistered hot-air balloons (which are consequently prohibited from making untethered flights), but this list includes only registered hot-air balloons capable of free passenger-carrying flight. Several of them are record-holders.

Number 1 is the balloon in which Richard Branson and Per Lindstrand crossed the Atlantic on 2/3 July 1987 – the first to do so in a hot-air balloon. Donald Cameron in Zanussi (a combined helium and hot-air balloon) almost achieved the same feat, but fell short by 166 km/103 miles on 30 July 1978 (shortly before Double Eagle II became the first helium balloon to cross the Atlantic.

The ICI balloon, Innovation, piloted by Julian Nott, and Nott's own balloon, both held the hot-air balloon altitude record at different times; in fact, the ICI record of 16,805 m/55,137 ft (over 16 km/10 miles) still stands.

The Nashua balloon holds the record for carrying the greatest number of people (50) in a hot-air balloon. The last two balloons in the list (and two other identical balloons) are used in Kenya to take passengers on safari.

Both Virgin balloons (the second of which was a practice balloon) were built by Colt; all the others were built by Cameron, the British company that is the world's largest, making some 45% of the world's hot-air balloons.

*Virgin*, the largest hot-air balloon ever flown, takes off on its Transatlantic crossing.

# THE FIRST 10 TRANSATLANTIC FLIGHTS

1. 16–27 May 1919
   Trepassy Harbour, Newfoundland to Lisbon, Portugal.
   US Navy/Curtiss flying boat *NC-4*.

*L*t-Cdr Albert Cushing Read and a crew of five (Elmer Fowler Stone, Walter Hinton, James Lawrence Breese, Herbert Charles Rodd and Eugene Saylor Rhoads) crossed the Atlantic in a series of hops, refuelling at sea. The Atlantic leg was part of an even longer journey; a convoy of three flying-boats, NC-1, NC-3 and NC-4, left Rockaway, Long Island, on 8 May, flying via the Azores to Portugal, but only NC-4 completed the distance; its final destination, Plymouth, England, was reached on 31 May after covering a total distance of 7,591 km/4,717 miles.

2. 14–15 June 1919
   St John's, Newfoundland to Clifden, Galway, Ireland.
   Twin Rolls-Royce-engined converted Vickers *Vimy* bomber.

*B*ritish pilot Capt John Alcock and navigator Lt Arthur Whitten Brown achieved the first non-stop flight, ditching in a bog after their epic 16 hr 27 min-journey. The first non-stop east-west crossing was made by Hermann Köhl on 12–13 April 1928.

3. 2–6 July 1919
   East Fortune, Scotland, to Roosevelt Field, New York.
   British R-34 airship.

*M*ajor George Herbert Scott and a crew of 30 (including the first ever transatlantic air stowaway, William Ballantine) made the first east-west crossing. It was the first airship to do so and, when it returned to Pulham, England, on 13 July, the first to complete a double crossing. The outward journey of 5,037 km/3,130 miles took 108 hr 12 min, and the return journey of 5,150 km/3,200 miles took 75 hr 3min.

4. 12–15 October 1924
   Friedrichshafen, Germany, to Lakehurst, New Jersey. *Los Angeles*, a renamed German-built ZR3 airship.

*P*iloted by its inventor, Dr Hugo Eckener, with 33 passengers and crew, this airship was acquired as part of the German war reparations and remained in service with the US Navy until it was decommissioned in 1932.

5. 23 January–5 February 1926
   Palos, Spain, to Buenos Aires, Argentina.
   *Plus Ultra*, a Dornier Wal twin-engined flying-boat.

*T*he crew of four (Ramon Franco, Druan, R. de Alda and Prata) achieved the first air crossing of the South Atlantic.

ABOVE Flying boat *NC-4* on the first ever Transatlantic flight. INSET Celebrating the first ever non-stop Transatlantic flight, a luncheon in honour of Alcock and Brown.

## AIR & SPACE

6. 13–24 February 1927
   Sardinia to Pernambuco, Brazil.
   *Santa Maria*, a Savoia-Marchetti 55 flying-boat.

*Francesco Marquis de Pinedo, Capt Carlo del Prete and Lt Vitale Vacchetti crossed in stages as part of a Fascist Italy goodwill trip to South America.*

7. 20–21 May 1927
   Long Island, New York, to Paris, France.
   *Spirit of St Louis*, a single-engined Ryan monoplane.

*Although Capt Charles Lindbergh is often erroneously said to have been the first to fly the Atlantic, his remarkable achievement was actually that he was the first to cross solo. He was, in fact, the 80th person to fly the Atlantic (or more than the 100th if the R-34's return journey is counted). The total distance covered was 5,810 km/3,610 miles in 33 hr 29.5 min.*

8. 23 May–11 June 1927
   Trepassy Bay, Newfoundland, to Lisbon, Portugal.
   *Santa Maria II*, a Savoia-Marchetti 55 flying-boat.

*The aeroplane with a three-man crew (Francesco Marquis de Pinedo, Capt Carlo del Prete and Lt Vitale Vacchetti) ran out of fuel and ditched in the sea 482 km/300 miles before its destination and had to be towed to port. As the trip was incomplete, it was overshadowed by Lindbergh's achievement.*

9. 4–6 June 1927
   New York to Eisleben, Germany.
   *Columbia*, a Giuseppe Bellanca.

*Clarence Chamberlain and his passenger, Charles A. Levine, established a new total distance record of 6,294 km/3,911 miles.*

10. 29 June–1 July 1927
    New York to Ver-sur-Mer, France.
    *America*, a Fokker tri-motor monoplane.

*Richard E. Byrd and his crew of three ditched in the sea off the French coast while attempting to reach Paris.*

Valentina Tereshkova, the first woman in space.

# THE FIRST 10 WOMEN IN SPACE

1. Valentina Vladimirovna Tereshkova (USSR), 16–19 June 1963, Vostok VI – the first and youngest (26) woman in space.

2. Svetlana Saviyskaya (USSR), 19 August 1982, Soyuz T7; on 25 July 1984 she also became the first woman to walk in space.

3. Sally Ride (USA), 18–24 June 1983, STS-7 Challenger Shuttle – the first American woman and the youngest (32) American in space; she also flew in the STS-41-G Challenger Shuttle (5–13 October 1984).

4. Judith A. Resnik (USA), 30 August–5 September 1984, STS-41-D Discovery Shuttle; she was killed in the STS-51L Challenger Shuttle disaster of 28 January 1986.

5. Kathryn D. Sullivan (USA), 5–13 October 1984, STS-41-G Challenger Shuttle; she was the first American woman to walk in space.

6. Anna L. Fisher (USA), 8–16 November 1984, STS-51-A Discovery Shuttle.

7. Margaret Rhea Seddon (USA), 12–19 April 1985, STS-51-D Discovery Shuttle.

8. Shannon W. Lucid (USA), 17–24 June 1985, STS-51-G; the oldest (42) woman in space.

9. Loren Acton (USA), 29 July–6 August 1985, STS-51-F Challenger Shuttle.

10. Bonnie J. Dunbar (USA), 30 October–6 November 1985, STS-61-A Challenger Shuttle.

*The only other woman in space to date was Mary L. Cleave (USA), STS-61-B Atlantis Shuttle, 26 November–3 December 1985, making a total of two Russian and nine American women.*

**AIR & SPACE**

Following in Neil Armstrong's 'small step for man' footprints, 'Buzz' Aldrin makes the second Moonwalk.

# THE FIRST 10 MOONWALKERS

| | Astronaut | Birthdate | Mission | Mission dates | Total EVA* (hr:min) |
|---|---|---|---|---|---|
| 1. | Neil A. Armstrong | 5 Aug 30 | Apollo 11 | 16–24 Jul 69 | 2:32 |
| 2. | Edwin E. Aldrin | 20 Jan 30 | Apollo 11 | 16–24 Jul 69 | 2:15 |
| 3. | Charles Conrad Jr | 2 June 30 | Apollo 12 | 14–24 Nov 69 | 7:45 |
| 4. | Alan L. Bean | 15 Mar 32 | Apollo 12 | 14–24 Nov 69 | 7:45 |
| 5. | Alan B. Shepard | 18 Nov 23 | Apollo 14 | 31 Jan–9 Feb 71 | 9:23 |
| 6. | Edgar D. Mitchell | 17 Sep 30 | Apollo 14 | 31 Jan–9 Feb 71 | 9:23 |
| 7. | David R. Scott | 6 Jun 32 | Apollo 15 | 26 Jul–7 Aug 71 | 19:08 |
| 8. | James B. Irwin | 17 Mar 30 | Apollo 15 | 26 Jul–7 Aug 71 | 18:35 |
| 9. | John W. Young | 24 Sep 30 | Apollo 16 | 16–27 Apr 72 | 20:14 |
| 10. | Charles M. Duke | 3 Oct 35 | Apollo 16 | 16–27 Apr 72 | 20:14 |

*Extravehicular activity (i.e. time spent out of the lunar module on the Moon's surface)

**E**ugene A. Cernan (b. 14 Mar 34) and Harrison H. Schmitt (b. 3 Jul 35) in Apollo 17 (7–19 Dec 72) were the last and only other astronauts to date who have walked on the surface of the Moon; both spent a total of 22 hours 4 minutes in EVA. The 12 moonwalkers brought back a total of 381 kg/840 lb of Moon rock samples.

LEFT John Glenn, the first American in space.

## AIR & SPACE

Gagarin, the first Russian in space.

# THE FIRST 10 PEOPLE IN SPACE

| | Name | Age | Date | Orbits | Duration hr | min | Spacecraft /country |
|---|---|---|---|---|---|---|---|
| 1. | Fl Major Yuri Alekseyevich Gagarin | 27 | 12 April 1961 | 1 | 1 | 48 | Vostok I USSR |
| 2. | Major Gherman Stepanovich Titov | 25 | 6–7 August 1961 | 17 | 25 | 18 | Vostok II USSR |
| 3. | Lt-Col John Herschel Glenn | 40 | 20 February 1962 | 3 | 4 | 56 | Friendship 7 USA |
| 4. | Lt-Col Malcolm Scott Carpenter | 37 | 24 May 1962 | 3 | 4 | 56 | Aurora 7 USA |
| 5. | Major Andrian Grigoryevich Nikolayev | 32 | 11–15 August 1962 | 64 | 94 | 22 | Vostok III USSR |
| 6. | Col Pavel Romanovich Popovich | 31 | 12–15 August 1962 | 48 | 70 | 57 | Vostok IV USSR |
| 7. | Cdr Walter Marty Schirra | 39 | 3 October 1963 | 6 | 9 | 13 | Sigma 7 USA |
| 8. | Major Leroy Gordon Cooper | 36 | 15–16 May 1963 | 22 | 34 | 19 | Faith 7 USA |
| 9. | Lt-Col Valeri Fyodorovich Bykovsky | 28 | 14–19 June 1963 | 81 | 119 | 6 | Vostok V USSR |
| 10. | Jr Lt Valentina Vladimirovna Tereshkova | 26 | 16–19 June 1963 | 48 | 70 | 50 | Vostok VI USSR |

*Number 2 was the youngest astronaut, aged 25 years 329 days.*
*Number 10 was the first woman in space. Among early pioneering flights, neither Alan Shepard (5 May 1961; Freedom 7) nor Gus Grissom (21 Jul 1961; Liberty Bell 7) actually entered space, achieving altitudes of only 115 and 118 miles respectively, and neither flight lasted more than 15 minutes. Glenn was the first American to orbit.*

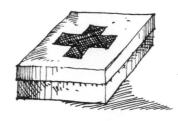

# Accidents
# & Disasters

· · · · · · · · · · · · · · · · · · · · · · · · · ·

## THE 10 COMMONEST TYPES OF FATAL ACCIDENT IN THE HOME

| Accident | Number |
| --- | --- |
| 1. Various falls | 1,852 |
| 2. Fall from stairs | 547 |
| 3. Uncontained fire | 510 |
| 4. Poisoning/inhalation | 480 |
| 5. Penetration by a foreign body | 322 |
| 6. Fall on same level | 161 |
| 7. Fall between two levels | 107 |
| 8. Contained fire | 95 |
| 9. Suffocation/choking | 80 |
| 10. Fall from building | 74 |

*There were a total of 4,485 fatal accidents in homes in England and Wales in 1985 (latest analysis available).*

## THE 10 COMMONEST TYPES OF NON-FATAL ACCIDENT IN THE HOME

| Accident | Number |
| --- | --- |
| 1. Falls | 825,200 |
| 2. Cuts | 361,600 |
| 3. Blows from an object or person | 345,500 |
| 4. Penetration by a foreign body | 96,800 |
| 5. Burns | 91,800 |
| 6. Blows from a falling object | 51,500 |
| 7. Poisoning | 40,000 |
| 8. Over-exertion | 25,400 |
| 9. Explosion | 4,200 |
| 10. Radiation | 2,800 |

*Based on estimates for 1987 by the Home Accident Surveillance System (HASS) at the Department of Trade and Industry. Falls, the leading category, includes everything from tripping over (233,800 cases) and falling on or down stairs (197,800) to falling off ladders (23,200) or buildings (8,400). HASS also lists 176,500 accidents of unknown cause and 79,100 'other'. Their figures cover only non-fatal accidents within homes and gardens, so exclude accidents at work, in traffic, and suchlike, and do not include self-inflicted/suspected suicide attempts or attack by other people.*

# THE 10 WORST RAIL DISASTERS IN THE UK

| Incident | Killed |
| --- | --- |

1. **22 May 1915, Quintinshill near Gretna Green.**
A troop train carrying 500 members of the 7th Royal Scots Regiment from Larbert to Liverpool collided head-on with a local passenger train. The 15 coaches of the troop train, 175 m/213 yards long, were so crushed that they ended up just 61 m/67 yards long. Barely a minute later, the Scotch express, drawn by two engines and weighing a total of 600 tons, ploughed into the wreckage. The gas-lit troop train then caught fire. The actual number of soldiers killed was never established, but was probably 215, as well as two members of the train's crew, eight in the express and two in the local train; 246 were injured, many very seriously. An inquiry established that the accident was caused by the negligence of the signalmen, George Meakin and James Tinsley, who were convicted of manslaughter.  **227**

2. **8 October 1952, Harrow and Wealdstone station**
In patchy fog, Robert Jones, the relief driver of the Perth to Euston express, failed to see a series of signal lights warning him of danger and at 8.19 a.m. collided with the waiting Tring to Euston train. Seconds later, the Euston to Liverpool and Manchester express hit the wreckage of the two trains. The casualties were 112 killed instantly, 10 who died later, and 349 injured.  **122**

3. **4 December 1957, Lewisham, South London**
A steam and an electric train were in collision in fog, the disaster made worse by the collapse of a bridge on to the wreckage, leaving many dead and 109 seriously injured.  **90**

4. **28 December 1879, Tay Bridge, Scotland**
As the North British mail train passed over it during a storm, the bridge collapsed, killing all the passengers and the crew of five. The bridge – the longest in the world at that time – had only been opened on 31 May the previous year, and Queen Victoria had crossed it in a train soon afterwards. The locomotive was salvaged from the bed of the Tay several months later.  **80**

5. **5 November 1967, Hither Green, South London**
The Hastings to Charing Cross train was derailed by a broken track. Apart from those killed, 78 were injured, 27 of them very seriously.  **49**

6. **28 February 1975, Moorgate Station, London**
The Drayton Park to Moorgate tube ran into the wall at the end of the tunnel, causing many deaths and injuring 74 in London Transport's worst rail disaster.  **43**

7= **12 December 1988, Clapham Junction, South London**
The 7.18 Basingstoke to Waterloo train stopped at signals outside Clapham Junction, the 6.30 train from Bournemouth ran into its rear and an empty train from Waterloo hit the wreckage leaving 113 injured.  **34**

7= **24 December 1874 at Shipton near Oxford**
The Paddington to Birkenhead train plunged over the embankment, badly injuring 65.  **34**

9. **20 August 1868, at Abergele, Wales**
Wagons from a goods train collided with the Irish Mail train. Barrels of paraffin on the goods wagons set the front three carriages on fire, and passengers locked inside them died.  **32**

10. **1 July 1906, Salisbury**
The Plymouth to Waterloo express, with passengers from the liner, *New York*, was derailed outside Salisbury while travelling at excessive speed and crashed into the rear of a milk train, killing 24 passengers and two crew on the express and two crew on the milk train, with a further eight injured.  **28**

The Tay Bridge disaster, though not the worst, was one of the most dramatic in British history.

Salvage attempts after the Bagmati River rail disaster, the world's worst.

# THE 10 WORST RAIL DISASTERS IN THE WORLD

| Incident | Killed | Incident | Killed |
|---|---|---|---|
| 1. **6 June 1981, Bagmati River, India**<br>The worst ever train crash | c.800 | 7. **29 September 1957, Montgomery, Pakistan**<br>A collision between an express and oil train | 250–300 |
| 2. **4 June 1989, Ufa, USSR**<br>Two passenger trains travelling on the Trans-Siberian railway, one of them laden with holidaymakers heading for Black Sea resorts, were destroyed by exploding liquid gas from a nearby pipeline. | 600+ | 8. **4 February 1970, near Buenos Aires, Argentina**<br>A collision between an express and a standing commuter train | 236 |
| 3. **12 December 1917, Modane, France**<br>A troop-carrying train ran out of control and was derailed | 543+ | 9. **22 May 1915, Quintinshill, Scotland**<br>Britain's worst rail disaster [see No. 1 in British list] | 227 |
| 4. **2 March 1944, Balvano, Italy**<br>A train stalled in the Armi Tunnel, many passengers suffocating | 521 | 10. **6 October 1972, near Saltilo, Mexico**<br>A train laden with religious pilgrims was derailed and caught fire; over 1,000 were injured | 204 |
| 5. **3 January 1944, Torre, Spain**<br>A collision and fire in a tunnel resulted in the loss of many lives; exact number unknown | 500–800 | | |
| 6. **3 April 1955, near Guadalajara, Mexico**<br>A train plunged into a ravine | c.300 | | |

## ACCIDENTS & DISASTERS

## THE 10 WORST AIR CRASHES IN THE USA

| Incident | Killed |
|---|---|
| 1. **25 May 1979, Chicago** An American Airlines DC-10 crashed on take-off | 275 |
| 2. **16 August 1987, Romulus, Michigan** A Northwest Airlines Macdonald-Douglas-82 crashed after take-off | 156 |
| 3. **9 July 1982, Kenner, Louisiana** A Pan Am Boeing 727 crashed after take-off, killing all on board and eight on the ground | 153 |
| 4. **25 September 1955, San Diego, California** A Pacific Southwest Boeing 727 collided in the air with a Cessna 172 light aircraft, killing 135 in the airliner, two in the Cessna and seven on the ground | 144 |
| 5. **16 December 1960, New York** A United Airlines DC-8 with 77 passengers and a crew of seven and a TransWorld Airlines Super Constellation with 39 passengers and four crew collided in a snowstorm. The DC-8 crashed in Brooklyn, killing eight on the ground, although one passenger survived; the Super Constellation crashed in Staten Island harbour, killing all on board | 134 |
| 6. **2 August 1985, Dallas-Fort Worth Airport, Texas** A Delta Airlines Boeing 747 crashed | 133 |
| 7. **30 June 1956, Grand Canyon** A United Airlines DC-7 and a TransWorld Airlines Super Constellation collided in the air | 128 |
| 8. **24 June 1975, JFK Airport, New York** An Eastern Airlines Boeing 727 crashed in a storm | 113 |
| 9. **4 September 1971, Chilkoot Mountains, Alaska** An Alaska Airlines Boeing 727 crashed | 111 |
| 10. **30 December 1972, Everglades, nr Miami, Florida** An Eastern Airlines Lockheed TriStar crashed during landing, but 75 on board survived | 101 |

*B*efore Lockerbie the United States' worst air disaster not occurring within US territory was the 12 December 1985 crash of a chartered Arrow Air DC-8 during take-off from Gander, Newfoundland, killing all 256 on board.

## THE 10 WORST AIR DISASTERS IN THE UK

| Incident | Killed |
|---|---|
| 1. **21 December 1988, Lockerbie, Scotland** [see No. 8 on World's Worst Air Crashes] | 270 |
| 2. **18 June 1972, Staines, Middlesex** A BEA Trident crashed after take-off | 118 |
| 3. **12 March 1950, Siginstone, Glamorganshire** An Avro Tudor V crashed while attempting to land at Llandow; two saved | 81 |
| 4. **23 August 1944, Freckelton, Lancashire** A US Air Force B-24 crashed on to a school | 76 |
| 5. **24 August 1921, off the coast near Hull** Airship R38, broke in two on a training and test flight | 62 |
| 6. **22 August 1985, Manchester Airport** A Boeing 737 caught fire on the ground | 55 |
| 7. **5 January 1969 near Gatwick Airport** Afghan Airlines Boeing 727 crashlanded | 50 |
| 8. **8 January 1989, M1 Motorway** A British Midland Boeing 737 attempting to land without engine power crashed on the M1 Motorway | 47 |
| 9= **6 November 1986, off Sumburgh, Shetland Islands** A Chinook helicopter ferrying oil rig workers ditched in the sea | 45 |
| 9= **15 November 1957, Isle of Wight** Following an engine fire, an Aquila Airlines Solent flying-boat struck a cliff | 45 |

Lockerbie: the wreckage of Pan Am Flight 103.

The wreckage of the KLM 747 after the world's worst air disaster.

## THE 10 WORST AIR DISASTERS IN THE WORLD

| Incident | Killed |
|---|---|
| 1. **27 March 1977, Tenerife, Canary Islands** Two Boeing 747s (KLM and Pan Am) collided on the runway | 583 |
| 2. **12 August 1985, Mt Ogura, Japan** A JAL Boeing 747 on an internal flight from Tokyo to Osaka crashed, killing all but four on board in the worst ever disaster involving only one aircraft | 520 |
| 3. **3 March 1974, Paris, France** A Turkish Airlines DC-10 crashed at Ermenonville immediately after take-off | 346 |
| 4. **23 June 1985, off the Irish coast** An Air India Boeing 747 on a flight from Vancouver to Delhi exploded in mid-air | 329 |
| 5. **19 August 1980, Riyadh, Saudi Arabia** A Saudi Arabian Airlines Lockheed Tristar caught fire during an emergency landing | 301 |
| 6. **3 July 1988, off the Iranian coast** An Iranian A300 Airbus was shot down in error by a missile fired by the USS *Vincennes* | 290 |

| Incident | Killed |
|---|---|
| 7. **25 May 1979, Chicago, USA** An American Airlines DC-10 crashed on take-off | 275 |
| 8. **21 December 1988, Lockerbie, Scotland** Pan Am Flight 103 from London Heathrow to New York exploded in mid-air by a terrorist bomb, killing 243 passengers, 16 crew and 11 on the ground in the worst ever United Kingdom air disaster | 270 |
| 9. **1 September 1983, off the Siberian coast** A South Korean Boeing 747 that had strayed into Soviet airspace was shot down by a Soviet fighter | 269 |
| 10. **28 November 1979, Mt Erebus, Antarctica** A New Zealand DC-10 crashed while on a sightseeing trip | 257 |

# ACCIDENTS & DISASTERS

## THE 10 MOST VULNERABLE ROAD-USERS IN GREAT BRITAIN

| Type of road user | Killed or seriously injured* |
|---|---|
| 1. Car and taxi drivers | 17,167 |
| 2. Adult pedestrians | 11,978 |
| 3. Car passengers | 11,919 |
| 4. Motor cycle riders | 9,989 |
| 5. Child (under age 14) pedestrians | 5,472 |
| 6. Adult pedal cyclists | 3,638 |
| 7. Moped riders | 2,251 |
| 8. Drivers of goods vehicles | 1,776 |
| 9. Child (under age 14) pedal cyclists | 1,458 |
| 10. Motor cycle passengers | 1,096 |

*1987 figures

*T*his list shows the total number killed and seriously injured on our roads, but does not reveal the relative danger of different types of vehicle. Such a list would show that for every 100,000,000 kilometres/62,000,000 miles driven, 249 motor cycle and moped users are killed or injured compared with just seven car drivers. Distance for distance, motorcyclists are thus almost 36 times more likely to be killed or injured than car drivers.

## ROAD CASUALTIES IN GREAT BRITAIN: THE 10 MOST VULNERABLE AGE GROUPS

| Age group | Killed or seriously injured* |
|---|---|
| 1. 15–19 | 13,752 |
| 2. 20–24 | 12,041 |
| 3. 60 and over | 9,081 |
| 4. 30–39 | 8,029 |
| 5. 25–29 | 6,854 |
| 6. 40–49 | 5,915 |
| 7. 50–59 | 4,566 |
| 8. 10–14 | 3,988 |
| 9. 5–9 | 3,219 |
| 10. 0–4 | 1,277 |

*1987 figures

*T*he peak age group of 15–19 is accounted for partly by recklessness and inexperience in controlling motor cycles and cars, although it has actually improved considerably since the late 1970s, when it was regularly over 20,000 per annum. Over the same period, the figures for deaths and serious injuries in the 20–24 age group have remained very similar, while those for all other groups have declined – particularly in the younger age groups.

Road traffic still causes over 60,000 deaths a year in Great Britain.

# THE 10 COUNTRIES WITH THE HIGHEST NUMBER OF ROAD DEATHS

| | | Deaths per | | |
| | Country | 100,000 population | 10,000 vehicles | Total deaths |
|---|---|---|---|---|
| 1. | United States | 19.0 | 2.6 | 46.056 |
| 2. | Japan | 10.0 | 2.4 | 12,112 |
| 3. | France | 21.7 | 4.8 | 11,947 |
| 4. | West Germany | 14.6 | 3.1 | 8,948 |
| 5. | Italy | 13.2 | 3.1 | 7,571 |
| 6. | Spain | 18.1 | 6.1 | 7,045 |
| 7. | United Kingdom | 9.9 | 2.5 | 5,618 |
| 8. | Poland | 12.4 | 7.3 | 4,667 |
| 9. | Yugoslavia | 18.8 | 11.8 | 4,414 |
| 10. | Canada | 15.8 | 2.6 | 4,017 |

*T*his comparison of international road death statistics for 1986 does not include the country with the highest number of road deaths per 100,000 population – Portugal, with 26.4. In other words, your chances of being killed on the road in Portugal are 3,788 to one, almost three times as great as in the United Kingdom.

# THE 10 WORST PRE-20TH CENTURY MARINE DISASTERS

| Incident | Killed |
|---|---|
| 1. *St George, Defence* and *Hero* British warships stranded off the Jutland coast, 24 December 1811 | c.2,000 |
| 2. *Sultana* A Mississippi River steamboat destroyed by boiler explosion near Memphis, 27 April 1865 – the USA's worst ever marine accident | 1,547 |
| 3. *Royal George* British warship wrecked off Spithead, 29 August 1782 – the worst ever shipwreck off the British coast | 800+ |
| 4. *Princess Alice* Pleasure steamer in collision with *Bywell Castle* on the Thames near Woolwich, 3 September 1878 | 786 |
| 5. *Queen Charlotte* British warship burnt in Leghorn harbour, 17 March 1800 | 700+ |

| Incident | Killed |
|---|---|
| 6. *Atlantic* British steamer wrecked off Nova Scotia, 1 April 1875 | 585 |
| 7. *Utopia* British steamer collided with British warship *Anson* off Gibraltar, 17 March 1891 | 562 |
| 8. *La Bourgogne* French steamer collided with British sailing vessel, *Cromartyshire*, off Nova Scotia, 4 July 1898 | 549 |
| 9. *Ertogrul* Turkish frigate wrecked off the Japanese coast, 19 September 1890 | 540 |
| 10. *City of Glasgow* British steamer, disappeared in the North Atlantic, 1854 | 480 |

The British troop ship *Lancastria*, which went down in 1940 with the loss of some 4,000 men.

# THE 10 WORST MARINE DISASTERS OF THE 20TH CENTURY

| Incident | Killed |
|---|---|
| 1. *Wilhelm Gustloff*<br>German liner torpedoed off Danzig by USSR submarine, *S-13*, 30 January 1945 | c.7,700 |
| 2. *Lancastria*<br>British troop ship sunk off St Nazaire, 17 June 1940 | c.4,000 |
| 3. *Provence*<br>French cruiser sunk in the Mediterranean, 26 February 1916 | 3,100 |
| 4. *Yamato*<br>Japanese battleship sunk off Kyushu Island, 7 April 1945 | 3,033 |
| 5. *Mont Blanc*<br>French ammunition ship collided with Belgian steamer *Imo* and exploded, Halifax, Nova Scotia, 6 December 1917 | 1,600 |
| 6. *Titanic*<br>British liner struck an iceberg in the North Atlantic, 14–15 April 1912 – the worst ever peace-time marine disaster | 1,503 |

| Incident | Killed |
|---|---|
| 7. *Dona Paz*<br>Ferry struck by oil tanker *MV Victor* in the Tabias Strait, Philippines, 20 December 1987; the loss of life may have been much higher (a figure of 3,000 has been suggested) due to excessive overcrowding, but no accurate records were kept | 1,500+ |
| 8. HMS *Hood*<br>British cruiser sunk by the German battleship *Bismarck* in the Denmark Strait, 24 May 1941 | 1,418 |
| 9. *Lusitania*<br>British liner torpedoed off the Irish coast by German submarine *U-20*, 7 May 1915 | 1,198 |
| 10. *Toya Maru*<br>Japanese ferry sunk in Tsugaru Strait, Japan, 26 September 1954 | 1,172 |

The submarine *Thetis* sinks in Liverpool Bay, June 1939

# THE 10 WORST SUBMARINE DISASTERS*

| Incident | Killed |
| --- | --- |
| 1. *Le Surcourf*<br>A French submarine accidentally rammed by a US merchant ship, *Thomas Lykes*, in the Gulf of Mexico on 18 February 1942. | 159 |
| 2. *Thresher*<br>A three-year-old US nuclear submarine, worth $45,000,000/£25,000,000, sank in the North Atlantic, 220 miles east of Boston on 10 April 1963. | 129 |
| 3= *Thetis*<br>A British submarine, sank on 1 June 1939 during trials in Liverpool Bay, with civilians on board. Her captain and two crew members escaped. *Thetis* was later salvaged and renamed *Thunderbolt*. On 13 March 1943 she was sunk by an Italian ship with the loss of 63 lives. | 99 |
| 3= *Scorpion*<br>This US nuclear submarine was lost in the North Atlantic, 250 miles southwest of the Azores. | 99 |
| 5. *I-67*<br>A Japanese submarine that foundered in a storm off Bonin Island to the south of Japan in 1940. | 89 |
| 6= *Ro-31*<br>A Japanese submarine lost off Kobe, Japan, on 21 August 1923 when a hatch was accidentally left open as she dived. There were five survivors. | 88 |
| 6= Soviet November Class submarine<br>Lost 70 miles off Land's End on 12 April 1970. | 88 |
| 8 *I-63*<br>This Japanese submarine sank on 2 February 1939 after a collision in the Bungo Suido (between Kyushu and Shikoku, Japan). Six crew were saved. | 81 |
| 9. *Dumlupinar*<br>A Turkish submarine in collision with a Swedish freighter in April 1953. Five survived. | 81 |
| 10. HMS *Affray*<br>A British submarine lost on 17 April 1951 in Hard Deep, north of Alderney. | 75 |

*excluding those lost as a result of military action

# Transport & Tourism

. . . . . . . . . . . . . . . . . . . . . . . . . . .

## THE WORLD'S TOP 10 CAR-PRODUCING NATIONS

| | Country | Total production |
|---|---|---|
| 1. | Japan | 7,891,087 |
| 2. | United States | 7,098,910 |
| 3. | West Germany | 4,373,629 |
| 4. | France | 3,051,830 |
| 5. | Italy | 1,713,300 |
| 6. | Spain | 1,402,572 |
| 7. | USSR | 1,329,000 |
| 8. | United Kingdom | 1,142,985 |
| 9. | Canada | 809,827 |
| 10. | Korea | 793,125 |

*The total world car production for 1987 was estimated to be 32,910,645. In that year Japan exceeded US production for the first time; in fact, one new car in four is now Japanese. The United Kingdom pushed Canada out of 8th position and Korea ousted Brazil from 10th.*

Robots do the work at Nissan, Japan.

## THE TOP 10 CAR MANUFACTURERS IN THE WORLD

| | Company | Country | Total car production |
|---|---|---|---|
| 1. | General Motors | USA | 6,508,491 |
| 2. | Ford | USA | 3,963,264 |
| 3. | Toyota | Japan | 2,752,875 |
| 4. | Volkswagen | West Germany | 2,605,369 |
| 5. | Nissan | Japan | 1,917,521 |
| 6. | Peugeot-Citroën | France | 1,697,945 |
| 7. | Renault | France | 1,633,781 |
| 8. | Fiat | Italy | 1,593,587 |
| 9. | Chrysler | USA | 1,325,039 |
| 10. | Honda | Japan | 1,263,562 |
| 17. | *Rover Group* | *Great Britain* | *404,454* |

Figures are for 1986 production, amalgamating worldwide production in all companies owned by manufacturers.

# THE 10 BESTSELLING MAKES OF CAR IN THE USA

| Make | Sales |
|------|-------|
| 1. Ford | 1,389,886 |
| 2. Chevrolet | 1,363,187 |
| 3. Oldsmobile | 714,394 |
| 4. Pontiac | 659,262 |
| 5. Lincoln-Mercury | 629,897 |
| 6. Buick | 557,411 |
| 7. Dodge | 348,294 |
| 8. Honda | 316,618 |
| 9. Chrysler | 294,125 |
| 10. Plymouth | 289,112 |

*T*otal sales in 1987 were down to 7,080,858 from a peak of 8,214,897 in 1986. It should be noted that Dodge, Plymouth and Chrysler are all part of the Chrysler Corporation, and that Lincoln-Mercury is owned by the Ford Motor Company. If sales by all the component companies of Ford are amalgamated, total sales amount to 2,019,783. US-built Hondas entered the Top 10 for the first time, ousting Cadillac, which previously held 10th position with sales of 261,284.

One of America's favourites – the Chevrolet Corvette

# THE 10 BESTSELLING ROLLS-ROYCE MOTOR CARS

| Model | Years manufactured |
|-------|--------------------|
| 1. Silver Shadow | 1965–76 |
| 2. Silver Shadow II | 1977–80 |
| 3. Silver Ghost | 1907–26 |
| 4. Silver Spirit | 1980– |
| 5. Silver Spur | 1980– |
| 6. 20/25 HP | 1929–36 |
| 7. Corniche convertible | 1971–87 |
| 8. 20 HP | 1922–29 |
| 9. Silver Shadow long wheelbase | 1965–76 |
| 10. Silver Cloud II | 1959–62 |

'*B*estselling' in Rolls-Royce terms does not mean the same as when applied to ordinary mass-market cars. To put it in perspective, the US giant General Motors produces about 100,000 cars a month – more than the total Rolls-Royce production since the firm started in 1904. Some 16,717 Silver Shadows, Rolls-Royce's number 1 bestseller, were sold in its 11 years of production, and fewer than 2,940 of the 20 HP. The Silver Ghost, in production for nearly 20 years, sold a grand total of 6,173 British models from 1907–25 and 1,703 of the model made under licence in the USA from 1921–26.

The majestic Corniche convertible.

## TRANSPORT & TOURISM

A Kawasaki ZX-10, the world's fastest production motorcycle.

# THE TOP 10 EXPORT MARKETS FOR ROLLS-ROYCE MOTOR CARS

1. United States
2. France
3. Japan
4. Germany
5. Canada
6. Switzerland
7. Australia
8. Saudi Arabia
9. Italy
10. Dubai

# THE 10 FASTEST* MOTOR CYCLES IN THE WORLD

|    | Make | Model | kph | mph |
|----|------|-------|-----|-----|
| 1. | Kawasaki | ZX-10 | 268.3 | 166.7 |
| 2. | Suzuki | GSX-R 1100 | 267.2 | 166.0 |
| 3. | Yamaha | FZR 1000 | 257.5 | 160.0 |
| 4. | Honda | RC 30 | 247.4 | 153.7 |
| 5= | Kawasaki | ZXR 750 | 244.6 | 152.0 |
| 5= | Suzuki | GSX 1100 F | 244.6 | 152.0 |
| 7= | Honda | CBR 750 | 243.0 | 151.0 |
| 7= | Yamaha | FZ 750 | 243.0 | 151.0 |
| 9= | Honda | VFR 750 | 241.4 | 150.0 |
| 9= | Suzuki | GSX-R 750 | 241.4 | 150.0 |

*based on 1989 production models

# THE 10 MOST EXPENSIVE CARS SOLD AT AUCTION

| | Car | Sale | Year | Price $ | Price £ |
|---|---|---|---|---|---|
| 1. | 1931 Bugatti Royale Type 41 Chassis '41.141' | Christie's, London | 1987 | 9,800,000 | 5,575,000 |
| 2. | 1929 Bugatti Royale Chassis '41.150' | Harrah, US, USA | 1986 | 6,500,000 | 4,300,000 |
| 3. | 1957 Aston Martin DBR2 | Christie's, Monaco, | 1989 | 3,700,000 | 2,178,000 |
| 4. | 1934 Alfa Romeo Tipo B Monopsto | Christie's, Monaco | 1989 | 3,300,000 | 1,971,000 |
| 5. | 1933 Alfa Romeo Tipo 8C 2300 | Christie's, Monaco | 1989 | 2,900,000 | 1,763,000 |
| 6. | 1936 Mercedes-Benz 500K Special Roadster | Christie's, Beaulieu | 1988 | 2,700,000 | 1,617,000 |
| 7. | 1962 Ferrari 196 SP | Christie's, Monaco | 1989 | 2,700,000 | 1,607,000 |
| 8. | John Lennon's Phantom V Rolls-Royce Limousine | Sotheby's, New York | 1985 | 2,900,000 | 1,600,000 |
| 9. | 1935/36 3.8-litre Alfa Romeo 8C-35 Grand Prix single seater | Christie's, Monaco | 1988 | 2,800,000 | 1,513,000 |
| 10. | 1961 Ferrari 250 GT SWB California Spyder | Oldtimer, Geneva | 1989 | 2,400,000 | 1,452,000 |

*calculated at rate prevailing at time of sale

*A*lthough these are the highest prices paid at public auction, it was reported in 1989 that the only surviving 1967 original ex-factory team Ferrari 330P4 sports prototype had been purchased privately by a Swiss collector for £5,800,000.

The 1931 Bugatti Royal Type 41 Chassis – a snip at nearly $10 million

TRANSPORT & TOURISM

# THE 10 COUNTRIES WITH THE MOST CARS

| Country | Cars |
| --- | --- |
| 1. United States | 135,431,112 |
| 2. Japan | 28,653,669 |
| 3. West Germany | 27,223,810 |
| 4. Italy | 22,000,000 |
| 5. France | 21,575,000 |
| 6. United Kingdom | 19,175,603 |
| 7. USSR | 11,800,000 |
| 8. Canada | 11,477,314 |
| 9. Brazil | 10,827,468 |
| 10. Spain | 9,643,448 |

*In 1986 the world total of cars registered was estimated to be 153,762,104. Based on the ratio of cars to people, most of the countries on the list would not have much of a problem (apart from the resultant traffic jams!) if the entire population decided to take to the road at the same time. The ratio of people per car ranges from 1.8 in the US (the world's lowest) to 2.9 in the UK and 4.2 in Japan. Brazil would have difficulties with its ratio of 13 people to every car, while the USSR would find the going very tough with its ratio of 24 people per car. These figures pale into insignificance, however, when compared with those of India, where the ratio is 554 per car, and China where there are 1,374 people per car.*

A freeway in California – the state where 'nobody ever walks'.

# THE 10 US STATES WITH THE MOST DRIVERS

| State | Licensed drivers |
| --- | --- |
| 1. California | 18,440,000 |
| 2. Texas | 11,352,000 |
| 3. New York | 10,098,000 |
| 4. Florida | 8,502,000 |
| 5. Pennsylvania | 7,782,000 |
| 6. Ohio | 7,460,000 |
| 7. Michigan | 7,384,000 |
| 8. Illinois | 7,186,000 |
| 9. New Jersey | 5,998,000 |
| 10. North Carolina | 4,328,000 |

*The United States is unusual in the world picture in both its high proportion of drivers (over 66% of the population) and in having almost as many women drivers (77,891,000) as men (84,084,000). In two states, Iowa and Kansas, women drivers actually outnumber men. With 18,440,000 licensed drivers, 15,978,000 cars and 4,630,000 trucks and buses on its roads, California's reputation as the state where nobody ever walks is well deserved. It is not surprising that it has more traffic deaths (5,500 in 1987) than any other state. However, the rate of fatalities per 100,000,000 miles driven is 2.4, which is below the national average of 2.6. Minnesota, is the safest (1.6 fatalities per 100,000,000 miles) and New Mexico the most dangerous state (4.1).*

## TRANSPORT & TOURISM

The long and winding road: a mountain stretch of the extensive Brazilian road system.

# THE 10 US STATES WITH THE MOST ROADS

| | State | km | miles |
|---|---|---|---|
| 1. | Texas | 460,211 | 285,962 |
| 2. | California | 281,783 | 175,092 |
| 3. | Illinois | 216,920 | 134,778 |
| 4. | Minnesota | 213,470 | 132,644 |
| 5. | Kansas | 213,467 | 132,642 |
| 6. | Missouri | 192,152 | 119,398 |
| 7. | Michigan | 189,362 | 117,664 |
| 8. | Pennsylvania | 186,142 | 115,663 |
| 9. | Ohio | 182,319 | 113,288 |
| 10. | Iowa | 181,048 | 112,498 |

*There are a total of 6,243,511 km/3,879,538 miles of rural and urban roads in the USA. If they were stretched out, they would encircle the world 155.8 times. Over 7% of them are in Texas (equal to 11.48 times round the globe). Hawaii has the least with 6,502 km/4,040 miles.*

# THE 10 COUNTRIES WITH THE LONGEST ROAD NETWORKS

| | Country | Total roads | |
|---|---|---|---|
| | | km | miles |
| 1. | United States | 6,243,511 | 3,879,538 |
| 2. | Brazil | 1,583,172 | 983,737 |
| 3. | India | 1,545,891 | 960,572 |
| 4. | USSR | 1,540,000 | 956,911 |
| 5. | France | 1,505,000 | 935,164 |
| 6. | Japan | 1,127,501 | 700,597 |
| 7. | China | 915,000 | 568,555 |
| 8. | Canada | 884,000 | 549,292 |
| 9. | Australia | 852,986 | 530,021 |
| 10. | West Germany | 490,045 | 304,500 |
| 11. | *United Kingdom* | *370,970* | *230,510* |
| | *World total* | *24,300,000* | *15,099,318* |

*At a constant 80 kph (50 mph), it would take 34 years 172 days to cover every road in the world, 8 years 312 days to drive over every road in the United States and a mere 193 days to traverse the entire United Kingdom road network. Unfortunately, in doing so you would be breaking the speed limit on a large proportion of them and would therefore probably lose your licence before completing your marathon rally.*

# GREAT BRITAIN'S 10 LONGEST MOTORWAYS

| | M/way | Between | Length km | miles |
|---|---|---|---|---|
| 1. | M6 | Rugby–Carlisle | 368 | 229.1 |
| 2. | M1 | London–Leeds | 301.4 | 187.6 |
| 3. | M4 | London–Port Abraham | 291.6 | 181.5 |
| 4. | M5 | Birmingham–Exeter | 265 | 165 |
| 5. | M25 | Encircles London | 194.4 | 121 |
| 6. | M62 | Liverpool–Humberside | 173 | 107.7 |
| 7= | M3 | London–Winchester | 81.9 | 51 |
| 7= | M11 | London–Cambridge | 81.9 | 51 |
| 9. | M8 | Edinburgh–Glasgow Airport | 78.2 | 48.7 |
| 10. | M42 | Bromsgrove–Tamworth | 65.9 | 41 |

*B*ritain's first motorway was the Preston
bypass section of the M6 (between junctions 29 and 32) opened on 5 December 1958. The
first section of the M1 did not open until 2 November 1959.

# THE WORLD'S 10 MOST EXPENSIVE CITIES FOR PETROL

| | City | Country | £/lt | £/gall |
|---|---|---|---|---|
| 1. | Abidijan | Ivory Coast | .62 | 2.82 |
| 2. | Tokyo | Japan | .62 | 2.81 |
| 3. | Milan | Italy | .57 | 2.59 |
| 4. | Naha | Okinawa | .55 | 2.48 |
| 5. | Dublin | Ireland | .51 | 2.30 |
| 6. | Paris | France | .49 | 2.23 |
| 7. | Oslo | Norway | .48* | 2.17* |
| 8. | Lisbon | Portugal | .45 | 2.06 |
| 9. | Amsterdam | Netherlands | .45 | 2.04 |
| 10. | Helsinki | Finland | .44 | 2.00 |

*price for self-service regular grade; all other prices are for full-service
regular grade. Prices correct as at March 1989

# THE WORLD'S 10 CHEAPEST CITIES FOR PETROL

| | City | Country | £/lt | £/gall |
|---|---|---|---|---|
| 1. | Caracas | Venezuela | .04 | 0.18 |
| 2= | Lagos | Nigeria | .05* | 0.23* |
| 2= | Quito | Ecuador | .05 | 0.23 |
| 4= | Kuwait | Kuwait | .08 | 0.37 |
| 4= | Riyadh | Saudi Arabia | .08* | 0.37* |
| 6. | Cairo | Egypt | .09 | 0.39 |
| 7. | Bogotá | Colombia | .09 | 0.40 |
| 8. | Santo Domingo | Dominican Republic | .09 | 0.41 |
| 9. | Warsaw | Poland | .12 | 0.53 |
| 10. | Jakarta | Indonesia | .13 | 0.59 |

*price for full-service supergrade; all other prices are for full-service regular
grade. Prices correct as at March 1989

# THE 10 LONGEST BRIDGES IN THE USA

| Bridge | Completed | Length of main span m | ft |
|---|---|---|---|
| 1. Verrazano Narrows, New York | 1964 | 1,298 | 4,260 |
| 2. Golden Gate, San Francisco, California | 1937 | 1,280 | 4,200 |
| 3. Mackinac Straits, Michigan, Missouri | 1957 | 1,158 | 3,800 |
| 4. George Washington, New York | 1931 | 1,067 | 3,500 |
| 5. Tacoma Narrows II, Washington | 1950 | 853 | 2,800 |
| 6. Transbay, San Francisco, California | 1936 | 704 | 2,310 |
| 7. Bronx–Whitestone, New York | 1939 | 701 | 2,300 |
| 8= Delaware Memorial, Wilmington, Delaware (twin) | 1951/68 | 655 | 2,150 |
| 8= Seaway Skyway, Ogdensburg, New York | 1960 | 655 | 2,150 |
| 10= Melville Gas Pipeline, Atchafalaya River, Louisiana | 1951 | 610 | 2,000 |
| 10= Walt Whitman, Philadelphia, Pennsylvania | 1957 | 610 | 2,000 |

TOP Verrazano Narrows, New York

ABOVE The Golden Gate, San Francisco.

*All are suspension bridges. The USA also has the longest steel arch bridge in the world, the New River Gorge Bridge, Fayetteville, West Virginia (1977), 518m/1,700ft – 9m/30ft longer than the next longest in the world, the Sydney Harbour Bridge (1932) 509m/1,670ft.*

• • • • • • • • • • • • • • • • • • • • • • • • • •

Humber Bridge, Britain's longest at 1,410 metres.

# THE 10 LONGEST BRIDGES IN THE UK

| Bridge | Completed | Length of main span m | ft |
|---|---|---|---|
| 1. Humber Estuary | 1980 | 1,410 | 4,626 |
| 2. Forth Road Bridge | 1964 | 1,006 | 3,300 |
| 3. Severn Bridge | 1966 | 988 | 3,240 |
| 4. Firth of Forth | 1890 | 521 | 1,710 |
| 5. Tamar, Saltash | 1961 | 335 | 1,100 |
| 6. Runcorn–Widnes | 1961 | 330 | 1,082 |
| 7. Clifton Suspension | 1864 | 214 | 702 |
| 8. Tyne Bridge, Newcastle | 1930 | 162 | 531 |
| 9. Menai Straits | 1834 | 176 | 579 |
| 10= Medway (M2 Motorway) | 1963 | 152 | 500 |
| 10= George Street, Newport | 1964 | 152 | 500 |

# THE 10 LONGEST BRIDGES IN THE WORLD

| Bridge | Completed | Length of main span m | ft |
|---|---|---|---|
| 1. Akashi-Kaikyo, Japan | under construction | 1,980 | 6,496 |
| 2. Humber Estuary, England | 1980 | 1,410 | 4,626 |
| 3. Verrazano Narrows, New York, USA | 1964 | 1,298 | 4,260 |
| 4. Golden Gate, San Francisco, USA | 1937 | 1,280 | 4,200 |
| 5. Mackinac Straits, Michigan, USA | 1957 | 1,158 | 3,800 |
| 6. Bosphorus, Istanbul, Turkey | 1973 | 1,074 | 3,523 |
| 7. George Washington, New York, USA | 1931 | 1,067 | 3,500 |
| 8. Ponte Salazar, Lisbon, Portugal | 1966 | 1,013 | 3,323 |
| 9. Forth Road Bridge, Scotland | 1964 | 1,006 | 3,300 |
| 10. Severn Bridge, England | 1966 | 988 | 3,240 |

# THE 10 LONGEST RAIL NETWORKS IN THE WORLD

| Country | Total rail length km | miles |
|---|---|---|
| 1. United States | 250,863 | 155,879 |
| 2. USSR | 246,400 | 153,106 |
| 3. Canada | 72,546 | 45,078 |
| 4. India | 61,230 | 38,047 |
| 5. China | 51,600 | 32,063 |
| 6. Australia | 38,943 | 24,198 |
| 7. Argentina | 36,185 | 22,484 |
| 8. France | 34,688 | 21,554 |
| 9. West Germany | 30,808 | 19,143 |
| 10. Brazil | 29,207 | 18,148 |
| 16. *United Kingdom* | *17,141* | *10,651* |
| *World total* | *1,300,000* | *807,782* |

# THE 10 LONGEST RAIL PLATFORMS IN THE WORLD

| Station | Platform length m | ft |
|---|---|---|
| 1. State Street Center Subway, Chicago, USA | 1,067 | 3,500 |
| 2. Khargpur, Bihar, India | 833 | 2,733 |
| 3. Perth, Western Australia | 762 | 2,500 |
| 4. Sonepur, India | 736 | 2,415 |
| 5. Bournemouth, England | 720 | 2,362 |
| 6. Bulawayo, Zimbabwe | 702 | 2,302 |
| 7. New Lucknow, India | 686 | 2,250 |
| 8. Bezwada, India | 640 | 2,100 |
| 9. Gloucester, England | 624 | 2,047 |
| 10. Jhansi, India | 617 | 2,025 |

The total length of the US railroad network just beats that of the USSR.

# THE 10 LONGEST RAIL TUNNELS* IN THE UK

| | Tunnel | County | km | m | miles | yd |
|---|---|---|---|---|---|---|
| 1. | Severn | Avon/Gwent | 7 | 13 | 4 | 629 |
| 2. | Totley | South Yorkshire | 5 | 697 | 3 | 950 |
| 3. | Standedge | Manchester/Yorkshire | 4 | 888 | 3 | 66 |
| 4. | Sodbury | Avon | 4 | 64 | 2 | 924 |
| 5. | Disley | Cheshire | 3 | 535 | 2 | 346 |
| 6. | Ffestiniog | Gwynned | 3 | 528 | 2 | 338 |
| 7. | Bramhope | East Yorkshire | 3 | 429 | 2 | 241 |
| 8. | Cowburn | Derbyshire | 3 | 402 | 2 | 182 |
| 9. | Sevenoaks | Kent | 3 | 157 | 1 | 1,693 |
| 10. | Morley | West Yorkshire | 3 | 81 | 1 | 1,609 |

*mainline, excluding London Underground system

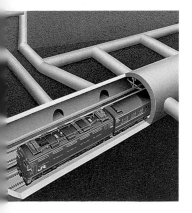

A cutaway section of the Seikan Tunnel, the longest in the world, connecting the Japanese islands of Hokkaido and Honshu.

# THE 10 LONGEST RAIL TUNNELS IN THE WORLD

| | Tunnel | Date completed | km | miles |
|---|---|---|---|---|
| 1. | Seikan, Japan | 1988 | 53.9 | 33.5 |
| 2. | Moscow Metro (Medvedkova/Belyaevo section) | 1979 | 30.7 | 19.1 |
| 3. | London Underground (East Finchley/Morden Northern Line) | 1939 | 27.8 | 17.3 |
| 4. | Dai-shimizu, Japan | 1979 | 22.3 | 13.8 |
| 5= | Simplon II, Italy/Switzerland | 1922 | 19.8 | 12.3 |
| 5= | Simplon I, Italy/Switzerland | 1906 | 19.8 | 12.3 |
| 7. | New Kanmon, Japan | 1975 | 18.7 | 11.6 |
| 8. | Apennine, Italy | 1934 | 18.5 | 11.5 |
| 9. | Rokko, Japan | 1972 | 16.3 | 10.1 |
| 10. | Henderson, USA | 1975 | 15.8 | 9.8 |

*The Channel Tunnel, scheduled for completion in 1993, will be 49.94 km/31.03 miles long, making it number 2 on the list.*

The British canal system, originally built for commercial traffic, has now largely given way to leisure uses.

## THE 10 OLDEST NAVIGABLE CANALS IN THE UK

| | Canal | Date navigable |
|---|---|---|
| 1. | Fossdyke Canal | c.AD 120 |
| 2. | Exeter Canal | 1751 |
| 3. | Bridgewater Canal | 1767 |
| 4= | Birmingham Canal | 1772 |
| 4= | Staffordshire and Worcestershire Canal | 1772 |
| 6= | Chesterfield Canal | 1777 |
| 6= | Trent and Mersey Canal | 1777 |
| 8. | Erewash Canal | 1779 |
| 9= | Coventry Canal | 1790 |
| 9= | Oxford Canal | 1790 |

## THE 10 LONGEST CANALS IN THE UK

| | Canal | Length km | miles |
|---|---|---|---|
| 1. | Grand Union Canal (main line) | 220 | 137 |
| 2. | Leeds and Liverpool Canal | 204 | 127 |
| 3. | Trent and Mersey Canal | 150 | 93 |
| 4. | Kennet and Avon Canal | 139 | $86^{1}/_{2}$ |
| 5. | Oxford Canal | 124 | 77 |
| 6. | Shropshire Union Canal | 107 | $66^{1}/_{2}$ |
| 7. | Caledonian Canal | 96 | 60 |
| 8. | Staffordshire and Worcestershire Canal | 74.2 | $46^{1}/_{8}$ |
| 9. | Llangollen Canal | 74 | 46 |
| 10. | Lancaster Canal | 68 | $42^{1}/_{2}$ |

# THE 10 BUSIEST LONDON UNDERGROUND STATIONS

| | Station | Passengers per annum |
|---|---|---|
| 1. | Victoria | 72,900,000 |
| 2. | King's Cross | 54,200,000 |
| 3. | Oxford Circus | 52,900,000 |
| 4. | Liverpool Street | 48,100,000 |
| 5. | Piccadilly Circus | 36,200,000 |
| 6. | Waterloo | 34,700,000 |
| 7. | Tottenham Court Road | 31,300,000 |
| 8. | Charing Cross | 28,900,000 |
| 9. | Paddington | 26,600,000 |
| 10. | Euston | 26,000,000 |

1987 figures, based on the estimated number of passenger journeys starting or ending at each station.

# THE 10 COMMONEST TYPES OF LOST PROPERTY ON LONDON TRANSPORT

| | Type | Number 1986/87 | 1987/88 |
|---|---|---|---|
| 1. | Umbrellas | 21,080 | 23,250 |
| 2. | 'Value items' (handbags, purses, wallets, etc.) | 21,940 | 19,868 |
| 3. | Books | 19,013 | 19,329 |
| 4. | Clothing | 16,497 | 15,211 |
| 5. | Cases and bags | 9,222 | 9,317 |
| 6. | Keys | 9,923 | 9,265 |
| 7. | Spectacles | 5,975 | 5,754 |
| 8. | Cameras, radios and jewellery | 5,550 | 5,304 |
| 9. | Gloves (pairs) | 5,625 | 4,402 |
| 10. | Gloves (odd) | 844 | 701 |

*T*here is a curious consistency in the numbers of articles handed in to London Transport's Lost Property Office in Baker Street from year to year, although, as the list shows, there have been some slight changes. Of late we are taking more care of our valuables and keys (or fewer have been handed in), but we are less careful with our umbrellas and clothing. Over a longer period, lost property is a fascinating barometer of changes in fashion. Gone are the days when hats were among the most common lost items; in are growing numbers of expensive electronic calculators and cameras. After the ten commonest items, the list continues with such articles as 'Smokers' Requisites', 'Perishables' (food items) and nearly 9,000 'Miscellaneous' objects, making a grand total of 121,816 for 1987/88. Over the years 'Miscellaneous' items have included such unlikely things as sets of false teeth, a box of glass eyes, an outboard motor, a 1.5-m/5-ft garden seat and a stuffed gorilla. On average, approximately one-third of all lost articles are returned to their owners.

# LONDON'S FIRST 10 UNDERGROUND LINES

| | Line | Date first section opened |
|---|---|---|
| 1. | Metropolitan | 10 January 1863 |
| 2. | District | 24 December 1868 |
| 3. | Circle | 6 October 1884 |
| 4. | Waterloo/Bank (BR) | 8 August 1898 |
| 5. | Central | 30 July 1900 |
| 6. | Bakerloo | 10 March 1906 |
| 7. | Piccadilly | 15 December 1906 |
| 8. | Northern | 22 June 1907 |
| 9. | Victoria | 7 March 1969 |
| 10. | Jubilee | 1 May 1979 |

*L*ondon's Underground system has grown to its present 409 km/254 miles by stages, usually fanning out from the centre, with suburban extensions being built as London expanded into the surrounding countryside. Many sections of line have been closed and there are consequently many 'ghost' lines and stations, such as the British Museum station which closed on 24 September 1933, the platforms of which can still be spotted by sharp-eyed travellers on the Central Line.

LEFT Building the world's first underground railway, London's Metropolitan line.

# THE 10 LARGEST OIL TANKERS IN THE WORLD

*Esso Mediterranean*, one of the 10 largest supertankers in the world.

| | Tanker | Year built | Shipyard | Length m | ft | Deadweight tonnage |
|---|---|---|---|---|---|---|
| 1. | *Seawise Giant* | 1979 | Japan | 458.45 | 1,504 | 564,739 |
| 2. | *Hellas Fos* | 1979 | France | 414.23 | 1,359 | 555,051 |
| 3. | *Esso Atlantic* | 1977 | Japan | 406.59 | 1,334 | 516,895 |
| 4. | *Esso Pacific* | 1977 | Japan | 390.13 | 1,280 | 516,423 |
| 5. | *King Alexander* | 1978 | Sweden | 364.02 | 1,194 | 491,120 |
| 6. | *Nissei Maru* | 1975 | Japan | 378.85 | 1,243 | 484,276 |
| 7. | *Stena King* | 1978 | Taiwan | 378.42 | 1,242 | 457,927 |
| 8. | *Stena Queen* | 1977 | Taiwan | 378.42 | 1,242 | 457,841 |
| 9. | *Esso Mediterranean* | 1977 | Japan | 378.39 | 1,241 | 457,062 |
| 10. | *Esso Caribbean* | 1976 | Japan | 378.39 | 1,241 | 456,368 |

*T*he Seawise Giant *is the largest ship ever built, being longer than 19 tennis courts laid end to end. On 5 October 1987, during the Gulf War, she survived an attack by Iraqi jets, but was so severely damaged in a second attack on 4 May 1988 that, although she remains afloat, she is no longer in seaworthy condition.*

• • • • • • • • • • • • • • • • • • • • • • • • • • • •

# THE 10 LONGEST DAYTIME LONDON BUS ROUTES

| | Route | Between | Length km | miles |
|---|---|---|---|---|
| 1. | K10 | Staines – Kingston | 40.72 | 25.30 |
| 2. | 105 | Heathrow Terminal 4 – Shepherd's Bush | 30.98 | 19.25 |
| 3. | 310B | Harrow – Enfield (Saturdays only) | 30.58 | 19.00 |
| 4. | 12A | Purley – Norwood Junction | 29.53 | 18.35 |
| 5. | 90B | Northolt – Kew Gardens | 28.49 | 17.70 |
| 6. | 226 | Golders Green – Burnt Oak | 28.40 | 17.65 |
| 7. | 21 | Swanley, Kent – London Bridge (weekday mornings only) | 28.00 | 17.40 |
| 8. | 140 | Harrow Weald – Heathrow | 27.92 | 17.35 |
| 9. | 25 | Becontree Heath – Victoria (Sundays only) | 27.76 | 17.25 |
| 10= | 221 | Edgware Station – King's Cross | 27.36 | 17.00 |
| 10= | 310Λ | Hertford – Enfield (weekdays only) | 27.36 | 17.00 |

# THE 10 LARGEST PASSENGER LINERS IN THE WORLD

| | Ship | Year | Built Shipyard | Gross tonnage |
|---|---|---|---|---|
| 1. | Sovereign of the Seas | 1987 | France | 73,192 |
| 2. | France/Norway* | 1961 | France | 70,202 |
| 3. | QEII | 1969 | Scotland | 66,450 |
| 4= | Celebration | 1987 | Sweden | 47,262 |
| 4= | Jubilee | 1986 | Sweden | 47,262 |
| 6. | Holiday | 1985 | Denmark | 46,052 |
| 7. | Canberra | 1961 | Northern Ireland | 43,975/ 44,807† |
| 8. | Royal Princess | 1984 | Finland | 44,348 |
| 9. | Seaward | 1988 | Finland | 42,276 |
| 10. | Westerdam | 1986 | West Germany | 42,092 |

*renamed      †tonnage altered during refitting

'Largest', in the case of passenger vessels, is usually based on a ship's gross tonnage. If the list were based on length, it would appear as follows:

| | Ship | Length m | ft |
|---|---|---|---|
| 1. | Norway | 290.66 | 954 |
| 2. | QEII | 270.39 | 887 |
| 3. | Sovereign of the Seas | 236.02 | 774 |
| 4. | Rotterdam | 228.18 | 749 |
| 5. | Canberra | 225.56 | 740 |
| 6. | Festivale | 213.37 | 700 |
| 7. | Starship Oceanic | 205.42 | 674 |
| 8. | Royal Viking Sun | 204.02 | 669 |
| 9. | Sky Princess | 203.03 | 666 |
| 10. | Royal Princess | 193.17 | 634 |

The largest liners in the world during the last 100 years were, progressively:

| Ship | Years in service | Gross tonnage |
|---|---|---|
| Great Eastern | 1858–88 | 18,914 |
| Oceanic | 1899–1914 | 17,274 |
| Baltic | 1904–33 | 23,884 |
| Lusitania* | 1907–15 | 31,550 |
| Mauretania | 1907–35 | 31,938 |
| Olympic | 1911-35 | 45,300 |
| Titanic* | 1912 | 46,232 |
| Imperator/Berengaria† | 1913–38 | 52,022 |
| Vaterland/Leviathan† | 1914–38 | 54,282 |
| Bismarck/Majestic/ Caledonia† | 1922–39 | 56,621 |
| Normandie/Lafayette*† | 1935–42 | 79,301/83,102‡ |
| Queen Mary | 1936–67 | 80,774/81,237‡ |
| Queen Elizabeth | 1938–72 | 83,673/82,998‡ |
| France/Norway† | 1961 | 66,348/70,202‡ |

*sunk   †renamed   ‡tonnage altered during refitting

*A*fter the fire and capsizing *of the* Queen Elizabeth *in Hong Kong harbour (9 January 1972), the* France, *later renamed* Norway, *remained the largest passenger vessel in service until the* Sovereign of the Seas *was launched.*

Sovereign of the Seas (left) and the QEII (above).

# **T**HE 10 MOST VISITED COUNTRIES IN THE WORLD

| | Country | Tourists per annum |
|---|---|---|
| 1. | Spain | 43,235,000 |
| 2. | France | 36,748,000 |
| 3. | Italy | 25,047,000 |
| 4. | United States | 21,018,000 |
| 5. | Austria | 15,168,000 |
| 6. | United Kingdom | 14,483,000 |
| 7. | Canada | 13,245,000 |
| 8. | West Germany | 12,686,000 |
| 9. | Hungary | 9,724,000 |
| 10. | Switzerland | 9,528,000 |
| | World total | 338,000,000 |

Spain attracts a greater number of tourists every year than its own population.

# **B**RITISH TOURISTS' 10 FAVOURITE OVERSEAS DESTINATIONS

| | Country | % of tourists visiting |
|---|---|---|
| 1. | Spain | 31 |
| 2. | France | 20 |
| 3. | Greece | 9 |
| 4. | Italy | 4 |
| 5= | West Germany | 3 |
| 5= | Austria | 3 |
| 5= | United States | 3 |
| 8= | Irish Republic | 2 |
| 8= | Netherlands | 2 |
| 8= | Switzerland | 2 |

20,000,000 British people took holidays abroad in 1987.

# **B**RITAIN'S 10 BUSIEST PORTS

| | Port | Goods handled per annum tonnes |
|---|---|---|
| 1. | Sullom Voe | 50,000,000 |
| 2. | London | 48,900,000 |
| 3. | Tees and Hartlepool | 33,900,000 |
| 4. | Milford Haven | 32,700,000 |
| 5. | Grimsby and Immingham | 32,200,000 |
| 6. | Forth | 30,000,000 |
| 7. | Southampton | 27,200,000 |
| 8. | Orkney | 17,100,000 |
| 9. | Felixstowe | 13,100,000 |
| 10. | Medway | 11,600,000 |

*I**n the mid-1980s, as a result of its handling of North Sea oil, Sullom Voe in Shetland overtook London as Britain's leading port. Liverpool, once Britain's second most important port, is now ranked 12th.*

## TRANSPORT & TOURISM

Santa Catalina in California, the USA's most popular tourist state.

# THE TOP 10 TOURIST STATES IN THE USA

| | State | Total visitors |
|---|---|---|
| 1. | California | 6,192,000 |
| 2. | New York | 5,382,000 |
| 3. | Texas | 5,032,000 |
| 4. | Florida | 3,853,000 |
| 5. | Hawaii | 2,203,000 |
| 6. | Washington (State) | 2,108,000 |
| 7. | Arizona | 1,982,000 |
| 8. | Nevada | 1,267,000 |
| 9. | Massachusetts | 1,253,000 |
| 10. | Michigan | 1,172,000 |

*This order of ranking applies to the total number of visitors to each state. Among overseas visitors, the order of popularity is rather different:*

1. California
2. New York
3. Florida
4. Hawaii
5. Washington, DC
6. Arizona
7. Texas
8. Massachusetts
9. Illinois
10. Nevada

# THE 10 LONDON BOROUGHS WITH THE MOST BLUE PLAQUES

| | Borough | Number of plaques |
|---|---|---|
| 1. | Westminster | 217 |
| 2. | Kensington and Chelsea | 97 |
| 3. | Camden | 91 |
| 4. | Wandsworth | 20 |
| 5. | Lambeth | 17 |
| 6. | Hammersmith | 14 |
| 7. | Tower Hamlets | 13 |
| 8. | Greenwich | 11 |
| 9. | Islington | 10 |
| 10. | Lewisham | 9 |

*Commemorating notable people by fixing a plaque on the wall of their former London residences was started in 1867 by the Royal Society of Arts. It was later taken over by the London County Council and its successor, the Greater London Council. Since the GLC was disbanded on 1 April 1986 (one of its last acts was to put up a plaque to itself in the entrance to County Hall), the erection of plaques has been the responsibility of English Heritage.*

*Early plaques vary in size and colour, but the familiar blue ceramic plaques with white lettering have now been standard for over 50 years. To qualify for a blue plaque, a person has to have been born more than 100 years ago or dead for over 20, should have made some worthwhile contribution to human welfare and happiness and be well known to the well-informed passer-by.*

*By 31 March 1989 over 430 plaques had been erected, including a number of 'unofficial' ones, such as that in South Street, W1, to Catherine 'Skittles' Walters (1839–1920), mistress of Edward, Prince of Wales, who is described on it as 'The Last Victorian Courtesan'. There are also occasional mistakes; for example, the one to Lillie Langtry (another of the Prince's mistresses) on the Cadogan Hotel in Pont Street, SW1, gives the wrong date of her birth (1852 instead of 1853), while some are believed to have been fixed on the wrong houses.*

*Westminster has by far the most blue plaques, largely because many politicians chose to live close to government offices and the Houses of Parliament. At the other end of the scale, several boroughs have only one plaque, while Barking, Enfield, Havering, Hillingdon and Kingston have none at all.*

## TRANSPORT & TOURISM

Fountains Abbey, visited by over 250,000 people every year.

## THE 10 MOST-VISITED NATIONAL TRUST PROPERTIES

| Property | Visitors |
|---|---|
| 1. Fountains Abbey and Studley Royal, North Yorkshire | 274,000 |
| 2. Stourhead Garden, Wiltshire | 214,000 |
| 3. Polesden Lacey House and Garden, Surrey | 186,000 |
| 4. St Michael's Mount, Cornwall | 176,000 |
| 5. Chartwell, Kent | 167,000 |
| 6. Corfe Castle, Dorset | 162,000 |
| 7. Quarry Bank Mill, Styal, Cheshire | 151,000 |
| 8. Bodnant Garden, Gwynedd | 150,000 |
| 9. Bodiam Castle, East Sussex | 147,000 |
| 10. Sissinghurst Garden, Kent | 141,000 |

***B**ased on 1988 figures for both paying visitors and National Trust members. Almost 70 National Trust properties are visited by 50,000 or more people a year.*

## BRITAIN'S 10 MOST POPULAR HISTORIC PROPERTIES

| Property | Visitors |
|---|---|
| 1. Tower of London | 2,289,354 |
| 2. Edinburgh Castle | 967,424 |
| 3. Roman Baths and Pump Room, Bath | 837,414 |
| 4. Windsor Castle, Berkshire | 709,446 |
| 5. Warwick Castle | 642,249 |
| 6. Stonehenge, Wiltshire | 617,295 |
| 7. Hampton Court Palace | 590,583 |
| 8. Leeds Castle, Kent | 518,248 |
| 9. Beaulieu, Hampshire | 513,481 |
| 10. Tower Bridge, London | 498,448 |

Once a prison and the last place anyone wanted to visit, the Tower of London is now consistently Britain's most popular historic site.

# BRITAIN'S TOP 10 TOURIST ATTRACTIONS CHARGING ADMISSION

| Attraction | Annual visitors |
|---|---|
| 1. Madame Tussaud's, London | 2,439,155 |
| 2. Alton Towers, Staffordshire | 2,300,000 |
| 3. Tower of London | 2,289,354 |
| 4. Blackpool Tower | 1,523,000 |
| 5. Kew Gardens, London | 1,335,690 |
| 6. London Zoo | 1,303,797 |
| 7. Magnum Leisure Centre, Irvine | 1,078,000 |
| 8. Thorpe Park, Surrey | 1,060,000 |
| 9. Bembom Brothers Theme Park, Margate | 1,000,000 |
| 10. Drayton Manor Park, Staffordshire | 972,000 |

1987 English Tourist Board figures

# THE 10 MOST-VISITED MUSEUMS AND GALLERIES IN GREAT BRITAIN

| Museum/Gallery | Annual visitors |
|---|---|
| 1. British Museum | 3,700,000 |
| 2. National Gallery | 3,566,568 |
| 3. Science Museum | 3,166,294 |
| 4. The Royal Armouries, Tower of London | 1,825,378 |
| 5. Tate Gallery | 1,725,084 |
| 6. British Museum (Natural History) | 1,290,648 |
| 7. Victoria & Albert Museum | 916,477 |
| 8. Jorvik Viking Centre, York | 886,855 |
| 9. Glasgow Art Gallery and Museum | 819,302 |
| 10. Design Centre, London | 773,760 |

1987 figures

## TRANSPORT & TOURISM

# BRITAIN'S 10 MOST-VISITED GARDENS

| Garden | Visitors |
|---|---|
| 1. Kew Gardens, London | 1,335,690 |
| 2. Duthie Park Winter Gardens, Aberdeen | 1,130,000* |
| 3. Stapley Water Gardens, Cheshire | 1,000,000* |
| 4. Royal Botanic Garden, Edinburgh | 761,145 |
| 5. Wisley Garden, Surrey | 614,693 |
| 6. Walsall Arboretum Illuminations, West Midlands | 327,950* |
| 7. Botanic Gardens, Glasgow | 300,000* |
| 8. Compton Acres, Dorset | 280,000* |
| 9. Stourhead, Wiltshire | 210,457 |
| 10. Blenheim Palace Grounds, Oxfordshire | 163,468 |

*estimated

# BRITAIN'S TOP 10 FREE TOURIST ATTRACTIONS

| Attraction | Annual visitors |
|---|---|
| 1. Blackpool Beach | 6,450,000* |
| 2. British Museum | 3,700,000 |
| 3. National Gallery | 3,566,568 |
| 4. Westminster Abbey | 3,500,000* |
| 5. Science Museum | 3,166,294 |
| 6. Albert Dock, Liverpool | 3,100,000* |
| 7. St Paul's Cathedral | 2,500,000* |
| 8. York Minster | 2,100,000* |
| 9. Canterbury Cathedral | 2,000,000* |
| 10. Tate Gallery | 1,725,084 |

English Tourist Board 1987 figures   * estimated

The Palm House at Kew, Britain's most-visited gardens.

# ACKNOWLEDGEMENTS

· · · · · · · · · · · · · · · · · · · · · · · · · · · · · ·

I would like to thank the following organizations and individuals who kindly supplied me with information to enable me to compile many of the lists in **THE TOP 10 OF EVERYTHING:**

Academy of Motion Picture Arts &
 Sciences
The ADT London Marathon
Alcohol Concern
American Kennel Club
The Arts Council
ASH
Association of British Insurers
The Association of the British
 Pharmaceutical Industry
Audit Bureau of Circulations Ltd
Automobile Association
The Bank of England
Beefeater Gin, Sponsors of the
 Oxford & Cambridge Boat Race
The Bell Foundry Museum,
 Loughborough
Bermans & Nathans Ltd
Birds Eye Wall's Ltd
A. & C. Black (Publishers) Ltd
*The Bookseller*
The Booksellers Association
The Boots Company Plc
The Brewers Society
The British Bloodstock
 Agency Plc
British Broadcasting Corporation
The British Film Institute
The British Library
The British Museum
The British Olympic Association
The British Pot Growers'
 Association
British Rail
British Rate & Data
The British Tourist Authority
The British Trust for Ornithology
British Telecom
The British Waterways Board
Burke's Peerage
Cadbury Ltd
Cameron Balloons Ltd
Capital Radio Plc
The Central Electricity Generating
 Board
Central Statistical Office
The Champagne Bureau
Charities Aid Foundation
Charities Commission
Chartered Insurance Institute
Christie's
Consolidated Gold Fields Plc
Thomas Cook Ltd
The Countryside Commission
Crown Berger Europe Ltd
Dayville Ltd
Department of Education and
 Science
Department of Employment
Department of the Environment
Department of Trade and Industry
Department of Transport
The Diamond Information Centre
Peter Dominic Ltd
Electoral Reform Society

English Heritage
The English Tourist Board
Euromonitor Ltd
Exhibitor Relations
The Farmhouse Cheese Bureau
Food and Agriculture Organization
 of the United Nations
The Football League
*Forbes Magazine*
Forbidden Planet
Foreign & Commonwealth Office
The Forestry Commission
Fortnum & Mason Ltd
*Fortune*
General Accident Insurance Group
The Geological Museum
The Halifax Building Society
Hamleys of Regent Street Ltd
Harlands of Hull Ltd
Harrods Ltd
The Hayward Gallery
Health and Safety Executive
H.J. Heinz Co Ltd
Hillier Parker International
The Historic Buildings Commission
Home Office
The House of Commons
The Huge Cheese Co
The Imperial War Museum
Independent Broadcasting
 Authority
The Institute of Sports Medicine
International Data Corporation
The International Racing Bureau
International Union for
 Conservation of Nature and
 Natural Resources
International Wine Auctions Ltd
ITV Association
The Jockey Club
Just Games
Kattomeat/Gallup
M.W. Kellogg Co
The Kellog Co of Great Britain Ltd
The Kennel Club
The Letter Box Study Group
Libertys
The Library Association
Littlewoods Pools
Lloyds Register
The London Coffee Information
 Centre
London Regional Transport
London Theatre Record
The London Tourist Board
MARC Europe Ltd
Marks & Spencer Plc
Medical Statistics Unit,
 Office of Population Censuses
 and Surveys
Milk Marketing Board
Miss World (UK) Ltd
Motorcycle News
Motor Vehicle Manufacturers
 Assoc. of the United States, Inc

MRIB
The Museums Association
National Aeronautics and Space
 Administration
The National Council for Voluntary
 Organizations
The National Federation of Self
 Employed and Small Businesses
The National Gallery
The National Maritime Museum
The National Portrait
 Gallery
National Spice Information Bureau
The National Trust
Newspaper Publishers Association
Nielsen Media Research
A.C. Nielsen Co Ltd
Office of Population Censuses and
 Surveys
Parker Brothers
Paxton & Whitfield Ltd
The Phobics' Society
Pizza Express
The Post Office
Proprietory Association of Great
 Britain
Public Lending Right
The Ramblers' Association
The Really Useful Group Plc
Relate National Marriage Guidance
The Reward Group
Rolls-Royce Motor Cars Ltd
The Royal Academy
The Royal Aeronautical Society
The Royal and Ancient Golf Club of
 St Andrews
The Royal Greenwich Observatory
The Royal Opera House
The Royal Shakespeare Company
The Royal Society for the
 Prevention of Accidents
The Royal Society for the
 Protection of Birds
The Royal Zoological Society
Runzheimer International
The Samaritans
H. Samuel Ltd
Sainsbury's
The Savoy Hotel, London
Peter Sawell & Partners Ltd
Scope Communications
 Management.
The Scottish Tourist Board
*Screen International*
The Shakespeare Centre Library,
 Stratford-upon-Avon
M. Shanken International Ltd
Siemens AG
*Slimming Magazine*
Smith's Crisps
Social Surveys (Gallup Poll) Ltd
Society of West End Theatres
Sotheby's
Spink and Son Ltd
Sports Council

Suttons Seeds Ltd
Tesco Stores Ltd
The Tate Gallery
Theatre Record
*The Times*
Titan Distributors
Trades Union Congress
Trinity House Lighthouse
 Service
*True Romances Magazine*
United Nations Educational,
 Scientific and Cultural
 Organization
United Nations
United States Travel & Tourism
 Administration
University Radio and Nescafe
*Variety*
The Victoria & Albert Museum
*Video Week*
Waddington Games Ltd
Woolworths Plc
The World Conservation Monitoring
 Centre
World Association of Girl Guides
 and Girl Scouts
World Health Organization
World Scout Bureau

John Alexander
John L. Amos
Tony Brown
Terry Charman
Simon Cooper
Luke Crampton
Paul Dickson
HRH Prince Edward
Harold Fisher
Christopher Forbes
Francesca Franchi
Darryl Francis
Sue Goddard
David Gore
Ron Hall
Dr M. Hutson
Hilary Kay
Gaynor Leigh
Salim Khoury
Karen Levi
Dr Benjamin Lucas
Andrew Maslem
Jo Moody
Peter Morgan
Simon Morley
Alan Noble
Peter Packer
David Preston
Alaric Pugh
Brian Riddle
Sandra Scott
Eric Syddique
David Thompson
Chris Ware
David Way
Sue Withers

# PICTURE CREDITS

· · · · · · · · · · · · · · · · · · · · · · · · · ·

# INDEX

INDEX